Frommer's®

25 GREAT drives in TUSCANY & UMBRIA

D1127184

WILEY

Wiley Publishing, Inc.

Touring Club Italiano
Chairman: Roberto Ruozi
Touring Editore
Managing director: Armando Peres
General manager: Marco Ausenda
Assistant general manager: Renato Salvetti
Editorial director: Michele D'Innella
Head of guidebooks: Anna Ferrari-Bravo
Editing: Cinzia Rando
Editorial production and layout: Studio editoriale Selmi
Written by: Stefano Baldi
Translated by: Barbara Fisher
Picture research : Rossella Barresi
Cover: *Federica Neeff* con *Mara Rold*
Maps: Graffito-Cusano Milanino
Revised maps: Sergio Seveso

Revised fifth edition published 2010
Revised fourth edition published 2008
Revised third edition published 2006
Revised second edition published 2004
First published 2002

Published by AA Publishing

Published in the United States by
Wiley Publishing, Inc.
111 River Street, Hoboken, NJ 07030

Find us online at Frommers.com

Frommer's is a registered trademark of Arthur Frommer.
Used under license.

ISBN 978-0-470-56026-6

Photolitho and photocomposition: Emmegi Multimedia, Milan
Printed and bound by : G. Canale & C. S.p.a., Torino, Italy

A04153

CONTENTS

ABOUT THIS BOOK

This book is not only a practical touring guide for the independent traveller, but is also invaluable for those who would like to know more about Tuscany and Umbria. It is divided into five geographical regions, with town visits and itineraries included for each one. Specific city tours are featured for Lucca, Florence, Siena and Perugia. Each tour has details of the most interesting places to visit en route. Boxes catering for special interests follow some of the main entries – for those whose interest is in history or walking or those who have children. There are also boxes which highlight scenic stretches of road and which give details of the natural environment, local traditions and gastronomy. Special features cover the Tuscan islands and coastline, oil and wine, spas and places associated with St Francis. The simple route directions are accompanied by an easy-to-use map at the beginning of each tour, along with a chart showing how far it is from one town to the next in kilometres and miles. This can help you decide where to take a break and stop overnight. (All distances quoted are approximate.)Before setting off it is advisable to check with the information centre listed at the start of the tour for recommendations on where to break your journey, and for additional information on what to see and do, and when best to visit.

⭐ This symbol on the maps represents other attractions seen along the routes, often mentioned in the panels.

Tour Information
See pages 167–176 for the addresses, telephone numbers and opening times of the attractions mentioned in the tours, including the telephone numbers of tourist information centres.

Accommodation and restaurants
Pages 160–166 list hotels, farm holiday centres and camping sites situated at the point of departure or along the route of each tour. Also listed are restaurants where you may like to stop for a meal. There are, of course, other possibilities to be found along the way.

Motoring
For information on motoring in Italy see pages 158–159.

Credit Cards
All principal credit cards *(carta di credito)* are accepted by most establishments, but not all petrol stations. Check before buying.

Currency
The unit of currency in Italy is the Euro (€). Euro bank notes are in denominations of €5, €10, €20, €50, €100, €200 and €500; coins are in denominations of 1, 2, 5, 10, 20 and 50 cents, and €1 and €2.

Customs Regulations
Items for personal or professional use may be brought into Italy free of charge, but take receipts for valuable articles to avoid paying duty on them. Travellers' allowances for Italy are the same as other EU countries. Check current guidelines.

Electricity
The current is 220 volts AC, 50 cycles, with two round-pin plugs. UK and North American visitors should check whether 110/120-volt appliances require a voltage transformer.

Emergency Telephone Numbers
Police tel: 113. Fire tel: 115. Ambulance tel: 118.

Entry Regulations
The only document necessary for UK, Commonwealth and US citizens is a valid passport for any stay of up to three months. Officially visitors from EU countries need only a national identity card to enter Italy, but in practice you will need a passport. However, passport and visa requirements are subject to change, so you should check prior to your visit.

Health
Health insurance is recommended, but visitors from EU countries are entitled to the health services available to Italians. This means obtaining, prior to travelling to Italy, the relevant documentation (EHIC – European Health Insurance Card).

The high cost of treatment makes insurance essential if you are a non-EU citizen. Keep all bills for medical treatment and medicines to claim back later.

Post Offices
Post offices are generally open 8–1.30/2 Mon–Fri and to 11.45 on Sat. On the last day of the month offices close at noon. Times vary from place to place.

Public Holidays
1 January – New Year's Day
6 January – Epiphany
Easter Monday
25 April – Liberation Day (1945)
1 May – Labour Day
2 June – Proclamation of Republic (celebrated on following Saturday)
15 August – Ferragosto (Assumption)
1 November – All Saints
8 December – Immaculate Conception
25–6 December – Christmas.

Roads
Tuscany and Umbria are served by a basic motorway network: the A12 from the border with Liguria to Rossignano

Marìttimo; the A11 from Florence to Pistoia, Lucca, Pisa and Versilia; the A1 from the Apennine border with Emilia to Florence, Arezzo and Orvieto, with the Florence–Siena and Bettolle–Perugia motorway link roads. The major state roads are: the SS1 Aurelia along the Tyrrhenian coast; the SS2 Cassia from Siena to the border with Lazio; the SS3 Flaminia from the border with Marche to Foligno, Spoleto and Terni; the SS3bis–E45 between Città di Castello, Perugia, Todi and Terni.

Motorways can always be used to cover certain sections of the tours quickly or for rapid returns, but tours generally use A roads and sometimes secondary roads. The few difficult routes

Typical Tuscan landscape

(coastal roads, for instance) are indicated so that you can choose whether or not to take them.

In Florence, Lucca, Siena, and Perugia the main problems are road congestion and parking. Some suggestions are given in the text; others can be obtained from tourist information offices.

Telephones

Most phone booths on streets and in bars, tobacco shops and restaurants take coins or a phone card *(una scheda telefonica)*, bought from post offices, stores or bars.

To call abroad, dial 00, then the country code, followed by the city code and number. The prefix for the UK is 0044; for Eire 00353; for the US and Canada 001; for Australia 0061.

Free phone numbers *(numeri verde)* usually begin with 800

and national call rate numbers begin with 848 or 199. Hotels tend to overcharge for long-distance and international calls, so it is best to make calls from public phones, using telephone cards. Rates are lowest on Sunday and between 10pm and 8am weekdays and Saturday.

Tourist Offices

The Italian State Tourist Office (ENIT) is represented in the following:
Australia: Level 24, 46 Market Street, Sydney NSW 2000 (tel: (02) 9262 1666).
Canada: Suite 907, 175 Bloor Street East, Toronto M4W 3R8 (tel: 416/925-4882).
UK: 1 Princes Street, London W1B 2AY (tel: 020 7408 1254).
US: Suite 1565, 630 Fifth Avenue, New York NY 10111 (tel: 212/245-5618).

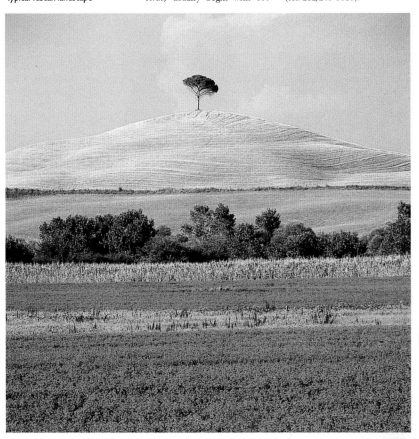

NORTHWEST TUSCANY

Spread over the provinces of Massa Carrara, Lucca, Pistoia and Prato, the northwestern part of Tuscany comprises territories with widely varying attractions. This is Apennine country, historically a place of travellers – peaceful or otherwise – as shown by its castles, fortified villages and wayfarers' hospices. Its air of remote transience couldn't be further from the seaside and society life of Versilia; straight, often sandy coastline that contrasts spectacularly with the Apuan Alps.

From the mouth of the Magra river in the north to the Serchio in the south, tourism has invaded the formerly unhealthy marsh areas, bypassed by the roads. Paralleling the coast, the rugged Apuan Alps, streaked with marble mines, form a dramatic backdrop to the wooded Garfagnana – the Serchio valley to the north of Lucca – bordered to the west of the river by the green and undulating Apennines. Monte Pisano is a geological extension of the Apuan Alps, a solitary peak that separates Lucca and the Serchio valley from the Pisa plain. In the 6th century BC Pisa overlooked the sea; now it lies 12km (7.5 miles) away. Woods and more woods are the prime feature of the Pistoian mountain landscape. This part of Tuscany contains a number of valleys that were once hotly fought over by Lucca and Florence. Last comes Prato, a town of industry and art, close to Florence, from which it was separated in 1992 to become a province, taking with it the Florentine Bisenzio valley, the route formerly followed by travellers crossing the Apennines to Bologna.

As is often the case in Tuscany, tourism is divided between nature – the glorious Tuscan landscapes – and art. Natural beauty draws the crowds to the seaside at Viareggio, Forte dei Marmi and other towns in Versilia; it offers the quieter pleasures of the *maquis*, dunes and Tyrrhenian flora and fauna at San Rossore and Migliarino; and it provides striking mountain views in the Apuan Alps and wooded hills and chestnut groves of the Garfagnana and the Lunigiana.

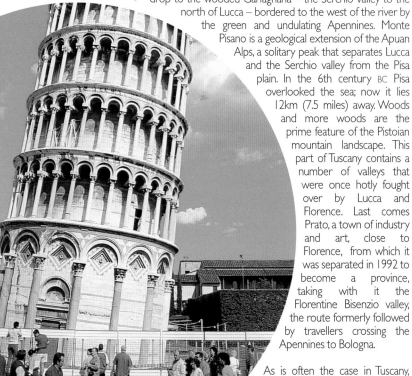

The Leaning Tower of Pisa, the town's most famous view

Tour 1

Marble quarries provide the theme for the initial stages of this tour, which passes through the blinding-white reflections of quarry debris and crystalline rock faces cut perpendicularly with wire. A brief detour into Liguria takes in the lovely town of Sarzana and deserted Luni, giving a glimpse of the present and past of the Lunigiana. This land is wedged in the Apennine ridge, on the border with Emilia and Liguria, and linking the Po plain to central Italy. Then it's time to relax and drive through the temples of summer seaside tourism along the beaches of Versilia.

Tour 2

Ancient Lucca 'of a hundred churches' is enclosed within its ring of walls and bastions – the monumental defences of an independence that lasted almost a thousand years. However, Lucca is a far from stern and forbidding fortress-town. Tree fronds grow from the tower-houses, the church fronts are softened by elegant loggias, and the entire urban layout bears the gracious mark of two forceful women – Elisa Baciocchi, a member of Napoleon's family, and the enlightened restorer Duchess Marie Louise of Bourbon.

Tour 3

From the villas, parks and spas that provided relaxation for Lucca's nobility and wealthy citizens, this tour climbs the upper Serchio valley between the steep mountain slopes and dense woods of Garfagnana, to enter the lunar scenery of marbled Monte Altissimo. After leaving behind the dazzling landscape of the Apuan Alps, you return to the coast to visit a quiet lakeside spot of subtle old-fashioned charm.

Tour 4

Marking the division between the lands of Lucca and Pisa, Monte Pisano was for centuries at the centre of disputes and parochial feuds that constantly erupted between the small states of Italy. Between spats, these were the societies that created, among other things, such gems as the Romanesque bell tower of San Piero a Grado, and the baroque Charterhouse of Calci. The itinerary starts with a journey along the Pisan coastline, where the San Rossore estate has preserved intact the blanket of foliage that covers the mouths of the Serchio and Arno rivers.

Tour 5

This tranquil tour takes you up mountains and down into valleys, through forests and

chestnut groves, taking in wonderful scenery as well as the legacies of generations of peasants, woodcutters and shepherds, displayed in the Pistoia mountains' ecomuseum. After passing through the lush, green Valdinièvole, with its Swiss-style charm, take a break at the Montecatini spa before heading back towards the increasingly built-up zones of the Arno plain to discover the artistic treasures of Prato.

Above: trekking in the Lunigiana
Below: Forte dei Marmi beach

Lunigiana
& Versilia

It's a short journey from the Apuan Alps to the golden sands – or, in summer, the multicoloured expanse of parasols – of Versilia. This itinerary never loses sight of either. The starting point is Massa, where the palace of the Cybo Malaspina family, the family tombs in the vaults of the Duomo (cathedral) and the Renaissance palace they added to the 14th-century scenic stronghold are all reminders of a supremacy that lasted from 1442 to 1741.

ITINERARY	
MASSA	▶ **Carrara (7km-4m)**
CARRARA	▶ **Colonnata (8km-5m)**
COLONNATA	▶ **Fantiscritti (5km-3m)**
FANTISCRITTI	▶ **Campo Cècina**
	(24km-15m)
CAMPO CÈCINA	▶ **Fosdinovo (15km-9m)**
FOSDINOVO	▶ **Sarzana (9km-5½m)**
SARZANA	▶ **Luni (8km-5m)**
LUNI	▶ **Forte dei Marmi**
	(19km-12m)
FORTE DEI MARMI	▶ **Marina di Pietrasanta**
	(3km-2m)
MARINA DI PIETRASANTA	▶ **Viareggio (11km-7m)**
VIAREGGIO	▶ **Massa (23km-14½m)**

2 DAYS • 132KM • 82 MILES

The grey-and-white striped façade of the Duomo of Carrara

i Viale Vespucci 24, Marina di Massa

▶ *Follow the signs to Carrara.*

1 Carrara

In its past, Carrara suffered a stormy succession of rulers. Finally, in 1442, it came under the governance of the Malaspina and Cybo Malaspina families, who reigned for 300 years. From their residence, now home to the Academy of Fine Arts, the medieval Via di Santa Maria (where Petrarch lived) leads to the Duomo (cathedral). Its marble façade, Romanesque at the bottom and Gothic at the top, is a reminder of its long building process (from the 11th to the 14th century). The house where Michelangelo stayed while collecting his marble is in the piazza. In this 'marble capital', a look at the Marble Museum is the best prelude to a visit to the quarries.

i Viale XX Settembre

SCENIC ROUTES

Before venturing into the massive quarry of the Colonnata 'canal' (always giving way to marble lorries!), you can enjoy a fine view of the Apuan Alps from the hilltop Bedizzano (276m/905 feet). The stretch of road leading to Fantiscritti is beautiful, and excellent views of Versilia are offered by the road that climbs to Campo Cècina with a panorama of quarries as far as the eye can see.

▶ *Travel northeast, following the signs to Colonnata.*

2 Colonnata

Accompanied by breathtaking views of the 22km (13-mile) railway line, a masterpiece of engineering that, between 1886 and 1964, linked the quarries to the port of Marina di Carrara, you reach the centre of the quarrying area famous for the black Colonnata marble. Since the times of the Roman slave colony that gave Colonnata its name, life has been harsh for the quarrymen of this rural village – as is particularly evident in the tablets on the walls of houses here, which proclaim the workers' anarchist ideals.

▶ *Descend from the Colonnata hill and take the road to Fantiscritti.*

3 Fantiscritti

This part of the route follows the viaducts of the 19th-century railway (the stunning 'Vara bridges'). To the right of a gallery cut through the marble slopes you'll find an immense fairy-tale hall carved into the polished marble. Further on, the Fantiscritti gorge (450m/ 1,476 feet) takes its name from a 3rd-century AD bas-relief found here in 1863 and now in the Accademia in Carrara. The *fanti*, or young men, are Jupiter, Hercules and Bacchus. Flemish sculptor Jean de Boulogne, better known as Giambologna, carved his name somewhat disrespectfully here in 1590, and in 1800 his example was followed by Antonio Canova. At the base of the gorge, tunnels

Curing *lardo* (fatty bacon) in the cellars of Colonnata

Walton quarries, named after the English entrepreneur who introduced new marble-processing technology in the first half of the 19th century.

▶ *Descend from Campo Cècina, following the signs to Fosdinovo.*

5 Fosdinovo

The 14th-century castle of Fosdinovo was built for Spinetta Malaspina, whose family ruled Lunigiana from 1306 to 1797. This served both as a military bastion and as an elegant residence. Redesigned during the Renaissance, it is one of the loveliest castles in this part of Tuscany. Italian poet Dante Alighieri is said to have stayed in one of the rooms in 1306.

▶ *From the village, take the road to the left that leads via Giucano to Sarzana.*

6 Sarzana

Geographically a part of Tuscany, the Ligurian town of Sarzana lies in the basin of the Magra river, inhabited since the

3rd millennium BC. The earliest residents were the Palaeo-Ligurians, who sculpted the enigmatic stelae-statues kept in the Piagnaro castle museum at Pontrèmoli (38km/24 miles north of Sarzana). Its position, at the point where the Cisa Pass road joins the Aurelia road made Sarzana a strategic base for the control of lower Lunigiana. Under Castruccio Castracani's rule, the people of Lucca built the splendid Sarzanello fortress here (1322); the Florentines, in Lorenzo d' Medici's era, erected the Cittadella (1488); and the Genoans gave it walls in the 1500s. A notable feature of Sarzana's rich artistic and monumental heritage is the splendid cathedral. Inside, the great cross painted in 1138 by Master Guglielmo is considered the

---

SPECIAL TO…

A fad among foodies, tasty Colonnata *lardo* (fatty bacon cured with herbs) has been made since Roman times and was once the staple meal of the quarrymen, who seasoned and spiced it before leaving it to cure for ten months in marble basins in their cellars. A visit to Colonnata is the best opportunity to taste the genuine articles.

---

branch out to the Ravaccione and Colonnata quarries and the splendid Quarry Museum shows the marble excavation, processing and transport techniques used from the Roman era to the present day, as well as a reconstruction of the everyday lives of quarrymen of the past.

▶ *Return to Carrara and take the* **SS446d***; after 9km (6 miles) turn right on to the road for Campo Cècina.*

4 Campo Cècina

The vast, open space of Campo Cècina (1,357m/4,452 feet) was already popular with the Romans during the golden age of the port of Luni (1st–2nd century AD). Today it is home to the Belvedere and Carrara refuge huts, used by hikers. Extending all around are the

---

RECOMMENDED WALK

An easy path leads from Campo Cècina to an ancient *via di lizza* – a formidable chute created in the sheer rock face, down which the blocks of marble were sent, tied to a sledge (*lizza*) made of sturdy planks bolted together. This was secured at the top by the workers' ropes. If the huge load broke loose, there was no escape for those who soaped the runners and inserted the rollers along the way. Now that the lethal sledge has disappeared, lorries zigzag up and down the white mounds of waste. Often there is no room to turn the bends and the lorries advance by alternating forward and reverse gears.

---

archetype of all similar Tuscan and Umbrian works.

▶ *Take the SS1 southbound to the Via San Pero turning, and turn right to Luni.*

7 Luni

Remains of the forum and the 'house of frescoes', sections of wall and an amphitheatre are among the few remains that tell of the rise and fall of Luni, which was founded as a seaport in 177 BC and subsequently exported marble all over the Roman Empire. After centuries of prosperity, the floods of the Magra River silted up the port. The coastline gradually retreated and is now about 2km (1 mile) away. Floods, malaria and feudal conflicts led to its final decline in the early 1200s. Both Dante and

writer Petrarch used Luni to symbolise the precarious state of human fortunes. At the centre of what is now an archaeological site is a national museum housing relics and documents.

▶ *After reaching the coast road, proceed southeast to Forte dei Marmi.*

8 Forte dei Marmi

In the 16th century there was a quay here, where marble from the quarries was loaded on to ships. Then, in 1788, Grand Duke Leopold I ordered the construction of the fort that still stands in the middle of the square. Today, elegant hotels and town houses – and famous entertainment nightspots such as the

Cutting marble in the Apuan Alps

Views of Viareggio: the seafront (left) and the carnival (above)

Pietrasanta in the Middle Ages after which the town was named). Leading from the canal are the art deco buildings Supercinema (now Caffè Liberty, Il '48 store, the Galleria del Libro bookshop, Gran Caffè Margherita and the Balena baths. A few steps from the sea, in a square named after him, is a bust of Percy Bysshe Shelley. The English poet drowned at the age of 29 off the Versilia coast and was cremated, in the presence of Byron, on the beach near Viareggio (1822). Happier scenes are conjured up by the famous local carnival, with its parade of comic and satirical papier-mâché floats.

⊡ *Viale Carducci 10*

▶ *Return to Massa on the SS1 northbound.*

Capannina – make Forte dei Marmi a seaside and holiday legend. Set on the fine sand of the Versilian beach, it is backed by pine woods, Mediterranean *maquis* and, beyond, by the Apuan Alps.

⊡ *Via Achille Franceschi 28d*

▶ *Continue along the coast road to the Capannina, then on the parallel Viale Morin to Fiumetto, in the comune of Marina di Pietrasanta.*

❾ Marina di Pietrasanta
Inland lies the Principe bridge, built by Leopold I in 1776, and to the left, before you reach the Fiumetto channel, stretch 80 hectares (198 acres) of the coastal forest that originally extended from the River Magra to the Livorno hills. Today, this makes up the lovely Versiliana Park, owned by the town authorities. In summer, exhibitions and

meetings are held here, continuing the tradition of Versilia's lively literary café society.

⊡ *Via Donizetti 14*

▶ *Back on the coast road, continue south to Viareggio.*

❿ Viareggio
The main axis of the town, one of Italy's pioneers of seaside holidays, is the beautiful flowered avenue on the seafront, lined with eclectic art deco and art nouveau hotels, town houses, cafés, restaurants, pavilions and shops. The first 'seaside homes' – segregating men and women – were built in 1828. Of the numerous wooden constructions, however, only Chalet Martini survived a disastrous fire in 1917. Above the Burlamacca canal rises the Matilda Tower (1544), erected by the people of Lucca near the Via Regia (the road which ran from Migliarino and

Lucca

1 DAY

Lucca has been the headquarters of many a political master: it was the capital of Lombard Etruria, then of the Carolingian marquisate of Tuscany, before becoming an autonomous *comune* in 1119. But between 1369 and 1799, this small model-state retained its independence, and established a quality of life that can still be seen in its brick and marble buildings, and in the streets and squares around the town.

Above: riding the ring of walls
Below: San Michele in Foro

ℹ️ *Piazzale Giuseppe Verdi, Lucca*

▷ *Enter the town through Porta Vittorio Emanuele and turn left on to Baluardo San Donato.*

❶ Baluardo San Donato

Only pedestrians and bicycles are allowed on the 4,200m-long (13,780-foot) ring of walls that still surrounds Lucca. Designed to resist heavy artillery, they stand 12m (39 feet) high, with large ramparts linking the 11 arrowhead bastions; but they remained unused until Marie Louise of Bourbon transformed them into a splendid tree-lined promenade during her stay between 1815 and 1824.

▷ *Follow Via San Paolino eastwards to the church of the same name.*

The narrow street on the left leads beyond Via Burlamacchi to the church of Sant' Alessandro. A turning to the right of the church takes you to Via Vittorio Emanuele; the left leads to Piazza Napoleone.

❷ Piazza Napoleone

Vast and shaded by plane trees, the square was opened in 1806; the site had already been established as the centre of municipal power under the rule of Castruccio da Castracani (1320–8) and Paolo Guinigi (1400–30). In 1578, Bartolomeo Ammannati designed the impressive Palazzo della Signoria, now home of the provincial offices (the right-hand wing was added in 1728) for the local authorities. It was later adapted for Elisa Baciocchi, Bonaparte's sister. The Duchess Marie Louise of Bourbon also lived there, and the monument in the centre of the square is dedicated to her. To the south is the Corte del Pesce, a delightful little medieval spot, leading to Via Pescheria.

▷ *Follow Via Vittorio Veneto northwards to Piazza San Michele.*

❸ Piazza San Michele

The former site of the Roman forum continued as the hub of medieval town life. Between 1070 and the 14th century, workmen from Pisa and Lucca constructed the fine church of San Michele in Foro in the centre of the square; the ornamental arches on columns and rows of loggias on the façade are their trademarks. In the 15th century, after the seat of secular power was transferred to what is now the Piazza Napoleone, the ancient forum became the meeting place for bankers and silk merchants.

▷ *Take Via Roma eastwards and turn left into Via Fillungo.*

❹ Via Fillungo

On the site of the main juncture of Roman Lucca, this is the favourite promenade and shopping street, marked since 1471 by a mechanical clock installed on the Torre delle Ore. Many of the shops between the palaces and towers still have their old signs and furnishings.

▷ *Pass Via dell'Anfiteatro on the right and turn left for Piazza San Frediano.*

❺ San Frediano

A large 13th-century mosaic adorns the façade of San Frediano, built between

Lucca's elliptical Piazza del Mercato

1112 and 1147 so close to the walls that its crenellated bell tower was used for military purposes. Inside is an unusual holy font (12th century), with a column in the form of a flame and imps, and a rich marble polyptych (1422) by Jacopo della Quercia. It also houses the tomb of Santa Zita (1218–78), venerated by the people of Lucca.

▶ *Return to Via dell'Anfiteatro and take one of the passages to Piazza del Mercato.*

6 Piazza del Mercato
This surprising elliptical square, enclosed between tall medieval houses, has its origin in the 2nd century AD, when an amphitheatre for 10,000 spectators stood here: sections of the two rows of arches that supported the auditorium are still visible along Via dell'Anfiteatro. Engulfed by houses and used for various purposes – over the centuries it has been a prison, salt warehouse and abattoir – it was cleared of its central buildings in 1830 and became a public square once more. Today, it's enlivened by meeting places and small shops.

▶ *Leave the square to the south and take one of the streets leading to Via Mordini. Follow this to the left, then turn right into Via Guinigi until you come to Via Sant'Andrea.*

7 Case dei Guinigi
Via Guinigi was where the palaces and towers belonging to this wealthy merchant family were concentrated, and they still form a fascinating ensemble of 14th-century Gothic architecture. At the corner with Via Sant'Andrea, climb to the top of the high tower, with its tiny garden of ilex trees, for the view.

▶ *Continue along Via Giunigi and Via dell'Arcivescovado, then turn right into Via del Battistero and left across Piazza Antelminelli to Piazza San Martino.*

8 Duomo di San Martino
Pilgrims marching along the Via Francigena would come to Lucca's cathedral, San Martino, to venerate the famous Volto Santo, a crucifix sculpted in wood by the Pharisee Nicodemus (today's crucifix is a 13th-century copy of a Syrian original, perhaps dating from the 8th century). Now most visitors are attracted to the church, which was rebuilt in the 13th century, to see the tomb of Ilaria del Carretto, the second wife of Paolo Guinigi, a medieval ruler of the city who died in 1405. Jacopo della Quercia even sculpted her little dog lying on the sarcophagus at her feet. Victory is symbolised by the 'Vizir's horse's tail', a bizarre trophy from a battle against the Turks, kept in a glass case.

▶ *Leave the square to the south to reach Corso Garibaldi, which to the left leads to Baluardo San Colombano. From here follow the walls east along Baluardo Santa Maria and Baluardo San Paolino to Porta Vittorio Emanuele.*

SPECIAL TO...

The delightful city of Lucca is the birthplace of one of the 20th century's most popular composers, Giacomo Puccini. He was born in 1858 in Casa di Puccini, close to Piazza Cittadella with its charming statue of him. He lived in Lucca until 1886, and later moved to Torre del Lago Puccini (see page 20), where he spent most of his life. Concerts of his music take place every year in Chiesa di San Giovanni, and the annual Puccini Festival is held at Torre del Lago.

Garfagnana &
the Apuan Alps

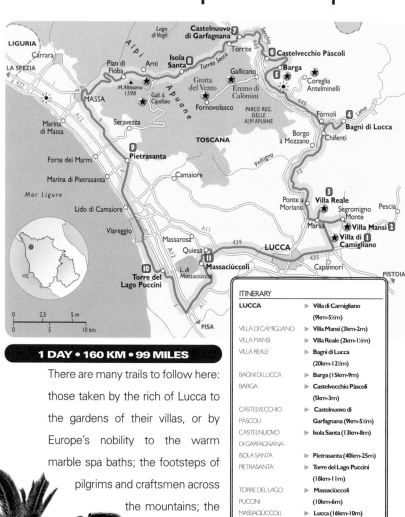

1 DAY • 160 KM • 99 MILES

There are many trails to follow here: those taken by the rich of Lucca to the gardens of their villas, or by Europe's nobility to the warm marble spa baths; the footsteps of pilgrims and craftsmen across the mountains; the escape routes of poets and musicians into a world of nature; and, of course, the trail of workers carrying crystalline rocks from the Apuan Alps to ports for transportation.

i Piazzale Giuseppe Verdi, Lucca

▶ *Leave Lucca to the east on the **SS435** to Pescia; just outside Borgonuovo turn left for Segromigno in Monte then right to Villa di Camigliano.*

❶ Villa di Camigliano

In the second half of the 17th century, this was the villa of Nicolao Santini, ambassador of Lucca at the court of Louis XIV. The baroque façade was inspired by Versailles, as were the gardens – the work of André le Nôtre, who created the gardens of the Sun King at Versailles. As well as the villa you can visit the spectacular Giardino di Flora, with grottoes, temples and water features. The rest of the park has been landscaped in keeping with romantic early 19th-century tastes.

▶ *Continue towards Segromino in Monte to Villa Mansi.*

❷ Villa Mansi

The Italian Renaissance gardens of Villa Mansi were redesigned in the 18th century by Filippo Juvarra, complete with a star-shaped wood, fishpond and theatre. There is also an English-style garden. The grand house was originally built in the late 16th-century but was transformed in the first half of the 17th century, and is rich in frescoes and fine furnishings.

▶ *Proceed towards Marlia to Villa Reale.*

❸ Villa Reale

In 1811 Elisa Baciocchi – the sister of Napoleon – bought a 16th- to 17th-century villa to convert into her country residence. Fortunately, the restructuring work left untouched the monumental yew and box hedges that form a series of garden rooms, as well as the lemon grove, the fountain and the water-grotto.

The woods, streams and lake of the romantic park were created in the first half of the 20th century. Past guests of Villa Reale (not open to visitors) include the great violinist and composer Paganini.

▶ *After reaching the Abetone-Brenner **SS12**, turn right for*

Villa di Camigliano, near Lucca

Ponte a Moriano and follow the road on the left of the rivers Serchio and then the Lima to Bagni di Lucca.

❹ Bagni di Lucca

At Borgo a Mozzano, the River Serchio is spanned by a staggering 14th-century hump-backed bridge known as the Maddalena. A shrine here once either contained a statue of the saint (now in the local parish church), or of the Devil. A little further on, the iron Ponte alle

SPECIAL TO…

Essayist Michel de Montaigne tried many spas in his attempts to relieve the pain of kidney stones, but (he wrote in 1581) only Bagni di Corsena (Lucca) helped. However, he took a sceptical view of the 'miraculous' waters. His advice to a friend worried about his wife's infertility was: 'If you want your wife pregnant, send her to Bagni and don't go yourself!'

RECOMMENDED
EXCURSION

The Civic Museum of Coreglia
Antelminelli, east of Barga, is
devoted to plaster figurines
and emigration – an unusual
theme that summarises the
area's still flourishing artistic
tradition, and the fate of its
figurine-sellers. From the 17th
century, the craftsmen migrat-
ed around the world in search
of buyers; they returned with
curiosities of all kinds, and
their haul is collected here,
along with more than a
thousand specimens of animals,
gods, busts and nativity scenes
produced between the 19th
and the early 20th century.

Catene crosses the Lima river,
linking Chifenti with Fònoli.

Made up of several hamlets,
Bagni di Lucca was once the
cosmopolitan haunt of Lucca's
aristocracy, and a magnet to
artists and scholars (including
Byron, Shelley, Dumas, Rossini,
Liszt, Verdi and Puccini).

Spas in the Bagni Caldi area
are still open; neo-classical
architecture and the remains of
abandoned spas can be seen at
Ponte a Serraglio and La Villa.

▶ *Return to the **SS12** and turn
right on to the **SS445** for
Barga.*

5 Barga
Barga was a Florentine outpost
on Garfagnana territory from
1341. Today, its Giardino district
is a flat expanse of modern
industry, but from here the
town's steep, narrow streets
climb to the Arringo, a paved
area at the top of the hill. The

SPECIAL TO...

An extraordinary spectacle can
be witnessed every 10–11
November and 30–31 January
in front of Barga's cathedral. At
dusk on these dates the sun
disappears behind the ridges of
the Apuan Alps and slips
perfectly into the great curve
of the 'pierced mountain',
Monte Forato
(1,150–1,175m/3,773–3,855
feet). This magical occurrence
can also be observed on different dates from other locations.
Perhaps the loveliest is on
6–10 October and 3–7 March,
near the church of San
Pellegrinetto, reached by car
via Gallicano and
Fornovolasco. On very clear
days remember to take a good
pair of sunglasses!

Bas-reliefs in Barga's Duomo

contours of the Apuan Alps and the Apennines frame the Romanesque sculptures of the façade of the Duomo (cathedral). Altered many times between the 9th and the 16th century, the building contains a splendid 12th-century *ambo* (oblong pulpit) resting on red marble columns.

The spa town of Bagni di Lucca

RECOMMENDED EXCURSION

From Gallicano (opposite Barga, across the River Serchio), climb westwards along the Tùrrite river to the turning for the Calòmini hermitage, a spectacular 11th-century sanctuary partially excavated in the sheer rock. Further on, near Fornovolasco, is the Grotta del Vento – 4km (2½ miles) of halls, tunnels, wells, lakes, siphons and subterranean rivers which can be visited along a marked route.

ⓘ *Via di Mezzo 45*

▶ *Follow the provincial road that leads via Ponte di Catagnana to Castelvecchio Pàscoli.*

❻ Castelvecchio Pàscoli

In a secluded spot just before you reach the village is the small house bought by poet Giovanni Pascoli (1855–1912) in 1895 with the proceeds from the medals won at a Latin poetry competition in Amsterdam. Local life is reflected in the pages of his *Songs of Castelvecchio*, published in 1903. The house is now a museum, preserved exactly as it was when Pascoli spent his holidays here in the company of his sister 'Mariù'. Both are buried in the annexed chapel.

▶ *Continue along the road and turn right on to the SS445 for Castelnuovo di Garfagnana.*

❼ Castelnuovo di Garfagnana

'Land of wolves and brigands' – this was how poet Ludovico Ariosto described wooded Garfagnana. Between the early 15th century and Italy's 19th-century unification, this area belonged (apart from a few brief intervals) to the Este family. Ariosto was obliged to act as governor, in service to the lords of Ferrara, and lived from 1522 to 1525 in the Rocca (stronghold), which still has a loggia overlooking the square of Castelnuovo.

In the 17th century another poet, Fulvio Testi of Ferrara, is said to have stayed there – again acting as governor (between 1640 and 1642) for the Este family of Modena. Today, the building houses a permanent exhibition on the ancient Ligurian civilization of the Upper Serchio Valley.

ⓘ *Piazza delle Erbe 10*

SPECIAL TO...

The rich marble deposits on the north side of Monte Altissimo were first exploited in the 1800s, after the opening of the Cipollaio tunnel. Among them, the disused Henraux quarry (reached by a high fissure at the exit from a tunnel just past Arni) stands as a beautiful amphitheatre of polished geometrical shapes cut into the marble.

Canoeing in the marshy waters of
Lake Massaciùccoli

▶ *Follow signs for Tòrrite
through a harsh landscape to
Isola Santa, in the heart of
the central Apuan Alps.*

8 Isola Santa

Isola Santa's dilapidated, stone-
roofed houses are usually the
only visible part of this village,
which grew up around a 13th-
century hospice serving travellers between Garfagnana and
Versilia. The rest of the crum-
bling community reappears
every ten years (next in 2014),
when the waters are drained
from the lake-reservoir that has,
since 1949, supplied the Tòrrite
hydroelectric station.

▶ *Continue (passing the turning
for the Cipollaio tunnel on the
left) via Arni and Pian della
Fioba to Massa; here take the
SS1 south to Pietrasanta.*

9 Pietrasanta

In 1255, Guiscardo Pietrasanta
founded a village to strengthen
Lucca's control of Versilia. From
its rectangular nucleus, this
settlement grew across the
Via Francigena, linked to the
forbidding Rocca di Sala (a
Lombard fort) by two wings of
crenellated walls. Today, the
village is renowned among

sculptors, mosaic-workers and
art lovers. At its entrance is the
Rocchetta, built in the 14th
century by Castruccio
Castracani and rebuilt in
1486–7. A little further on is the
cathedral (13th–14th century)
and, before it, the Marzocco
column (1514) and the lion,
symbol of Florence. In the
background are the Apuan Alps.

ⓘ *Piazza Statuto*

▶ *After reaching Viareggio on
the SS1, continue along Viale
dei Tigli to the turning on the
left for Torre del Lago Puccini.*

10 Torre del Lago Puccini

A faded holiday atmosphere
hangs around this peaceful
village, which was chosen in
1891 by Luccan composer
Giacomo Puccini (1858–1924) as
the site for his lakeside villa.
Puccini spent long periods of
time writing several works in
the village, and is buried here.
His furniture and curios are on
display in Villa Puccini. Every
year, the open-air theatre on the
shores of the lake hosts a highly
regarded Puccini festival.

▶ *Return to the SS1 and follow
it southbound; immediately
before the Pisa Nord slip road
of the A12, a secondary road*

*to the left leads to
Massaciùccoli.*

11 Massaciùccoli

Swampy Lake Massaciùccoli is
the last remnant of an ancient
lagoon formed by the Arno and
Serchio rivers, and provides the
ideal habitat for more than 250
species of migratory and non-
migratory birds. On the eastern
shore is the small village of
Massaciùccoli, where the
Romans built a villa and, higher
up, the spa known as Bagno di
Nerone (1st–2nd century AD).
At the foot of the village, long
footbridges lead over the water
to birdwatchers' hides.

▶ *Continue northwards to
Quiesa and then turn right
on to the SS439 to Lucca.*

SCENIC ROUTES

Staggering views of mountains
half-eaten by quarries mark the
beginning of the descent to
Massa. The route leads to a
chapel with a stone commem-
orating the dramatic events of
World War II, when the
Germans fortified the 'Gothic
line' here. The best view of
Monte Altissimo is enjoyed
from the Cipollaio road, just
after passing through the
tunnel of the same name.

The Sea
& Monte Pisano

Tucked into a corner of Pisa's walls are the glories of the Piazza del Duomo (popularly known as Campo dei Miracoli). Visitors come to see the marble wonders of the Duomo (cathedral, 1064), baptistery (1152) and cemetery (1277), and, of course, the famous leaning bell tower (1173).

1/2 DAYS • 110 KM • 69 MILES

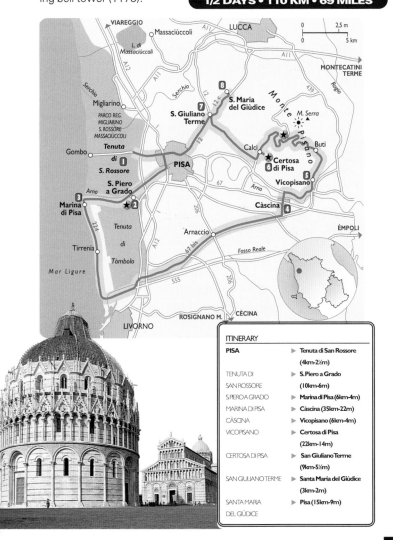

ITINERARY		
PISA	▶	**Tenuta di San Rossore**
		(4km-2½m)
TENUTA DI	▶	**S. Piero a Grado**
SAN ROSSORE		**(10km-6m)**
S. PIERO A GRADO	▶	**Marina di Pisa (6km-4m)**
MARINA DI PISA	▶	**Càscina (35km-22m)**
CÀSCINA	▶	**Vicopisano (6km-4m)**
VICOPISANO	▶	**Certosa di Pisa**
		(22km-14m)
CERTOSA DI PISA	▶	**San Giuliano Terme**
		(9km-5½m)
SAN GIULIANO TERME	▶	**Santa Maria del Giùdice**
		(3km-2m)
SANTA MARIA	▶	**Pisa (15km-9m)**
DEL GIÙDICE		

ⓘ *Piazza dei Miracoli;*
Piazza Vittorio Emanuele II, 16;
Pisa Airport

▶ *Leave Pisa to the west on Viale delle Cascine to the Trombe bridge and the entrance to San Rossore.*

❶ Tenuta di San Rossore

During Roman colonisation the entire 'plain of Pisa', from Viareggio to Livorno, was a succession of sea straits, dunes, woods and marshes. The Medici

Dense pinewood on the San Rossore estate

family continued the centuries-old struggle to regulate the Serchio and Arno delta, and at the same time large hunting reserves were developed, which were later passed on to the Lorraine and Savoy families, and – as in the case of San Rossore – to the Republic.

The estate's history of leisure use has prevented its development; today, guided tours can be taken to some areas. In this way, one of the most unspoiled and precious plant landscapes on the Tyrrhenian coast has been safe-guarded against reclamation.

▶ *Return towards Pisa, cross the Arno and follow its left bank towards Marina di Pisa to the turning on the left for San Piero a Grado.*

❷ San Piero a Grado

St Peter himself is said to have disembarked here in AD 44, during his voyage from Antiochia to Rome. Today, it has a fine Romanesque church, built in Livorno tufa and black and white San Giuliano marble, a solitary landmark in open countryside. There was once a port at the mouth of the Arno and, in the 4th century, a Christian basilica drew pilgrims here. The present church was built over the basilica in the 10th and 11th centuries. An important cycle of frescoes in the nave was commissioned for the Jubilee of 1300, and a Gothic ciborium, or shrine, marks the spot where the apostle is said to have preached to the faithful. The church's design is extremely unusual: three eastern apses and a western apse replacing the original façade, which was destroyed when the River Arno flooded in the late 12th century.

▶ *Return to the bank of the Arno and follow it to Marina di Pisa.*

❸ Marina di Pisa

After passing the picturesque Bocca dell'Arno, dotted with

> ### BACK TO NATURE
>
> It's not unusual, while strolling through the pines and oaks of San Rossore, to see cormorants and herons; you may also spot fallow deer, roe deer, boar, hares, rabbits, martens and foxes. Further north, across the Serchio, the woods of the estate extend into the Mediterranean *maquis* of Migliarino. Here tamarisks, myrtle, juniper, ferns and broom line a splendid sandy beach, against a background of pinewoods and ancient ilex groves (great for birdwatching).

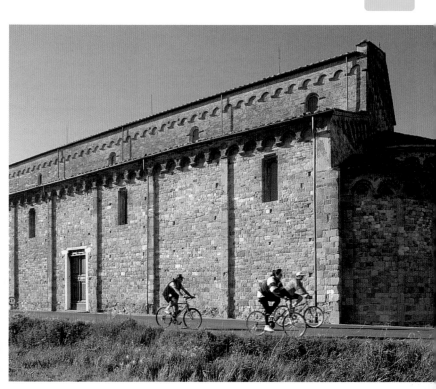

Basilica of San Piero a Grado

stilted huts and the characteristic *retoni* (fishing nets), you come to Marina di Pisa, the oldest of Pisa's seaside resorts, with its gracious art nouveau buildings. More late 19th-century architecture can be seen further south, at Tirrenia. Behind it stretches the flat Tòmbolo estate, which was established as a 23,000-hectare (56,832-acre) nature park in 1979, along with Migliarino, San Rossore and Massaciùccoli (see Tour 3). After centuries of neglect by its ecclesiastical owners, the Tòmbolo area was finally reclaimed by the Lorraine family in the early 19th century. They planted the pinewoods where, at the end of World War II, the Americans set up a military base.

▶ *Continue along the SS224 southbound, then eastwards to the slip roads leading to the SS67 bis for Càscina.*

4 Càscina

The turreted walls and square layout of the village, arranged around a long, porticoed street, mark Càscina as one of the 'new lands' designed in the Middle Ages as a Pisan outpost against Florence, which still managed to capture it in 1406. Càscina is now given over to the manufacture of furniture, knitwear and bricks; to the west, the grandiose Romanesque parish church of San Casciano has doorways carved in 1180.

▶ *Follow signs for Vicopisano.*

5 Vicopisano

The Florentines called on architect Filippo Brunelleschi (1435–9) to restore Vicopisano's towers and fortifications, having captured the village from the Pisans in 1407. The towers are dotted along the walls near Palazzo Comunale, and on the keep that dominates the rings of narrow village streets, providing Vicopisano with its distinctive

skyline. The defences were originally developed in the Middle Ages to control the River Arno, which, in those days, passed close to its walls.

FOR HISTORY BUFFS

One day in 1364, a group of Florentine soldiers taking a swim in the Arno near Càscina was ambushed by Pisans. They quickly retrieved their arms, however, and emerged victorious from the ensuing clash. In 1504, Republican Florence, led by Piero Soderini, commissioned Michelangelo to create a fresco depicting this episode in Palazzo Vecchio, beside a representation of the victory of Anghiari against the Milanese in 1440, which was assigned to Leonardo da Vinci. But the two works were never finished: only the cartoons (initial drawings) appeared, which were received enthusiastically by contemporaries.

FOR CHILDREN

The museum housed in the Certosa (Charterhouse) di Pisa will fascinate children, with its skeletons of whales, dolphins and porpoises. This is the most important cetacean collection in Italy.
Alternatively, the classic attractions of Fantasilandia amusement park are set amid the pine trees and *maquis* vegetation of the Migliarino-Massaciùccoli Park, just 700m (770 yards) from the main square of Tirrenia, and give direct access to the free beach.

i *Via Lante 1a*

▶ *Proceed northwards to Buti, then follow the signs for Calci and the Certosa di Pisa.*

⑥ Certosa di Pisa

Rich in marble, frescoes, paintings and stucco work, this huge charterhouse, founded in 1366, is a triumph of 16th- to 17th-century baroque style. The church, cloisters, gardens, fountains, priory and guest rooms used by grand dukes were abandoned by the Carthusian monks as recently as 1969. Today the charterhouse is also home to the Museum of Natural and Territorial History, whose collection of relics was first begun by the University of Pisa in 1591, at the behest of Grand Duke Ferdinand I.

i *Via Roma 9, Calci*

The Charterhouse of Pisa at Calci

▶ *Follow the signs for San Giuliano Terme.*

⑦ San Giuliano Terme

Dominating the village square, on the lower slopes of Monte Pisano, is the 18th-century Palazzo delle Terme and its extensive park. The wide avenues of the village, lined with plane trees, are a reminder of the 18th- and 19th-century golden age, when the hot springs of San Giuliano were renowned throughout Europe and drew visitors such as Byron, Shelley, Gustav III of Sweden, George IV of England, Louis Bonaparte, Paolina Borghese and Charles Albert of Savoy.

i *Piazza P B Shelley*

▶ *Take the **SS12c** northbound to the turning on the left for Santa Maria del Giùdice.*

⑧ Santa Maria del Giùdice

This charming mountainside village has two churches of note. The Pieve Vecchia (11th–12th century), just outside the village, has a façade in the Romanesque style of Lucca and a bell tower with two rows of double-mullioned windows. The parish church of Santa Maria Assunta, built in or around

SCENIC ROUTES

The best views of Monte Pisano are between Buti and Calci. Turn right at the Passo Prato Ceragiola and you will come to Monte Serra, at 917m (3,008 feet), the highest in the range. From the top, the view sweeps across from the Apuan and Apennine ridges to the settlements on the plain and the sea. The descent from Santa Maria del Giùdice to San Giuliano Terme is stunning.

1166 in Pisan Romanesque style, features an unusual octagonal bell tower set on a semicircular apse.

▶ *Go back along the **SS12c**, then take the **SS12** to Pisa.*

The Pistoia
Mountains & Prato

Before surrendering to Florence in **2 DAYS • 216KM • 134 MILES** 1401, Pistoia was a free and wealthy *comune*; its statute of 1117 is one of the earliest recorded in Italy. During this era its main monuments were built in the distinctive zebra stripes of the Pisan Romanesque style, alternating white marble with intense green – executed to perfection in the church of San Giovanni Fuoricivitas.

Above: the Acquerino forest, northeast of Pistoia
Right: an orchid in the Campolino Nature Reserve

ℹ️ *Piazza del Duomo 4, Pistoia*

▶ *Take the SS66 Abetone road to Le Piastre.*

❶ Le Piastre

Along the Reno river, just past the village of Le Piastre, a thatched and tiled roof on the right covers a truncated, cone-shaped structure. This is the Madonnina ice-house, where the ice that formed during winter in the nearby canals and lakes was preserved until spring (hence the area's title of 'cold valley'). Once the weather had changed, the ice was retrieved to be sold in the local towns.

▶ *Continue along the SS66 to the Passo di Oppio; turn right for Gavinana-Maresca, then left for Gavinana.*

❷ Gavinana

A 20th-century equestrian monument in the square of Gavinana commemorates Francesco Ferrucci, who led the Florentines here in 1530 against the Duke of Orange and his imperialist forces. Ferrucci was wounded, captured and publicly killed by Fabrizio Maramaldo of Calabria. His defeat marked the end of the republic and the return of the Medici family to Florence. A small museum is dedicated to the battle.

ℹ️ *Via Marconi 70, San Marcello Pistoiese*

▶ *Descend towards San Marcello Pistoiese, then turn right on to the SS66 to La Lima. Turn right again on to the SS12 to the turning on the right for Cutigliano.*

❸ Cutigliano

Set in dense woods, this is the best-preserved village in the Pistoia Apennines. In 1368, Cutigliano was the seat of the mountain commanders of the local militia *(Capitani del Popolo)* under Pistoian rule. The coats of arms of the seven governed *comunes*, together with many others, adorn the façade of Palazzo Pretorio. Opposite is

> ### FOR HISTORY BUFFS
>
> This is how the 16th-century historian Benedetto Varchi related Francesco Ferrucci's fate: 'Fabrizio had him brought before him, and after having him disarmed in the square and addressing him with insults and abuse, to which Ferruccio always responded boldly, he thrust some say a sword, some say a dagger and some a sort of spear, some say into his chest and some into his throat. "You kill a dead man," said his victim, after which Fabrizio ordered his men to finish him off.' The ferocious Calabrian captain won the dubious honour of having his name enter the Italian language as a term for the disgraceful arrogance of someone who acts cruelly towards the defenceless.

an elegant 15th-century loggia, where the commander administered justice from a stone bench.

i *Piazza Catalina*

▶ *Back on the SS12 continue your ascent to the Passo dell'Abetone.*

❹ Passo dell'Abetone

This renowned ski resort has been active since the early 20th century, when winter sports became popular. The 1,388m (4,554-foot) pass is named after a large fir tree which was felled to make way for the road built

The Castruccio bridge at Popiglio

for the Grand Duke of Lorraine Peter Leopold (1767).

Francesco III d'Este, who was also involved with the project, wanted a proper triumphal arch to celebrate the undertaking, but had to make do with two stone pyramids bearing the coats of arms of Este (to the right of the summit) and Lorraine (to the left). The posthouse, inn and customs post on the Grand Duke's road, together with a small church (1784), were built just before the pass, at Boscolungo.

i *Piazza Piramidi 501, Abetone*

▶ *Return along the SS12 and turn right for Popiglio, bearing right after Pian degli Ontani at the asphalted junction with a sign for two farm B&Bs (agriturismo).*

❺ Popiglio

About 21km (13 miles) after leaving the SS12, a few minutes' walk in the woods leads to the Torri di Popiglio (signposted), impressive and scenic ruins of Roman fortifications. The route then reaches Popiglio, apparently named after a commander of the Roman garrison, and the lovely 13th-century parish church of Santa Maria Assunta. The nearby Museum of Holy Art

contains furnishings, sculptures and hangings from mountain churches.

▶ *Continue to the right on the SS12 to the road signposted on the left that climbs to Lucchio.*

❻ Lucchio

Clinging to the side of a breathtaking spur, the village is so steep that women are said to have secured their children with ropes when they were playing on the street outside. The climb culminates in the remains of a medieval stronghold, a fantastic eyrie with sweeping views over the winding Lima river valley.

▶ *Back on the SS12, return to La Lima and turn right on to the SS66. After a short*

stretch, turn right for Piteglio and Prunetta, then right again on to the SS633 and follow the signs to Pescia.

7 Pescia

Five districts called *quinti* – four on the right and one on the left of the river – form this little town, the capital of Valdinièvole. Pescia's reputation as a trading and manufacturing centre first began to spread in the 14th century. Arriving from the north, you can still see the old paper mills, recognisable by the countless openings of the top-floor drying-rooms. The 'long market' was held in Piazza Mazzini, between Palazzo dei Vicari (13th to 14th century) and the church of the Madonna di Piè di Piazza (1447). A huge flower market has been held here since the 1970s. Carnations are a local speciality.

i *Piazza Castello 118*

▶ *Follow the signs for Collodi.*

8 Collodi

Towering at the foot of this picturesque hilltop village is the large, baroque Villa Garzoni. Its 18th-century gardens, embellished with steps, terraces, statues and water features, are considered among the finest in Italy. A modern Butterfly House has been built to display hundreds of butterflies from all over the world. Lower down is Pinocchio Park, which recreates episodes from the famous story. The author of *Pinocchio's Adventures: Story of a Puppet* (1880), Carlo Lorenzini of Florence, spent his childhood at Collodi, from which he took his pen name.

Villa Garzoni (above) and Pinocchio Park (below) at Collodi

FOR CHILDREN

Children will find that the exciting crossing of the metal bridge, reached from the SS12 just before Popiglio, partially makes up for the numerous bends along the way. This dramatic 1922 structure, less than 1m (3 feet) wide, 220m (722 feet) long and 36m (118 feet) high, is suspended over the Lima river bed. Younger visitors will enjoy exploring the paths of the Pinocchio Park, and unexpected encounters with the characters of the story of the puppet.

▶ *Back at Pescia, follow the signs for Montecatini Terme.*

9 Montecatini Terme

Long before Grand Duke Peter Leopold encouraged their modern exploitation in the latter part of the 18th century, the sodium-chloride-sulphate-alkaline waters of Montecatini and their healing powers were known to the ancient Romans. A 'canopy' covered the bath in which Florentine noblemen and gentlemen practised water therapy in 1417. Today, a refined early 20th-century atmosphere surrounds the spas and grand hotels of this airy garden-town. For a real taste of the spa experience, visit the Tettuccio, with its travertine-stone colonnades and the sumptuous tap-rooms rebuilt in 1925; the classical-style Terme Leopoldine, built in 1777; and the art nouveau baths of the Excelsior (the former town casino, converted to a spa in 1915). A scenic route (there is also a funicular railway) climbs to Montecatini Alto.

i *Viale Verdi 66–68*

▶ *After taking the A11 motor-way towards Florence, exit at Pistoia and take the SS66 to Poggio a Caiano.*

🔟 Poggio a Caiano

Designed by Giuliano da Sangallo (*c*1445–1535), the splendid Medici villa of Poggio a Caiano was the prototype for new aristocratic residences. The formerly inaccessible fortress was transformed to open on to the landscape, with a wide ground-floor portico and a loggia on Ionic columns surmounted by a tympanum (the glazed terracotta frieze is a copy of the original, inside). The decoration is rich with humanistic references to the classical period: characters from ancient Rome are shown in frescoes in the central hall, overshadowing the man who commissioned the work, Lorenzo il Magnifico, and his father Cosimo.

The villa has witnessed its share of drama. In 1587, the Grand Duke Francesco I and his beloved second wife Bianca Cappello died here just a few hours apart; she was unpopular with her subjects and there was

Water, marble and paintings at the Terme Leopoldine

talk of poison (although the true cause of death may have been malaria). After Italian unification, King Vittorio Emanuele II (1820–78) stayed here with Rosa Vercellana (the famous 'Bella Rosina'), who became his wife.

i *Piazza dei Medici*

▶ *Follow the signs for the town of Prato.*

1️⃣1️⃣ Prato

The symbolic figure of Prato is merchant banker Francesco di Marco Datini (1330–1410), who created a financial empire with branches all over Europe. His mansion is a remarkable example of a pre-Renaissance residence, its exterior once entirely covered in frescoes. The industrious modern town – seems to have inherited the manufacturing genius of the 13th century, when this was the Tuscan capital of wool cloth, a tradition revived in the 19th and 20th centuries and celebrated in the impressive museum.

Art treasures adorn the Romanesque-Gothic Duomo (13th–14th century). The external pulpit by Michelozzo (1396–1472) has dancing *putti* on its parapet, sculpted by Donatello (*c*1386–1466). Inside

are fresco cycles by Agnolo Gaddi (1333–96), Paolo Uccello (*c*1396–1475) and Fra' Filippo Lippi (1406–69). The mighty turreted walls of the Castello dell'Imperatore, built by Frederick II between 1237 and 1248, are reminiscent of the Swabian castles of Puglia and Sicily. A few steps away is Santa Maria delle Carceri, a perfect example of a Greek cross church, built by Giuliano da Sangallo between 1485 and 1505.

i *Piazza Duomo 8*

▶ *Return to Pistoia along the road running at the foot of the hills, via Montale.*

SCENIC ROUTES

Much of the route between Pistoia and Pescia is scenic. If you have an off-road vehicle, you can cut out numerous winding miles by turning left, just before Lucchio, on to the rough cart track to Pontito. From here an asphalt road descends to Pescia. This is a magnificent excursion – also recommended from Pescia – through picturesque fortified villages perched on both sides of the valley.

FROM MAREMMA TO THE SEA

Maremma, in Tyrrhenian Tuscany, stretches from the mouth of the Cècina river to Tarquinia (in Lazio) and beyond, along a sweep of sandy coastline, mainly flat but punctuated with the heights of the Piombino headland, Punta Ala and mounts Uccellina and Argentario. It extends across no fewer than three provinces – Livorno, Pisa and Grosseto – and encompasses a variety of landscapes. In the northern hinterland are the Mediterranean *maquis* and evergreen wood vegetation of the beautiful Livorno hills, parallel to the coast. Central inland Maremma runs to the slopes of the metalproducing hills, where it reaches the greater heights of the Cornate di Girifalco and Poggio di Montieri, which rise above 1,000m (3,280 feet), cloaked with chestnut and other trees.

The region flourished in Etruscan and Roman times, before marshland encroached on the protective dunes of the coastal plain and drove the inhabitants away. In subsequent centuries Maremma was a desolate, malarial wetland, where the average life span before 1840 was less than 20 years. The 20th century brought reclamation (with the Cècina, Cornia, Bruna, Ombrone and Albegna rivers serving as outfall drains), and created the new geometric pattern of roads, canals and hydraulic engineering works that today seems part of the natural landscape. Malaria is a thing of the past, and the Maremma coastline has re-established itself as a holiday area; but the region's traditional image of silent pools, horses and 'cowboys', reeds and marshy ground beneath *maquis*, water, sky and wind can still be found, preserved in the Uccellina Park.

Volterra, Massa Marittima, Sovana and Pitigliano are just some of the memorable Tuscan locations that provide intriguing insights into the medieval way of life. Off the coast, beyond the Piombino channel, the isle of Elba – the most famous and largest island in the Tuscan archipelago – attracts seaside and other tourism with its extraordinary mosaic of natural scenery.

The wild boar, an animal typical of Maremma (and its cuisine)

Tour 6

Maremma's Livorno coastline is high and rocky as far as Castiglioncello; from there to the Piombino headland it's flat and sandy, and often protected by pinewoods. Having rid itself of its gloomy past as a deserted malarial zone, it has transformed itself into a splendid seaside location. The tour leaves the coast at Cècina and heads for Volterra, before venturing into the metal-producing hills amid the white industrial vapours of the 'Valley of Hell'. Back on the coast, ancient Etruria and the feudal Middle Ages are conjured up by the fascinating remains of two mining centres – Populonia and Rocca San Silvestro – before the tour heads for a poet's birthplace and an ancient coastal sanctuary.

Tour 7

An arm of wind-blown sea, just over 8km (5 miles) wide, separates Piombino from the isle of Elba – an island of beauty and light with a surprisingly mild climate. At 27km (17 miles) long and 18km (11 miles) wide – but less than 4km (2 miles) wide at its narrowest point – this is the largest and most famous tourist destination in Tyrrhenian Tuscany. Starting from Portoferraio, this tour visits the lesser known features – tiny sanctuaries, inland villages, romantic churches, strongholds and fortresses, mountain springs, chestnut groves and disused mines – without neglecting Elba's two best-known attractions: the beaches and Napoleon Bonaparte.

Tour 8

The Etruscans and the Romans managed to do for Maremma what the medieval feudal power of Pisa and Siena could not do. They saved it from disintegrating into marshland by creating *tombolos* (sand dunes) to obstruct the river flow. As the marshes took over during the later period of neglect, the populated centres were abandoned, and their inhabitants withdrew to the hills. The wild Uccellina Park, where this tour begins, is all that survives of that marshy

Sweeping view of Marciana and Capo Sant'Andrea, Elba

world, which was subsequently erased by 19th- and 20th-century reclamation. After exploring the coastline, the route turns inland to retrace the glorious path of a thousand-year history in the magnificent city of Massa Marìttima and the ancient stones of Vetulonia and Roselle.

Tour 9

This tour combines the evocative legacies of a medieval past – at Sovana, Sorano and Pitigliano – with the charm of a landscape covered with *maquis*, furrowed by ravines and gullies and scattered with the Etruscan 'ways' and burial grounds of the 'tufa lands'. On reaching the sea, at Orbetello and the Argentario, the Etruscan and Roman remains blend with the pinewoods and protected wetlands, and provide a contrast with the more obvious attractions of seaside holiday beaches and tourist marinas.

The Maremma
around Livorno

With its sunny squares and breezy seafront, Livorno is the newest Tuscan city – in more than one sense. Originally created in 1577 by Grand Duke Francesco I de'Medici, it was built anew nearly 400 years later, after being badly damaged by World War II bombing.

3 DAYS • 324KM • 201 MILES

Above: Castiglioncello's beach
Below: alabaster plaque

ℹ️ *Piazza Cavour 6; Piazza del Municipio 6; Porto Mediceo, Livorno*

▶ *Follow Viale Italia along the shore, southbound to Ardenza.*

❶ Ardenza

Drive past the houses and 19th- and 20th-century kiosks and bathing establishments, many built in art nouveau style. Continue beyond the Accademia Navale (1878) and hippodrome (1869) to the semicircular neo-classical Casini d'Ardenza, built in 1844 to the model of the 18th-century Royal Crescent in Bath. Its several self-contained units were originally rented holiday houses. The great seaside holi-day boom was just beginning at this time, in a revival of the 18th-century tradition of summer escape captured in Carlo Goldoni's *Villegiatura Trilogy* (1761), set on the Montenero hill (see Tour 13).

▶ *Continue along the coast road to Castiglioncello.*

❷ Castiglioncello

With its inlets, sandy shores and rocks shaded by pine and ilex trees, this is the headland of the seaside resort of Castiglioncello, guarded by a Medici watch-tower. The most notable sights are the Pasquini castle (an annual theatre and dance festival is held in its grounds) and the National Archaeological Museum – an Etruscan temple reconstructed between 1912 and 1914.

ℹ️ *Via Aurelia 967*

▶ *Travel south to the SS1. Drive towards Grosseto as far as the exit for the SS68 and Volterra.*

❸ Volterra

Severe, grey Volterra perches 531m (1,742 feet) on its hill overlooking the subsiding Cretaceous chasm of the Balze. In the 5th and 4th centuries BC, the original Velathri had 25,000 inhabi-tants – twice as many as the town now has. It was one of the 12 great Etruscan towns, exporting wheat, iron and alabaster all over the Mediterranean. Exceptional funerary urns (including the famous Sposi urn, 1st century BC) and the bronze Ombra della Sera (3rd century BC) can be seen in the Mario Guarnacci Etruscan Museum, part of which dates from 1732. The free *Comune* proclaimed in 1193 built the Duomo (cathedral) and octagonal baptistery facing it, as well as the nearby square on which stands the Palazzo dei Priori, begun in 1208, and considered the oldest town hall in Tuscany. After sacking the town during the War of Volterra (1472–5), the Florentines consolidated their power by adding the Rocca Nuova to the 14th-century

A spectacular view of the Balze, the landslide close to Volterra

Rocca Vecchia. The whole complex is now used as a prison, and is not open to the public.

Two of Volterra's artistic treasures should not be missed – the Gothic chapel of the Croce di Giorno in San Francesco, entirely frescoed in 1410 by Cenni di Francesco Cenni, and the *Deposition* (now in the Art Gallery and Civic Museum), painted for the same chapel by Rosso Fiorentino in 1521.

i Via G Turazza

▶ Return along the **SS68** to Saline di Volterra and turn left on to the **SS439**. After Pomarance turn left for San Dalmazio and follow the signs to the Rocca di Sillano.

4 Rocca di Sillano

After passing the ruins of a 13th-century parish church on the right, the road reaches a barrier and a steep dirt track that leads to the considerable remains of the Rocca di Sillano stronghold; its high tower is visible from afar. During the 1200s, it belonged to the bishops, then to the *comune* (municipality) of Volterra. Modernised in the 15th century by the Florentines, it is owned by the *Comune* and has been restored. The original three rings of walls can be made out, but the central polygonal construction survives and the top (reached with caution) offers a superb view of the ravines below.

▶ Return to the **SS439** and continue southwards to Montecèrboli.

5 Montecèrboli

Clustered around a Romanesque brick parish church, this village sits like a medieval balcony over the steaming landscape of the 'Valley of Hell'. Boric acid fumeroles rise amid the flaring silhouettes of an electric power station's cooling towers, some up to 75m (246 feet) high, and a great spider's web of silver-coloured pipelines spreads over valley and hill as far as the eye can see.

▶ Drive on and turn left almost immediately for Larderello.

6 Larderello

The Museum of Geothermal Energy, housed in the ENEL (National Electricity Board) management offices while it awaits transfer to the Palazzo de Larderel, is the first stop on a visit to a geothermal power station and its covered lake. The Larderello plants originally extracted boric acid from the lake waters, but since 1905 this work has been increasingly supplemented by the conversion of steam energy into electricity. Boric acid production continues, but now uses colemanite, a boric mineral imported from Turkey and Argentina. It's worth a visit to the unusual church built in 1956–8 by Giovanni Michelucci for the modern residential centre constructed by ENEL.

i Museum of Geothermal Energy, Piazza Leopolda

▶ Return to the **SS439** and follow it to the **SS398**, which leads to the right via Suvereto to Venturina.

BACK TO NATURE

Northeast of Piombino, between the Vignale-Riotorto road and the sea, past an intimidating cluster of smokestacks, lies the well-equipped Sterpaia Park, criss-crossed with paths that venture into the lush vegetation of the dunes behind the beach.

7 Venturina

Two large open-air thermal pools are the reason for a stop here. The Terme di Caldana waters maintain a temperature of 32°C (90°F), and the small, crystal-clear, gravel-bed Calidario lake is overlooked by the remains of the old ironworks and the paper mill that exploited the spring waters. Open all year round until late at night, the pools provide a refreshing solution to the strain of long hours at the wheel.

i *Via Roma, Campiglia Maríttima*

➤ *Continue on the SS398 to the southwest to Piombino.*

FOR HISTORY BUFFS

François-Jacques de Larderel set up his boric acid extracting factory in 1818. In 1827 he had the ingenious idea of building a brick dome over the bubbling 'lake' and using the steam to heat the boilers where the boric solution was concentrated. Grand Duke Leopold II was sufficiently impressed to make him Count of Montecèrboli in 1837; the village that grew up around the plant – an enlightened example of industrial paternalism – was given the name of Larderello in 1846.

The 15th-century Rocca dominates Populonia

8 Piombino

The expansion of the metal and steel industry and the great movement of people and goods to the isle of Elba have practically erased all trace of Piombino's past. From 1399 to 1815 this was the capital of the small independent state run by the Appiani family of Pisa and their descendants. To rediscover it you must climb to Piazza Citadella, converted to a residence by the Appiani family in 1465–70. Near the scenic Piazza Bovio, protruding into the sea, are the 12th-century port and the marble water fountains of the Canali springs, dated 1248.

i *Via de Amicis 23*

➤ *Drive back along the SS398 and go left for San Vincenzo; turn at the junction signposted on the left for Populonia.*

9 Populonia

At the foot of the Populonia headland, the road skirts the pine-shaded dunes that edge the charming Baratti gulf before arriving, on the left, at the necropolis site (7th–6th century BC), the only large Etruscan centre right on the sea. Here, from the 6th century BC to the

3rd century AD, workers processed the haematite that was brought across from the isle of Elba. The huge mounds of slag that accumulated on various types of tombs (including trench, chamber, tumulus and tambour) were removed by companies exploiting their high mineral residue between the 1920s and 1960s. On the rise behind the site is an Etruscan sandstone quarry, reused as a necropolis in the Hellenistic period (4th–2nd century BC).

The Larderello boric acid fumarole, with vapours pouring out of the cooling towers

Modern Populonia, set 170m (558 feet) up, is a tiny village dominated at the entrance by a 15th-century stronghold constructed by the Appiani family. There are fantastic views from the large grass clearing before it and even better ones from the top of the central tower.

▶ *After reaching San Vincenzo to the north, turn right for Campiglia Marittima and drive to Madonna della Fucinaia; here an unsurfaced road on the left leads to the Temperino Mining Park.*

10 Rocca di San Silvestro
A shuttle service leaves from the Temperino Mining Park visitor centre to pass through working quarries to the Rocca di San Silvestro, a spectacular fortified village at the top of an isolated spur. A return on foot allows you to visit mines dating from Etruscan times to the 20th century. The structures of the Rocca are quite clearly visible, thanks to recent excavations. The village was built in the 10th century to exploit the local copper, silver and lead, and was abandoned in the mid-14th century. After the guided tour of the Temperino mine, visit the Etruscan foundry furnaces (5th–4th century BC) on the left at the point where the park road meets the road to Campiglia.

i *Via Roma, Campiglia Maríttima (seasonal)*

RECOMMENDED WALK

A path descends from the clearing on the left of the road up to Populonia to reach the sea in less than an hour, passing close to the vast Buche delle Fate necropolis (3rd–1st century BC), not equipped for visitors and still plundered by grave robbers (though with extreme care you can enter numerous underground chamber tombs). Along the coast below, wind and water have eroded the rocks into amazing shapes.

▶ *Back on the asphalt road, continue via Campiglia Marittima to Cafaggio; turn left on the **SS398** to Suvereto and go left again via Sassetta to Castagneto Carducci.*

11 Castagneto Carducci
Coats-of-arms, arches and sculpted decorations are among the numerous reminders in Castagneto of the period between the 13th century and 1749, when the della Gherardesca family ruled the village. Their castle, greatly altered, still stands at the top of the village. Since the last century, however, this rich medieval history has been over-shadowed by memories of celebrated poet Giosuè Carducci (1835–1907), who lived in Castagneto with his family in 1848–9, until his father, Michele, local doctor and member of the independence movement, was dismissed and moved to Florence. An archive museum and the Carducci Centre are dedicated to the poet's memory.

i *Via della Marina 8, Marina di Castagneto-Donoràtico (seasonal)*

▶ *Follow the **SS329** to the **SS1**; turn right and skirt the dual*

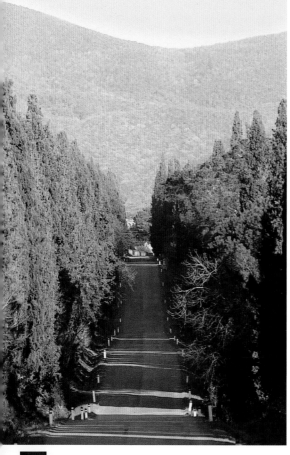

The famous cypress-lined avenue that climbs to Bòlgheri dall'Aurelia

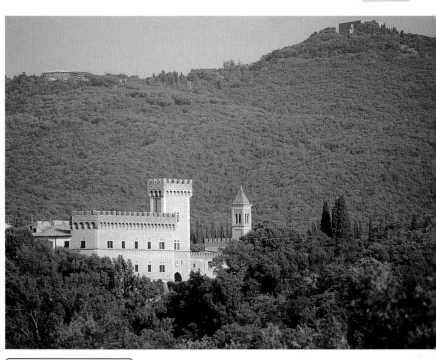

carriageway to San Guido, then right again to Bòlgheri.

12 Bòlgheri

The fame of this village, where Giosuè Carducci spent his childhood from 1838 to 1848, is concentrated in the straight tree-lined avenue that climbs from the Via Aurelia. Its cypress trees, lauded by the poet in a famous work of 1874, still rise to meet travellers between the octagonal oratory (1703),

named after the hermit saint Guido della Gherardesca (10th–11th century), and the rural farming village of Bòlgheri. A turreted gate provides access to the castle, which, since the late 19th century, has incorporated Palazzo della Gherardesca and a Romanesque church.

▶ *Return to the SS1 and drive towards Livorno to the turning signposted on the left for the Santuario di Montenero.*

13 Santuario di Montenero

In 1345, a local shepherd found a picture of the Virgin Mary, brought it to this spot and found himself miraculously cured of a serious illness. The small oratory, consecrated in 1575, was extended and given a baroque-style interior in the 18th century. In the sacristy, a rich collection of votive offerings, mainly from sailors, provides an interesting illustration of the themes of popular devotion. From the church square, 193m (633 feet) up, the

Bòlgheri, in the woody hinterland of Livorno

view sweeps over Livorno and the sea. On a rock off the coast is the Meloria tower, on the site of a naval battle won in 1284 by the Genoese – a victory that marked the decline of Pisa as a seafaring power.

▶ *Follow signs for Livorno centre.*

TUSCAN ISLANDS & BEACHES

Elba, Gorgona, Capraia, Pianosa, Montecristo, Giglio and Giannutri – when the neck-lace adorning Venus' delicate throat broke, its splendid pearls are said to have fallen into the Tyrrhenian Sea and created the seven islands of the Tuscan archipelago. This 'ecological corridor' of islands between the peninsula, Corsica and Sardinia, has been part of a national park since 1989 – one of the largest marine parks in Europe. Despite their popularity, they can still offer havens of peace along the coast, especially in June and September.

Elba, at 223sq km (87 square miles), is the largest and most varied island in the archipelago and the subject of Tour 7.

Gorgona is the northernmost island – 34km (21 miles) from Livorno – as well as the smallest (2.23sq km/0.8 square miles) and greenest. It's entirely mountainous and has been home to a prison farming complex since 1869. Gorgona is only accessible on guided nature excursions from Livorno (Cooperativa Parco Naturale Gorgona, tel: 0586 899760).

Capraia lies 53km (33 miles) from Piombino and is volcanic, elliptical in shape and mountainous, culminating in 44m (144-foot) Monte Castello. Most of its coastline is rocky and inaccessible. The rich Mediterranean *maquis* consists of marine rock-rose, myrtle, lentiscus and rosemary mixed with oleander and arboreal euphorbias. The wild goats that gave the island its name are now extinct, as is the colony of monk seals that once settled here. From the 15th century onwards the island belonged to Genova (Genoa), but in 1815 it passed to the Kingdom of Sardinia. The only inhabited centre, Capraia Isola, features the Genoese fortress of San Giorgio. There is a lovely walk to the Stagnone, a small lake surrounded with buttercups in spring.

Pianosa is low and flat. A neighbour of the isle of Elba,

The gulf of Baratti, just north of Populonia

14km (9 miles) away, it has been a prison since 1858 and is not accessible to the public.

Montecristo, 40km (25 miles) south of Elba, is a granite mass bizarrely sculpted and smoothed by erosion and culminating in 645m (2,116-foot) Monte Fortezza. Wild and inhospitable, it has never been permanently inhabited apart from a settlement of Benedictine and, later, Camaldolensian monks. Their wealth was spirited away after devastating raids by Barbary pirates in 1553, giving rise to the legend of the buried treasure that inspired Alexander Dumas'

1844 novel *The Count of Monte Cristo*. The Savoy family turned the island into a hunting preserve and it is now a marine and land nature reserve, allowing access to no more than 1,000 visitors per year on organised guided trips (Ufficio Forestale di Follònica, tel: 0566 40019).

Giglio, 14km (9 miles) from the Argentario (ferry service from Porto Santo Stefano, also to Giannutri), is almost entirely mountainous, with a generally high coastline that is rugged to the west and in the east has sandy coves equipped for seaside tourism (Giglio Campese). Fragrant *maquis* alternates with rock, and the cultivated vine terraces produce a strong, prized wine called *Ansonica*. The main commercial centre is Giglio Porto and the *comune* is based at Giglio Castello, 6km (4 miles) from the port in the centre of the island. This charming maze of narrow streets, steep steps and medieval houses is dominated by the Pisan Rocca. It was rebuilt after 1544 when the notorious Barbary pirate Barbarossa (Khair-ed-Din) devastated the island and deported the 700 survivors as slaves.

Giannutri, part of the *comune* of Giglio, 16km (10 miles) away, is the southernmost island in the Tuscan archipelago. Its crescent-shaped coastline is nearly all rocky, with two short pebble beaches. Having served as a Roman commercial port, a sanctuary for monks and a Pisan naval base, it is now a private residential estate. Visitors can land on it but may not stay overnight unless invited.

From Viareggio to the Argentario
Tuscany has approximately 300km (186 miles) of coastline, much of which gets crowded in the summer holiday months, especially July and August. Immediately inland, however, from the Apuan Alps to the historical villages in the Livorno hills, there are many rewarding distractions.

The coastline is generally low and sandy, with large beaches and bathing establishments. The terrain rises briefly to the south of Livorno, then again after Baratti in the Piombino headland, at Punta Ala, after Bocca d'Ombrone in the Uccellina mountains, and in Monte Argentario. Stretches of the original coastal dune

landscape can be seen near the Migliarino *maquis* (see Tour 4), in the Uccellina Park (see Tour 8) and around Orbetello (see Tour 9). The principal seaside (and society) resorts are Forte dei Marmi, Viareggio, San Vicenzo and the Baratti gulf, Castiglioncello, Punta Ala and Castiglione della Pescaia, Porto Santo Stefano and Porto Èrcole on the Argentario.

Sun and sea at Punta Ala

The Isle
of Elba

Just an hour's ride on the ferry from Piombino to Portoferraio will bring you to the incredible mosaic of natural scenery that is Elba – gulfs, headlands, precipitous coastline, peaceful bays, Mediterranean *maquis*, abandoned mines, woody mountains and terraced vineyards; and, all around, the deep, blue sea.

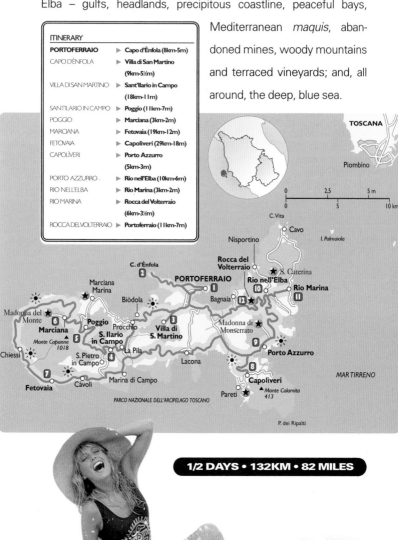

1/2 DAYS • 132KM • 82 MILES

Sansone beach, near Portoferraio

house between 1814 and 1815, and adopted it as his country residence. In fact, he used it only as a stopover during his walks, and never slept here.

▶ *Back on the main road, continue west to Procchio, then left to the Pilà (airport) and right for Sant'Ilario in Campo.*

◆ Sant'Ilario in Campo

Leaving the sandy shores of the Biùdola and Procchio gulfs to the right, climb to the village of Sant'Ilario in Campo (202m/ 663 feet). About 3km (2 miles) further on, towards Poggio, the road passes through fine scenery close to the largest Romanesque church on Elba, the roofless parish church of San Giovanni (12th century). Near by, on a huge granite mound, stands a Pisan defence tower.

▶ *Continue to Poggio.*

◆ Poggio

After passing the charming hamlet of Poggio, you will come to the Fonte di Napoleone, set in a cool wood surrounded by granite rocks. This tiny spa is no longer in use, but if you want to test the diuretic properties of the water – sampled by Napoleon himself when he visited the sanctuary of Marciana – you can buy it bottled, or use the highly popular fountain along the road.

◆ Portoferraio

Cosimo de'Medici and Napoleon Bonaparte were the two men who shaped this town's destiny. In 1548, the former transformed the medieval mining port of Ferraia into the impregnable Cosmopolis, defended on its seaward boundary by three mighty forts – Linguella, Falcone and Stella – and on land by the grand Fronte d'Attacco bastions. The exiled Napoleon landed in the capital of Elba on 3 May, 1814. The Palazzina dei Mulini was adapted for him, and he lived there until 26 February, 1815, when he set out to try and regain power and face his old enemy at Waterloo.

ⓘ *Calata Italia 26*

▶ *Travel west on the coastal road to Capo d'Ènfola.*

◆ Capo d'Ènfola

A strip of land links the island with this sheer, rocky headland (135m/443 feet), covered with shrubbery and edged with the splendid Acquaviva beach. On the approach is a large 18th-century fishery that was in use until a few decades ago.

▶ *Return along the same route and follow the signs for Marciana Marina; turn left for Villa di San Martino just past the Porto Azzurro junction.*

◆ Villa di San Martino

Napoleon added a small two-storey neo-classical building to this originally unpretentious

---

FOR CHILDREN

At San Giovanni, near Portoferraio, a pleasant stop can be made at Elbaland, where horses, goats, sheep, donkeys, peacocks, deer, rabbits, ostriches, ducks, geese and swans live in harmony with visitors beside a toddlers' playground.
In the evenings Amadeus is a delightful amusement park, overlooking the Barbarossa gulf at Sassi Turchini.

▶ *Follow the signs to Marciana.*

⑥ Marciana

Set on the slopes of Monte Capanne (at 1,018m/3,340 feet the highest peak on the island, reached by cableway or path), lies Marciana, a pretty village with narrow winding streets, dominated by the picturesque ruins of the castle taken by the Appiani family of Piombino in 1399. From the village, a road and then a path with a Via Crucis (Way of the Cross) of 14 chapels lead in 45 minutes to the medieval Sanctuary of the Madonna del Monte, rebuilt in the 16th and 17th centuries. In 1814 Napoleon was often a guest at the nearby hermitage; on one visit he was accompanied by Maria Walewska, his Polish lover.

▶ *Return to the coast road and follow it around the west of the island to Fetovaia.*

⑦ Fetovaia

On the way here the route passes a sheer, rugged coastline

RECOMMENDED EXCURSION

South of Capoliveri a fast road leads to Pareti and the Innamorata Bay, surrounded by dazzling marine landscapes and monuments of industrial archaeology. In the early 20th century, this was a fully equipped quay for the export of minerals; now it's a modern ruin, corroded by wind and salt.

Along the coast near Marciana

SPECIAL TO...

At the foot of Marciana is Marciana Marina, at just over 5sq km (2 square miles), the smallest *comune* in Tuscany. It forms a crescent along the beach, with its convenient harbour guarded by a round Pisan tower, 25m (82 feet) high.
Between Marciana Marina and Procchio stretches the delightful Paolina beach, where Napoleon's enigmatic sister indulged in the then scandalous practice of nude sunbathing.

and, not far from Chiessi, the lovely 13th-century church of San Bartolomeo, well worth a visit. At the foot of a rocky outcrop you reach the spectacular sandy beach of Fetovaia, framed by pine trees. Also of note, a short distance further to the east, is the Càvoli beach, a popular area that can get crowded.

▶ *Continue east towards Porto Azzurro to the turning on the right for Capoliveri.*

⑧ Capoliveri

At the Roman Caput Liberum, preceded by the remains of the Romanesque church of San Michele (late 12th century), you enter Elba's mining territory. Nowadays, in fact, the local economy relies mainly on tourists from all over the world. A scenic road high above the sea offers views of the former iron mines of Monte Calamita (413m/1,355 feet), at the foot of which lie some of the island's wildest and most unspoiled beaches.

▶ *Return the same way, following signs for Porto Azzurro.*

Porto Azzurro

Porto Azzurro lies on a fiord in the Mola Gulf, an area which, during the 17th century, was garrisoned by the Spanish. They built the Focardo fort, to the southeast, and the mighty star-shaped Longone fortress (now used as a prison; the town was called Porto Longone from 1863 to 1947) at the opposite end of the bay. North of Porto Azzurro, today a renowned holiday resort with a leisure-boat marina, a path climbs to the Sanctuary of the Madonna di Monserrato

spurs raised by the Appiani family in the 16th century. To the north of the village is the hermitage of Santa Caterina, surrounded by fragrant rose bushes.

▶ *Descend eastwards to Rio Marina.*

Rio Marina

Protected by a 16th-century hexagonal tower, the small bay overlooked by Rio Marina – once a mining centre – is enclosed within red-ochre

ferrous rocks. In the village, where the houses shine with specks of iron, the Elba Mineral Museum displays minerals extracted on the island. Near by, enthusiasts can search for haematite and magnetite crystals among the gigantic tiers of an old open-air mine. The famous beaches of Bagnaia, Nisporto and Nisportino lie to the west of the village.

▶ *Back at the Rio nell'Elba junction, proceed eastwards to the Rocca del Volterraio.*

The Volterraio stronghold

(1606), where a copy of the Black Madonna of the monastery of Monserrat in Catalonia is venerated.

▶ *Continue northeast to Rio nell'Elba.*

Rio nell'Elba

Reddish rocks near Rio nell'Elba bear witness to the ancient mining activities of this area. Etruscans came here seeking supplies of iron minerals for the furnaces of Populonia. The church at the centre of the village is defended by fortified

RECOMMENDED WALK

Terranera is an emerald-green lake of sulphurous sodium chloride, sodium iodide and bromine waters. This surreal place is surrounded by red rocks and yellow broom, and separated from the sea by a strip of light-coloured sand. Take the road from Porto Azzurro to Rio nell'Elba and turn right just after the turning for the Madonna di Monserrato, at the sign 'Residenza Reale'. The final descent is on foot; the spectacle of the lake and its setting is without equal.

Rocca del Volterraio

After a few kilometres the ruins of the Volterraio stronghold appear, perched on their rock. The complex developed around a Pisan watch-tower (built, according to legend, by the Etruscan Queen Ilva), and its arches, wells, vaults and military patrol walks can be reached along a footpath. Splendid views of the coast accompany the descent to Le Grotte and the remains of a Roman villa dating from the 1st century AD, arranged around a large pool.

▶ *Follow the signs west back to Portoferraio.*

The Maremma
near Grosseto

3 DAYS • 248KM • 154 MILES

Grosseto, the commercial and administrative hub of Maremma, is a modern-looking town, though the old centre still survives, enclosed within the strong hexagonal walls erected by the Medici family in 1564–93. A delightful half-hour walk takes you all the way round.

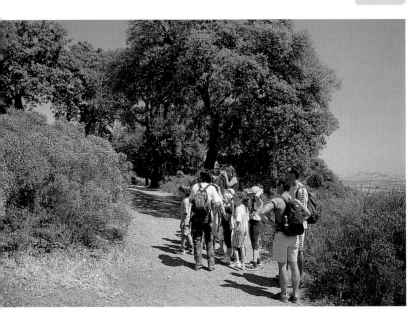

The Maremma Park in Alberese

ℹ️ *Viale Monterosa 206, Grosseto*

▶ *Follow the SS1 southbound to Santa Maria di Rispescia, then signs for Alberese and the Maremma (or Uccellina) Nature Park Visitor Centre.*

❶ Parco Naturale della Maremma

The Uccellina mountains, the Marina di Alberese pinewood, the mouth of the Ombrone river and the Trappola marsh make up Uccellina Park, a microcosm of classic Maremma, where cowboys on horseback oversee the grazing cattle – distinctive for their long lyre-shaped horns – and horses roam half-wild. Paths in the park include a 6km (4-mile) circular walk (5 hours) across *maquis* and hills to the ruined abbey of San Rabano (11th to 12th century), and a 5km (3-mile) circular walk (3 hours) to the watch-towers (13th and 16th century), taking in all the major ecosystems en route. A 12km (7-mile) walk (6 hours) runs from the coast to the splendid beach of Cala di Forno.

ℹ️ *Via del Fante*

▶ *Return to Grosseto and take the SS322 west to Castiglione della Pescaia.*

❷ Castiglione della Pescaia

Climb from the picturesque port-canal, crowded with fishing vessels and leisure craft, to the medieval district, perched on a spur of rock. The formidable ring of Pisan walls and towers (12th to 13th century) was reinforced during the occupation of the Aragonese (1446–60) with the restoration of the triangular stronghold. Today, Castiglione is a renowned seaside resort; to the southeast, it boasts an endless sandy shore framed by the large pines and dunes that skirt the Diaccia Botrona nature reserve.

ℹ️ *Piazza Garibaldi 6*

▶ *Continue along the SS322 to the turning on the left for Punta Ala.*

Sunset in the Maremma Park

'*Butteri*', Maremma's cowboys

3 Punta Ala

Until 1932 this resort was known as Capo Troia. It acquired its new name, which means 'Wing Point', when the entire area was bought by the Fascist government member and aviator Count Italo Balbo (1896–1940). A luxury tourist zone, with lavish apartments and a glitzy marina, has developed among the dense *maquis* that covers the headland, and, slightly further north, is Cala Violina, a beautiful bay with sand that crunches musically beneath your feet. The Hidalgo or Barbiere tower (1577) is an outpost of the State of Piombino, on the border with the Grand Duchy of Tuscany; there's also a contemporary tower, known as the Troia (or Balbo castle).

▷ *Back on the SS322, continue northwards to Follònica.*

4 Follònica

The highly unusual church of San Leopoldo sits in the centre of town. Its portico, bell tower, altar, candelabra and pulpit all feature extensive use of ornately fashioned cast iron, produced between 1836 and 1838 by the old foundries of Great Duke Leopold II, who encouraged the industry as part of the Maremma reclamation programme. Once a

---

RECOMMENDED WALK

On the road from Grosseto, a small turning on the right, just before the bridge over Castiglione della Pescaia canal, leads to Casa Rossa Ximenes. This houses a multimedia museum that gives a fine introduction to the Diaccia Botrona nature reserve. Cameras placed in the reserve relay live film to the museum enabling unprecedented observation of the birds and animals, without any disturbance to the fragile ecosystem.

simple hamlet, Follònica is now the second major urban centre of Grosseto province and a popular beach resort.

i Via Giacomelli 11–13

▶ Take the **SS439** to the foot of Massa Marìttima; turn left and follow the signs for the Centro Carapax.

Punta Ala, the Cala Violina beach

this, a breathtaking arched bridge, 22m (72 feet) long, connects the Sienese keep to the older Candeliere tower with a fine view from the top. The Città Vecchia boasts a splendid, sloping medieval square, overlooked by the buildings of episcopal and lay power. By a skilful play of perspective, the arches on the façade of the magnificent 12th–13th-century Romanesque-Gothic Duomo

origins. The mineral reserves were exploited in neolithic times and made the city the most prosperous in the region. Its wealth produced its many superb buildings, but also attracted the attentions of the Sienese, who conquered it in 1335. Later it was decimated by plague and poverty, and only recovered in the 19th century.

i Via Todini 3–5

5 Centro Carapax
This European centre for the protection of tortoises and turtles has recently closed.

▶ Return to the junction with the SS439 and follow the signs to the centre of Massa.

6 Massa Marìttima
Massa Marìttima has two separate centres. The lower Città Vecchia is the hub of civic activities, while the Città Nuova, a development started in 1228, sits higher up. Between the two is the fortress built by Siena to control the people of Massa after their subjugation in 1335. To pass from one centre to the other you must go through the Silici Gate; near

(cathedral) of San Cerbone seem to grow narrower as you walk towards the end of the square. Opposite is the Palazzo Pretorio or Podestà (1225–35), which houses an archaeological museum containing fossils from the Miocene era, as well as Roman and Etruscan finds from the local area. The Museo di Arte Sacra houses one of the most impressive altarpieces in the area, the colourful *Majesty* created in 1340 by Ambrogio Lorenzetti, and celebrating the figures of Faith, Hope and Charity, as well as depicting the 6th-century saint Cerbone with his flock of geese.

A few steps away, the Mining Museum commemorates Maremma's mining

SPECIAL TO...

At Massa Marìttima, the recent restoration of the Fonti dell'Abbondanza (1265, named after the public granary above) uncovered a fresco of a 'fertility tree' with male penises hanging from its branches. Women converse beneath its foliage; two are fighting over one of the unusual 'fruits', while another chases the crows that are about to eat them. This is an exceptionally rare find in Italy: most representations of this theme are more circumspect, depicting men and women hanging from the branches.

▶ *Back at the junction, continue along the SS439 towards Follònica; enter Valpiana and follow the signs to the left for Lago dell'Accesa. At La Pesta a short unsurfaced road leads to the lake.*

7 Lago dell'Accesa

Clear blue waters flow under-ground at a constant temperature of 20°C (68°F) in a hollow surrounded by meadows and wooded hills. The pale sand bed plunges at the centre to a depth of 45m (148 feet). This unspoiled corner of Maremma is a haven for the swimmers who venture into the marsh grass, sedge and water lilies of its shores.

▶ *Drive on and take the provin-cial road on the left to Ribolla; shortly after the junction, turn right on to an unsurfaced estate road and proceed for 2.6km (1.5 miles) to a derelict farm on the right.*

Piazza Garibaldi in Massa Marittima; on the left are the steps leading up to the Duomo

8 Castello di Pietra

Leave the car and in just a few minutes you can climb to the precipitous ruins of a castle, whose presence was first recorded in 1067. During the 13th century it belonged to the Pannocchieschi family; one of them – Nello – is said to have brought his Sienese wife, Pia dei Tolomei, here and killed her so that he could marry the power-ful Margherita Aldobrandeschi. The unfortunate Pia makes an appearance in Dante's *Inferno*, and an ominous sign among the ruins marks the spot known as the Countess's Leap.

▶ *Back on the provincial road, proceed right via Ribolla towards Roccastrada to the turning on the left for Montemassi.*

9 Montemassi

You will already have seen the crenellated silhouette of Montemassi castle. This Pannocchieschi fortress was besieged in a daring campaign by Guidoriccio da Fogliano,

> SPECIAL TO...
>
> In the 15th century, the Tolomei family of Siena – who had a mansion near by – had a bell cast in gold, silver and bronze in memory of their relative Pia (see Castello di Pietra). The bell was installed in Montepescali's clock tower and connected to a mechanical wheeled clock with a single face. A second 'inverted' face was used to correct the time from the inside. This can still be seen engraved on the wall – but all trace of the bell and clock has been lost.

captain of the Sienese army. In 1328 Simone Martini celebrated his victory in a fresco in the Palazzo Pubblico in Siena. Behind the captain, he shows the temporary wood and stone structure erected by the Sienese in the course of the siege. Only the ruins of the stronghold, with its unmistakable octagonal tower, now survive.

Detail of the frescoes at the Fonti dell'Abbondanza, Massa Marittima

marked the beginning of a crisis, when nearby Populonia seized its monopoly of the iron and maritime trades. The ruins of its 5km (3 miles) of polygonal-block walls are all that survive of past grandeur in the town itself; archaeological sites at the entrance to the town and near the cemetery date from Roman times (2nd–1st century BC). Even the name was lost for a while – it became known as Colonna di Buriano, until a royal decree of 1887 restored the name of Vetulonia.

On the northeastern slopes of the hill are the impressive tombs of a necropolis called Via dei Sepolcri. The Pietrera tumulus (7th century BC) measures 60m (197 feet) in diameter.

▶ *Return to Braccagni and follow the old Aurelia road southbound, turning left for the SS223 Siena-Grosseto; to the north, this leads to the turning signposted on the left for Roselle.*

13 Roselle

The history of Etruscan Roselle mirrors that of Vetulonia. Situated on the opposite shore of Lake Prile, it flourished from the end of the 6th century BC as its rival declined, and based its fortunes on farming. Conquered by the Romans in 294 BC, it continued to prosper until the 1st century BC and was not abandoned until 1138, when the bishop of Roselle moved to Grosseto.

Straddling two deserted hills, gigantic Etruscan walls surround considerable Roman remains – streets, a medieval tower, the imperial forum, outline of the amphitheatre, and spa (reused as a church in the 5th and 6th centuries), as well as the foundations of houses and public buildings.

▶ *Back on the SS223 travel southwards to Grosseto.*

▶ *Return to the last junction and continue towards Roccastrada for approximately 5km (3 miles). Turn left at the signpost for Tecnobay and drive 200m (220 yards) to the agriturismo at San Guglielmo.*

10 Abbazia di Giugnano

The ruins of the abbey dedicated to San Salvatore comprise a splendid Romanesque crypt and a colonnade with cross vaults on four columns. You must descend underground to reach it, as the original plan was 3m (10 feet) lower than at present.

Near by stand the Gothic remains of a church. A stone hydraulic structure, also in the area, indicates the site of a former foundry. The name of the centre, San Guglielmo, probably derives from Wilhema of Bohemia, who had a strong following in 13th-century Maremma.

▶ *Continue to Roccastrada, then turn right on the SS73 and drive towards Grosseto until you come to Braccagni; from here proceed to Montepescali.*

11 Montepescali

Montepescali, set in a dominant position on the plain leading to Grosseto, was a feudal territory

belonging to the Aldobrand-eschi family throughout the 13th century. Ultimately, though, it fell within the orbit of Siena, and the city finally took possession of it around 1300. Of considerable note here are the 14th-century church of San Lorenzo (the square which it overlooks has a sweeping view of Maremma and the Giglio island), and the Romanesque San Niccolò (12th–13th century).

▶ *Descend to Braccagni again and travel westwards following the signs for Buriano and then Vetulonia.*

12 Vetulonia

It may seem unlikely now, but Etruscan Vetluna was a seafaring town. In a sculpture dating from the 1st century AD the town is personified as a young man with an oar on his shoulder, and indeed at that time Vetulonia overlooked the large lagoon that extended to the sea and which the Romans called Lake Prile. This was a centre of primary importance in the 8th and 7th centuries BC; it was here that many of the Romans' symbols of power were devised – the *curule* chair (seat of office for Roman officials), the purple-edged toga, the *fasces* (symbolic rod denoting a magistrate's power), and the trumpet of war. But the early 6th century BC

The Tufa Lands
& the Argentario

The name Maremma derives from *mare* – the sea. But there is also an inland Maremma – the Maremma of impenetrable *maquis* and shady gorges, of strongholds and rocky sites, of Etruscan burial places and 'quarry ways' cut into the thick layer of tufa, volcanic rock produced when Monte Amiata and the Bolsena mountains spewed lava over the land where the Albegna now flows.

3 DAYS • 267KM • 166 MILES

ℹ️ *Viale Monterosa 206, Grosseto*

▶ *Follow the SS322 to Scansano.*

❶ Scansano

Until 1897, this village was invaded every year from May to September by Grosseto's leading civil, military and religious authorities. This was the 'summering' – an administrative holiday instigated by the Grand Duke of Lorraine, Leopold II, known as 'Canapone' for his thick red hair. The purpose of the annual exodus was to avoid the worst of the malaria season – an equivalent of the British flight to the Indian hills during the monsoon. In winter the whole process went into reverse, as shepherds and woodcutters descended from the mountains to the coast. The air really is good up here, 500m (1,640 feet) above sea level in the Maremma countryside. From Scansano you can see Monte Amiata and the sea, from the isle of Elba to Civitavecchia in the distance. The wine is also rather good: production of the local tipple *(Morellino)* is celebrated with a grape festival in September.

▶ *Continue along the SS322 to Montemerano.*

❷ Montemerano

The narrow streets and tiny squares of this village clustered on a 303m (994-foot) hillock form a charming medieval picture of one of the most well-preserved centres in the Albegna valley. The fine church of San Giorgio (14th century) has an unusual panel, the 15th-century *Madonna della Gattaiola*. It has survived despite years of use as a granary door, complete with a hole at the bottom to let the cat through. The church is full of treasures, including a superb polyptych.

▶ *Go back to the turning for Saturnia.*

❸ Saturnia

As you arrive in the valley at the foot of Saturnia (294m/964 feet),

Relaxing in the warm waters of Saturnia's natural pools

your nostrils are assailed by a strong smell of sulphur. It emanates from the warm, whitish-blue waters of the Gorello falls, which fume and bounce off perfect natural basins of white travertine stone. Enthusiastic bathers flock here summer and winter, day and night.

A little further on to the right, Via delle Terme leads to two magnificent pools, where the water flowing from a rocky spring is even hotter, at 37°C (99°F). Higher up, on a plateau, is a quiet 19th-century farming village, with good visitor amenities. Marks left by the iron rims of ancient cartwheels are still visible in the paving of Via Clodia, which crosses the monumental Etruscan–Roman south gate (ancient Saturnia was destroyed by Silla in 82 BC). From here a 30-minute walk along a lovely path leads to the spa pools (156m/512 feet).

▶ *Proceed eastwards following
the signs for Sovana.*

4 Sovana
Beyond a tunnel visitors are
confronted by mysterious 'eyes'
hollowed in the tufa rock.
These are the first signs that
you have reached the isolated
town of Sovana, birthplace of
Hildebrand, who became Pope

Pitigliano's houses are built into
the tufa hills

Gregory VII (1073–85). At one
end of the village stand the
ruins of the Rocca
Aldobrandesca (13th–14th
century); at the opposite end is
the solitary Romanesque
Duomo (cathedral, 12th–14th
century). Between the two
stretches the brick-paved village
street. Grouped in the fascinating square are the Palazzo
Pretorio (12th–13th century),
the adjacent Loggia del
Capitano, the Palazzo Archivio,
the ruins of an early-Christian
church (possibly 4th century)
and the Romanesque Santa
Maria (12th–13th century).
All around Sovana lie large
Etruscan necropolises, inter-
laced with beautiful nature
walks. Among the mysterious
'quarry ways' cut precipitously
in the tufa is that of San
Sebastiano, near the Sirena
tomb.

ⓘ *Palazzetto dell'Archivio*

▶ *Follow the signs for Sorano.*

5 Sorano
Watching over the village is the
mighty stronghold built by
Niccolò IV Orsini in 1552 – one
of the most impressive military
structures in Maremma. The
defensive ring of walls that

protect it are reached via a
gateway that displays the
emblems of the Aldobrandeschi
and Orsini families. At its foot,
the village, full of unusually
decorated old buildings,
extends towards Sasso
Leopoldino. This remarkable
rock was incorporated in the
18th century into a sloping wall
surrounded by houses built in
tufa. Huddled together or
perched on the slope, these are
linked by steep streets, covered
and underground passages and
steps. The whole district,
known as Rocca Vecchia, has
suffered the worst of the landslides which have threatened
the existence of Sorano for
nearly 200 years.

Wildfowl in the Monte Argentario nature reserve

i *Piazza Busati*

▶ *Follow the signs to Pitigliano.*

6 Pitigliano

The best place to view this extraordinary spectacle is from the Sanctuary of the Madonna delle Grazie, at the first left-hand bend on the SS74 for Marciano. Even at night, when it's illuminated with floodlights, Pitigliano is an amazing sight.

FOR CHILDREN

Tarot-card characters and mystic visions inhabit the Giardino dei Tarocchi, the park created by Niki de Saint-Phalle in 1979 in an abandoned quarry. The brightly coloured reflecting surfaces of the Wheel of Fortune, the Magician and the High Priestess, the Tower and the Empress combine fun and fairy-tales with an unsettling air of sorcery and spirits. The park is reached along an unsurfaced lane that branches off the Aurelia junction for Pescia Fiorentina.

Its houses sit on the edge of a sheer tufa mass, filled with cavities and dominated by the grandiose arches of the aqueduct (1543–5), designed by Antonio da Sangallo for Gian Francesco Orsini. Set 313m (1,027 feet) up, it was built to a typically Etruscan plan: a spur surrounded on three sides by ravines and fortified on the fourth, with 'quarry ways' leading from the foot of the site. It acquired its medieval-Renaissance appearance thanks to the Orsini family, who ruled between 1293 and the 16th century. They were responsible for the palace-fortress that now houses the Diocesan Museum of Holy Art and the Civic Archaeological Museum. In a side street, a small synagogue (1589) with an unleavened-bread oven is a reminder of the Jewish community that formed here after the expulsion of Jews from Rome by the Papal bull of 1569. The Jewish population diminished as people emigrated to Livorno and Florence, and vanished altogether after the Fascist persecutions. The local

Tha Abbadia bridge across the Fiora river at Vulci

economy now relies heavily on the production of its prized white Pitigliano wine.

i *Piazza Garibaldi 51*

▶ *Take the SS74 to Manciano where you turn left on to the provincial road to Ponte dell'Abbadia (Vulci).*

7 Ponte dell'Abbadia

Anyone crossing the bridge over the Flora river had to pass under the arched walls and tower of the

The bay and port of Porto Ercole

Badia castle, a 12th-century Cistercian building restructured in the 16th century. This formed the customs post between the Papal State and the Grand Duchy of Tuscany; today it houses the Vulci National Museum. Vulci was – especially in the 7th and 6th centuries BC – one of southern Etruria's main trading and manufacturing centres. The museum houses

---

FOR HISTORY BUFFS

In 1557 Philip II, the King of Spain, yielded his Sienese territory to Cosimo I de'Medici, although he maintained control of a number of fortresses on the Tyrrhenian coast. Thus was born the administrative area known as Stato dei Presidi, comprising Orbetello, the capital, Porto Ercole, Monte Argentario and Porto Santo Stefano. The Presidi then passed to the Austrians (1714) and the Bourbons of Naples (1738) before eventually being incorporated in the Kingdom of Etruria (1801) and then in the reconstituted Grand Duchy of Tuscany (1815).

---

what little remained after Lucien Bonaparte started excavating in 1828.

Near by, you can visit the town's remains and necropolis, including the maze-like Cuccummella tumulus and the tomb of François (4th century BC), once famous for containing the only cycle of wall paintings with an 'historical' subject handed down by the Etruscans. The paintings were removed in the 1800s and most of the cycle is on display in the Torlonia collection of Villa Albani in Rome.

▶ *Follow the signs for Montalto di Castro to the SS1 (Aurelia); turn right on to this and exit at Pescia Romana to reach the coast, which leads westwards to Ansedonia.*

8 Ansedonia
Ansedonia does not exist – it was totally destroyed by the Sienese in 1330. Today's elegant resort is made up of villas and visitor amenities dotted across the slopes of a hill, at the top of which stand the ruins of the flourishing Roman town of Cosa, founded in 273 BC. Remains of the old quays crumble into the waves, but the silting of the port at the foot of the rise is

prevented by the regulation of the flow and ebb of waters, using the so-called Tagliata Etrusca (Etruscan Channel). Before the Romans dug this tunnel from the rock, drainage was guaranteed by the breathtaking Spacco della Regina Channel, on the other side of the Tagliata and now blocked in its final section. The nearby Torre della Tagliata (15th century), along with the remains of a Roman villa, was occupied by Puccini when composing part of his opera *Tosca*.

▶ *Continue across the Ansedonia hill (signposted to the right is the Cosa archaeological site) and return to the SS1; after 3km (2 miles), turn left for Orbetello.*

9 Orbetello
Orbetello perches on a strip of land extended by a dam built in 1842 and now reaching the Argentario, dividing the lagoon in two. The town's military past is preserved in the remains of Etruscan walls and 15th-century Sienese and 16th- to 18th-century Spanish fortifications. At the town library is the terracotta pediment of the Etruscan temple of Talamone (2nd century BC). It is not known

whether the Argentario ('silver') headland (then an island) was named after the shiny rocks or the office of *argentarii* (bankers) exercised by the Romans who governed the area.

⌐i⌐ *Piazza della Repubblica 1*

▶ *After reaching the Argentario, follow the signs to the left for Porto Èrcole.*

⑩ Porto Èrcole
This seaside resort and tourist marina sits on a bay overlooked by a circle of 16th-century forts and bastions. A splendid old village occupies the foot of the headland, where the Rocca (fort) looms. A pointed gate leads to a maze of covered passages, low arches and steps hewn into the rock. The powerful defence system of Porto Èrcole (founded by the Romans) comprises the quadrangular Filippo fort (1558, private) and the original Stella fort.

⌐i⌐ *Via Caravaggio 78*

▶ *Drive around the edge of Monte Argentario, following the signs for Cala Piccola and Porto Santo Stefano, on a splendidly scenic but winding road, with a difficult unsurfaced section approximately 4km (2.5 miles) long immediately after Porto Ercole. Those wishing to avoid this section can go back along the SS440 to the Tombolo della Giannella.*

⑪ Porto Santo Stefano
A group of Genoese sailors was shipwrecked here in the 15th century and stayed put to live as fishermen. This is the centre that suffered most damage during the bombing raids of World War II. Its post-war reconstruction spared the old centre, clustered around the 17th-century stronghold, and the village is now kept alive by the busy tourist trade passing through the port, that serves the Giglio and Giannutri islands.

⌐i⌐ *Corso Umberto 55*

▶ *Take the SS440 towards Orbetello and turn left for the Tombolo della Giannella as far as the SS1; drive 8km (5 miles) towards the Grosseto exit at Fonteblanda to reach Talamone to the west.*

⑫ Talamone
This was called Tlamu by the Etruscans and Telamon by the Romans, when it was the main port of the Albegna valley towns. At that time it extended between the Bengodi and Talamonaccio hills. The site of today's lively fishing village was established in the Middle Ages, and is dominated by the mighty Rocca, erected by the Sienese in the 15th century.

⌐i⌐ *Piazzale del Porto (seasonal)*

▶ *Take the SS1 back to Grosseto.*

Fishing in the Orbetello lagoon

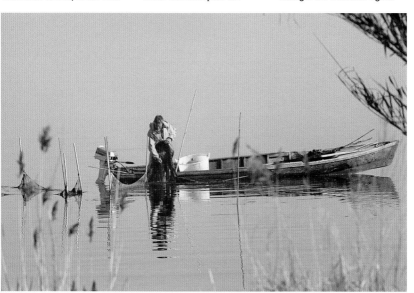

NORTHEAST TUSCANY

This area was historically part of Florence's first dominion; today it lies within the provinces of Florence and Arezzo. Mugello, northeast of the regional capital, is a vast hollow in the mountains, crossed by the Sieve river, which flows through the valley of the same name into the Arno. The hills around Florence gradually dissolve into the alluvial plain of the lower Valdarno, and the river basins of the Elsa and Era also flow into the Arno. Val d'Elsa (the Elsa Valley), wedged between the Chianti hills, which separate it to the east from Val di Pesa and the ridge of heights that extend from San Gimignano to San Miniato, was once one of the main through-routes between northern and southern Tuscany.

Between the upper Valdarno and the Sieve are the rounded meadow-covered hills of the Pratomagno. To the west lies the Casentino, a deep hollow in the upper reaches of the Arno, with a landscape of turreted hill-villages, castles and parish churches, climbing from the vineyards and olive groves of the valley floor to chestnut groves, meadows and extensive, ancient fir woods. On the plain, you travel through the Upper Val Tiberina, the Tuscan stretch of the Tiber Valley, past mountain springs and Sansepolcro. After an excursion to Città di Castello in Umbria, you cross the farming region of Valdichiana, southwest of Arezzo.

Of the rich and varied attractions found in this part of Tuscany, the foremost are those in Florence; a remarkable Renaissance showpiece, crammed with the very best of that exceptional era's artistic output. In Tuscany a city is wherever there is a square, a church and a mansion; other splendid examples include San Miniato, tiny Certaldo, San Gimignano and Cortona. Out in the countryside there are more treasures: the Medici villas, monasteries and hermitages hidden in the silent, dark green woods. Art is omnipresent, and deserves its own tours – such as that of Piero della Francesca, from Arezzo to Anghiari and Sansepolcro.

Palazzo Pitti seen from the Bòboli gardens in Florence

A wolf in the Casentino forest

Tour 10

Florence is one of the world's most famous cities, a treasure trove of art and architecture. This tour explores it on two circular routes which converge to form a figure of eight on Piazza della Signoria. Make sure you take into account the vast crowds of visitors to museums, churches and chapels (best to book where possible) as well as the incredible wealth of things to see. The Uffizi alone would take several long visits to do it justice.

Tour 11

West of Florence, the urbanised Arno plain was, and still is, a manufacturing, craft and industrial centre. The hunting and the grape-harvests that brought the Medici family here on their holidays are, however, things of the past. Visit the lofty stronghold of the imperial San Miniato before heading south across Val d'Elsa, dotted with its 'dual' towns – the monuments of nobility and power on the hill-tops, the merchant houses and markets lower down. Medieval San Gimignano is an exception, its ancient towers and streets forming an irresistible whole. Monteriggioni, near Siena, and the Charterhouse of Galluzzo, close to Florence, illustrate the themes of secular force and religious spirit that recur, often in fierce opposition, throughout the history of this area.

Tour 12

The centuries-old practice of 'colonisation' conducted by the Florentine capital in the Mugello hills, northeast of the city, created a dense network of parish churches, villas and castles around the vast valley of the Sieve, a crucial tributary of the Arno. The Medici came here for amusement, but also to attend to their affairs. Today's visitors can indulge their fantasies as they explore ancient 'walled lands' and the scenic delights of the hill of Fiesole, Etruscan precursor of Florence.

Tour 13

This tour winds through one of Tuscany's most extensive and unspoiled 'green lungs', home to numerous hermitages and religious settlements entrusted with care of the majestic fir and beech woods that cover the area. The Franciscan site of Verna and the Benedictine complex at Camàldoli, protected by the turreted castles of the Guidi counts, are followed by the long, rounded mountain ramparts of the Pratomagno hills, watched over by Vallombrosa. Parish churches, abbeys and 14th-century settlements accompany the return to Arezzo.

Tour 14

After passing the small centres of the Arezzo hinterland on the edge of the Romagna-Marches Apennines, this tour crosses into Umbria which, especially at Città di Castello, seems so very Tuscan. It follows a section of the upper reaches of the Tiber, then passes through quiet countryside to emerge in the Chiana Valley and Cortona, on its eastern edge, standing amid olive groves.

The Medici villa at Artimino

Florence

Florence is one of the world's great cities. The sheer concentration of great art – in churches, mansions and museums – almost defies belief, and is matched only in Rome and Venice. The beauty of the city itself, set amid the gentle slopes that descend to the River Arno, is another element in its uniquely Tuscan magic.

3 DAYS

ⓘ *Via Cavour 1r; Piazza della Stazione 4a*

Portrait of a Man by Sandro Botticelli in the Uffizi Gallery

▶ *Go to Piazza della Signoria on foot or by public transport. The closest large car-parks are to the northwest, beneath Piazza del Mercato and the Santa Maria Novella railway station.*

❶ Piazza della Signoria

This became the home of secular power when, in the early 14th century, Arnolfo di Cambio built the Palazzo dei Priori. It was later known as Palazzo Signoria in the 15th century, Palazzo Ducale in 1540, when Cosimo I (1537–74) took up office here, and Palazzo Vecchio when he later moved to the Palazzo Pitti (1565). Parliament sat in the Palazzo Vecchio from 1865 to 1871, when Florence was the capital of Italy. Today, this massive structure, crowned by a gallery built for the lookout patrol (the design was based on the tower, 94m/308 feet high), serves as the city hall, and contains splendid rooms.

The square before it, scene of great political events, was adorned over the years with symbolic sculptures (most have been replaced with copies) – Donatello's *Judith and Holofernes* (here since 1495) and Michelangelo's *David* (1504) mark the victory of democracy over tyranny, whereas *Hercules and Cacus* (1534), created for the first Duke, Alessandro (1532–7), represents victory over the Medici's enemies. Ruler Cosimo I was portrayed in it on horseback by Giambologna (1594–8). Far less visible, near the Neptune fountain (known as *il Biancone* to the Florentines), an inscription indicates the place where religious and political reformer Girolamo Savonarola was hanged and burnt at the stake in 1498 with two fellow Dominican friars.

▶ *To the south of the square is the entrance to the Uffizi Gallery, at the top of the loggia on the left.*

❷ Galleria degli Uffizi

Duke Cosimo I planned to take the state into his own hands, uniting 13 magistratures (*uffizi*) in an annexe of Palazzo Vecchio. Giorgio Vasari (1511–74) designed two long wings, connected by a short block overlooking the Arno. When Cosimo moved to Palazzo Pitti, Vasari created a corridor running from there via Ponte Vecchio and the Uffizi, providing the Duke with discreet and safe access to the Palazzo Vecchio along a covered passageway. On completion of the work (1560–80), the Grand Dukes started to fill the building with all sorts of 'artifices' produced by man and nature. Today the gallery's internationally renowned art collections are besieged by visitors. Botticelli's *The Birth of Venus* is one of the Uffizi's most popular paintings. Mention of only the best-known painters becomes a roll-call of the masters of Italian art from the 12th to the 18th centuries.

Piazza della Signoria with Palazzo Vecchio and Arnolfo tower

▶ *Cross Piazzale degli Uffizi to the Lungarno and continue to the right to the Ponte Vecchio.*

❸ Ponte Vecchio

The *madielle* (glass cases) of the shops on Florence's most famous bridge, which crosses the Arno at its narrowest point, are filled with gold. Because of them, the river can be glimpsed only where the bridge widens at the centre. Butchers, fishmongers and greengrocers originally installed themselves on the three solid arches built in 1345, but they were forced out in 1593 by Grand Duke Ferdinando I, who considered gold- and silversmiths more appropriate tenants. His preference may also have had something to do with the fact that they paid higher taxes.

▶ *Across the bridge follow Via de' Guicciardini to Piazza de' Pitti.*

❹ Palazzo Pitti

A far smaller version of the Palazzo Pitti was commissioned in or around 1458 by the merchant and banker Luca Pitti, but due to his financial ruin it was never completed. Cosimo I bought it in 1549 to turn it into a palace; it subsequently became the official residence of the Medici Grand Dukes (until 1737), those of Lorraine (1737–1800 and 1814–59) and Vittorio Emanuele II (1865–71). Extended over the centuries, Pitti is the largest palace in Florence and its façade is 205m (672 feet) long. Visit the Royal Apartments, the Costume Gallery and the amazing collections in the Silver Museum.

The Ponte Vecchio, with its shops

The greatest attraction, however, is the Palatina Gallery, originally an annexe for the overflowing collections of the Uffizi. It contains a superb range of work by Raphael, Andrea del Sarto and Titian.

▶ *Cross Sdrucciolo de'Pitti and Via de' Michelozzi to Piazza Santo Spirito (the elegant interior of the church of the same name is by Filippo Brunelleschi); south of the square, Via Sant'Agostino and Via San Monaca lead to Piazza del Carmine.*

❺ Cappella Brancacci

The frescoes painted by young Masaccio in the Brancacci chapel were said to have 'schooled the

Brunelleschi's great dome stands out against the Florence skyline

SPECIAL TO...

'Rising high above the heavens, wide enough to cast shade over all the Tuscan peoples' – this was how Leon Battista Alberti described the octagonal dome of Santa Maria del Fiore. The difficulty in making it so high and so wide (42m/138 feet in diameter and almost 87m/285 feet from the ground) lay in the supporting framework, considered technically impossible, until Brunelleschi devised a double spherical vault capable of supporting itself during construction. The exhausting steps that climb to the top of the dome (91m/298 feet) offer unexpected views of the Baptistery and Duomo, as does the top of the bell tower (nearly 85m/279 feet) begun by Giotto in 1334 and completed more than 20 years later.

world' and were studied by all the Renaissance painters. The more traditional Masolino da Panicale helped decorate the chapel (1423–27), which can also be reached from the church of Santa Maria del Carmine. The work was completed by Filippino Lippi in 1480.

▶ *North of the square, turn into Borgo San Friediano, left into Via de' Serragli, right into Lungarno Guicciardini, left on to the San Trinità bridge (the finest in Florence) into Via de' Tornabuoni, right into Via Porta Rossa (picturesque medieval Palazzo Davanzati, now the Museum of the Old Florentine House) and left into Via de' Calzaiuoli to Orsanmichele.*

6 Orsanmichele

The origin of Orsanmichele is unusual, although appropriate to its function as church of the guilds (*arti*). Its name was inherited from the now-vanished Oratory of San Michele in Orto, but the building was initially a loggia designed by Arnolfo di Cambio as a grain market (1290). The arches were walled in and it was raised another two storeys when converted to a church at the end of the 14th century. Still visible inside are the loading and unloading apertures of the granaries above. All around are statues of the patron saints of the guilds, commissioned in the 15th century.

▶ *Continue along Via de' Calzaiuoli to Piazza del Duomo, adjacent to Piazza San Giovanni.*

7 Piazza del Duomo

The great octagonal Baptistery – Dante's 'bel San Giovanni' (he also claimed to have broken one of its fonts to save 'one who was drowning in it') – dates perhaps from the 11th century. The decoration of this symbol of the city became a competition between its patron, the powerful Merchants' Guild, and the Wool Guild.

Vying for prestige, the Wool Guild undertook work on Santa Maria del Fiore, opposite, and may be said to have won, given the exceptional quality of the three bronze doors (the south door is by Andrea Pisano, about 1330; the north and east doors by Lorenzo Ghiberti, 1403–24) and the inlaid marble floor (1207).

The Duomo (cathedral) or basilica of Santa Maria del Fiore was conceived in the late 13th century by Arnolfo di Cambio as a place where the entire community could gather – not only for worship, but also for secular events. Readings of the *Divine Comedy* are still a popular non-religious occasion here. He made it big enough for 30,000 people: 153m (502 feet) long, 90m

(295 feet) wide at the transept and 38m (125 feet) at the aisles. The erection of the dome was completed by Brunelleschi in 1436. The much-debated façade was not finished until 1887.

The Museo dell'Opera exhibits pieces never used in, or removed from, the Duomo, the Baptistery and the bell tower, such as the façade sculptures begun by Arnolfo di Cambio and dismissed in 1587 as 'unfashionable'; and the choirs by Luca della Robbia (1431–8) and Donatello (1433–9).

▶ *Go northwards along Via de' Martelli and Via Cavour to the Palazzo Medici-Riccardi.*

8 Palazzo Medici Riccardi

The area around today's Via Cavour became the 'headquarters' of the Medici family in the 15th and 16th centuries. Michelozzo constructed this prototype (1444–62) of the aristocratic Renaissance residence for Cosimo the Elder, and it served as the family residence until 1540. In 1659 it was purchased and then enlarged by the Riccardi family, although

the figures of the old proprietors still appear in the chapel, in the *Procession of the Magi* wall fresco, created by Benozzo Gozzoli in 1459–60.

▶ *To the left of the Palazzo, take Via de' Gori to Piazza San Lorenzo.*

9 Basilica di San Lorenzo

In 1418 the Medici family began to transform what had been Florence's first cathedral (4th–7th century) into the family church. Brunelleschi designed the interior for them but the façade was left in rough stone. The old sacristy (1421–6) was completely finished – a Brunelleschi cube decorated by Donatello. Michelangelo then intervened to create the new sacristy (1520–56; it serves as the funeral chapel of the family of Lorenzo il Magnifico), which became the prototype for mannerist architecture, made all the more dynamic by the great man's intense sculptures. During the same period, Cardinal Giulio de' Medici commissioned Michelangelo to build the Medici Laurenziana

library for the collection of manuscripts begun by Cosimo the Elder. The Chapel of the Principi, conceived by Cosimo I, is sheer opulence – the Opificio delle Pietre Dure workshop was created in 1588 specifically to fashion the precious materials required, and it remains a leading presence in the field of restoration.

▶ *Continue along Via Cavour to Piazza San Marco.*

The stone façade of San Lorenzo

da Fiesole (better known as Fra' Angelico). Nearly all his works in Florence are in the rooms of the convent-museum.

▶ *Go south along Via Ricasoli to the Galleria dell'Accademia.*

🔢 Galleria dell' Accademia

The students of the Academy of Fine Arts needed examples of sculpture for reference, and in 1784 Grand Duke Pietro Leopoldo decided that they should have only the greatest Florentine masterpieces. The

> **FOR CHILDREN**
>
> To celebrate the nativity of the Virgin Mary, Piazza dell'Annunziata is illuminated on the night of 7 September with the flickering lights of lanterns (*rificolone*) hanging from the tops of sticks. They are carried by worshippers on their way to pay homage to the Madonna of the sanctuary, lighting their way as did the citizens of the past, and by children all over the city.

Above: Piazza della SS Annunziata
Bottom right: the old 'pharmacy' of Santa Maria Novella

🔟 Chiesa e Museo di San Marco

In 1437, Cosimo the Elder called on his trusted architect, Michelozzo di Bartolomeo Michelozzi, to restructure the 14th-century complex of San Marco for the Dominicans. The church apse and sacristy were revamped and the convent layout proved one of the most practical and rational of its time. The undertaking cost more than 40,000 florins, but it's doubtful whether the commissioner was ever recompensed. His inept great-nephew Piero, son of Lorenzo il Magnifico, was chased from the city by the followers of one of San Marco's priors, reformer Savonarola, considered by some the master of the city and a guiding spirit of

the Florentine Republic (1494–1512). Cosimo, who had reserved a double cell for himself in the convent, never saw the sublime frescoes created there by Fra' Giovanni

> **SPECIAL TO...**
>
> In Via della Scala, you can buy perfume, spirits, soap, balsam and lotions in the neo-Gothic surroundings of the 'Officina profumo-farmaceutica di Santa Maria Novella', owned by the Dominican friars until 1866. Just a few steps away, a visit to the Chiesa di Santa Maria Novella (1278) is a must both for its exemplary façade (1458–78), by Leon Battista Alberti, and the frescoes by Paolo Uccello (from 1425–30, in the church museum), Masaccio (1427) and Domenico Ghirlandaio (1485–90).

choice was obvious: in time the gallery became a 'Michelangelo museum', also housing the casts of works on display elsewhere. Four of the gigantic *Prisoners* are here – powerful figures sketched for the tomb of Pope Julius II and half imprisoned in the stone itself. They provide a startling contrast to the refined

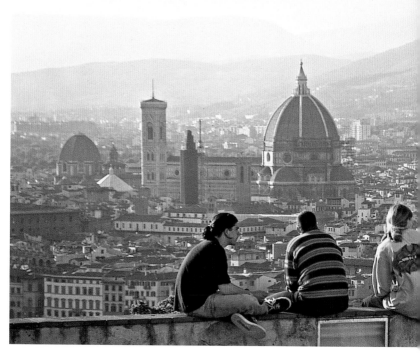

original *David* moved from Piazza della Signoria.

▷ *Back in Piazza San Marco, turn right into Via Battisti and follow it to Piazza della SS Annunziata.*

12 Piazza della SS Annunziata

The Ospedale degli Innocenti (1419–45), built by Brunelleschi and financed by the Silk Guild, is a masterpiece of precise symmetry: in the portico, the width of the arches is equal to the height of the columns and the depth of the bays. It provided a blueprint for Renaissance architecture, but the building served a daily practical function, too. The abandonment of children was a persistent problem, and the creation of a 'Hospital of Innocents' was the city's way

of addressing the issue. From 1660 to 1875 the children were collected from a rotating stone – 'the wheel' – situated in the Ospedale's portico. Opposite the Ospedale, the Loggiato dei Serviti (1516) imitates Brunelleschi's arches. Between the two is the basilica of the Annunziata (1444–77). To the east of the square, a large vault leads to the Archaeological Museum. Here you can see the oldest Tuscan art – that of the Etruscans – including famous pieces such as the bronze sculptures *Chimera di Arezzo* (5th–4th century BC) and the *Arringatore di Perugia (Orator of Perugia)*, an example of Etruscan realism.

▷ *Walk south along Via de' Servi, around the apse of the Duomo and down Via del Proconsolo to Palazzo del Bargello.*

13 Museo del Bargello

You pass through the 13th-century Volognana tower, whose bell rings only for the passing of a century, to the first public building (13th–14th century) of communal Florence. In 1574 it became the seat of the *shirro*, or the police, and prison. The museum arranged in the rooms of the Bargello comprises works by Donatello (two Davids), Michelangelo, Pollaiolo, Verrocchio and Cellini. It even offers the opportunity to judge between the two bas-reliefs of the *Sacrifice of Isaac*, entered in the 1401 competition between Brunelleschi and Ghiberti to decorate the north door of the Baptistery. Ghiberti won.

▷ *Continuing along Via del Proconsolo you come to Piazza San Firenze (fine late-baroque Palazzo San Firenze,*

The classical view of Florence from San Miniato al Monte, with the Fièsole hills in the background

> with the twin façades of the church and oratory of San Filippo Neri); turn left into Via dell'Anguillara and walk to Piazza Santa Croce.

14 Chiesa di Santa Croce

The Church of Santa Croce was begun by Arnolfo di Cambio in 1295 for the Franciscans in a heavily populated quarter of wool-workers. The grandiose Gothic style is at its height on the sides and on the apse (the façade is 19th-century neo-Gothic); the solemn interior contains the tombs of many notable Florentine citizens. Giotto created his last fresco cycles (1320–5) in the Peruzzi and Bardi chapels. The adjacent Pazzi Chapel is Brunelleschi's masterpiece (1429, included in the Museum of Works of Santa Croce). Hanging in the refectory is a great crucifix by Cimabue, which suffered in the 1966 flood.

EXCURSION

> ▶ To the west of the square, Via Borgo de' Greci and Via de' Gondi lead back to Piazza della Signoria. Take your car or public transport to Piazzale Michelangelo, south of the Arno.

Piazzale Michelangelo e San Miniato al Monte

Admiring the view from this large square, built in 1875 and well connected to the Firenze Sud motorway exit, is an excellent way to take leave of the city. Even better, drive up Viale Galilei (or climb the steps) to San Miniato al Monte (1018–1207). Together with the baptistery – which it echoes in its distinctive white and green marble – this church is the greatest masterpiece of Florentine Renaissance style.

A Florentine football match, in Piazza Santa Croce

From Val d'Arno
to Val d'Elsa

Visiting the borderlands of Florence, Pisa and Siena, this tour travels along two important ancient routes: Via Pisana, which follows the Arno, and Via Francigena, the only medieval channel of communication across the peninsula and seen here on its stretch along the Elsa river. Traffic, farming and industry enriched the people who lived along these routes, enabling them to build walls around their splendid towns.

2/3 DAYS • 193KM • 120 MILES

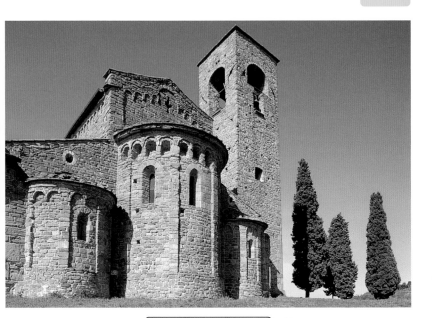

Church of San Leonardo, Artimino

▶ Take the **SS67** westbound to
Lastra a Signa.

1 Lastra a Signa

The countryside hereabouts has
been heavily urbanised from the
Middle Ages on. Florentine
expansion took the form of new
'walled lands', of which Lastra a
Signa is a classic example. In
1424 Brunelleschi worked on the
ring of walls originally built on
the instruction of the Florentine
authorities in 1377. Below the
village is the starting point of the
narrow Golfolina gorge, Arno's
route to the Tyrrhenian sea.

i Piazza IV Novembre 8

▶ Continue along the **SS67**,
then cross the Arno and
follow the signs to Artimino.

2 Artimino

Good wine and an abundance
of game attracted the Medici
family here every autumn. In
1594, Grand Duke Ferdinand I
asked Bernardo Buontalenti to
erect a 'hunting and grape-

SPECIAL TO...

Florence is famous for its
elegant straw hats, first
introduced at Signa in 1718,
when a man from Bologna
planted 'March wheat' to be
harvested before the ear
ripened. This was then used to
weave hats of far superior
quality to those made using
ripe wheat straw. A cottage
weaving industry flourished
during the 19th century and
the province of Florence had
100,000 workers, living on
starvation wages. In the early
20th century, traveller Edward
Hutton noted: 'One of the
finest ladies' sun hats...costs
15 lire, and the woman who
makes it only gets 2 or 3'.

harvesting' villa on a hill site.
Bizarre chimneys in various
shapes and sizes adorn the roofs,
and the view sweeps over the
Arno Valley to Florence and
Pistoia. Not far away is the
lovely Romanesque church of
San Leonardo, founded in 1107.

▶ Back on the **SS67**, continue
westwards to Montelupo
Fiorentino.

3 Montelupo Fiorentino

A marketplace developed at the
point where the Pesa river flows
into the Arno, and in the late
Middle Ages Montelupo
became a flourishing ceramic
centre. Before yielding to temp-
tation in the craft shops, visit the
restored Palazzo Podestà and see
pottery produced over the
centuries by local kilns, and now
on display in the Archaeological
and Pottery Museum.

i Via Baccio Sinibaldi 43

▶ Take the Florence-Livorno-
Pisa dual carriageway
eastbound, exit at San

FOR HISTORY BUFFS

The Florentines were vexed
by the presence of Capraia, an
outpost of their Pisan rivals
nestling on a rugged crag
across the Arno. They decided
that 'a wolf (lupo) is needed to
destroy this goat (capra)'. So in
1203 they created their wolf –
the castle of Montelupo,
whose ruins can be glimpsed
at the top of a hill southeast
of the village.

FOR HISTORY BUFFS

When poet and Nobel prize-winner Giosue Carducci (1835–1907) taught 'eloquence' in the local grammar school, the town was called San Miniato al Tedesco ('German San Miniato'). It had been the seat of representatives of the Holy Roman Empire since the 10th century; one imperial vicar was Bonifacio, Marquis of Tuscany and father of Countess Matilda, who was born here in 1046. Several German emperors made their homes here: Henry IV, who was excommunicated by Pope Gregory VII and later deposed him; Barbarossa (between 1178 and 1195); Otto IV (1206); and Frederick II (around 1226). In 1291 the *Comune* allied itself with the papal Guelph faction, opposing the power of the German emperors and their Ghibelline league. It came under Florentine protection in 1347.

down towards the coast. San Miniato Basso (26m/85 feet), the lower, modern town, is now a busy leather-processing centre. The four original districts on the ridge were restructured and fortified in 1226 by Frederick II. Of the stronghold he built at the highest point (192m/630 feet) only the tower survives, rebuilt after bombing in 1944. This is probably the scene of the tragic downfall of jurist, poet and king's representative Pier delle Vigne (*c*1190–1249), who fell into disgrace, was blinded and – according to Dante – committed suicide to 'escape contempt'. Two spectacular squares are linked by steps around the 13th-century cathedral. In November, the town is packed for the national white truffle fair.

[i] *Piazza del Popolo 3*

▶ *After descending to the foot of San Miniato, travel east to the* **SS429**, *which to the right leads to Castelfiorentino.*

5 Castelfiorentino
Like other towns in Val d'Elsa, Castelfiorentino consists of a modern and industrialised centre on the plain and an older settlement on the hill. Roman in origin, it was a Carolingian fief before coming under Florentine influence and taking its present name in 1149. Two visits are especially worthwhile. The

RECOMMENDED EXCURSION

About 20km (12 miles) or so north of Montelupo and San Miniato, on the lower slopes of Monte Albano, stands Vinci. The great artist and inventor Leonardo (1452–1519), illegitimate son of Ser Piero, the notary, took the name of his birthplace. Inside the almond-shaped castle of the Guidi counts (12th-century) is the Leonardo Museum, exhibiting models of the machines designed by this brilliant Renaissance man. From his flying machines to the bicycle, it represents the best of 15th-century science fiction.

Church of Santa Verdiana, a showpiece of early 18th-century architecture and painting, has an underground cell where Verdiana (1178–1242), patron saint of the town, lived the last 34 years of her life – in the company of two snakes, according to legend. In the town's Cultural Centre you can admire two fresco cycles by Benozzo Gozzoli (1420–97) and his assistants, depicting the life of the Virgin Mary.

[i] *c/o Railway Station, Via Rudolfo 1*

▶ *Proceed south, following first the signs for Montaione and then those for San Vivaldo.*

6 San Vivaldo
In 1320, a Franciscan monk, Vivaldo Stricchi, who had retired here to lead a hermit's life, was found dead in the hollow trunk of a chestnut tree. He was later canonised and a small church was built for him and consecrated in 1416. The Franciscans, guardians of the Holy Places in Palestine, arrived in the 16th century, and created a 'holy mount', reproducing the sanctuaries of Jerusalem and marking stages in the life of Jesus. A large group of chapels was built around 1515, of which about half still remain. They contain large tableaux fashioned

Miniato and follow the signs to the town.

4 San Miniato
The nucleus of the old town is distributed on three rises overlooking the Arno plain, with wide views over the valley and

One of the chapels of San Vivaldo, at Montaione

in multicoloured terracotta by local artists of the Robbia school.

▶ *Go back and take the road signposted on the right for Gambassi Terme and Certaldo.*

7 Certaldo

In the 13th century Certaldo's low-lying *borgo* (village) began to develop around Via Francigena; this commercial and residential area is now known as Certaldo Basso. Up on the hill, the institutions of power centred around the castello, and this area, Certaldo Alto, is the most interesting quarter for visitors today. The warm tones of its medieval brick architecture have survived the tribulations of centuries, not least the destruction wrought by World War II. Rich in scenic views, the upper town culminates in Palazzo Pretorio, revamped in the 15th century. Inside, the walls of the cells used for a men's prison (there is also a women's version) still bear messages written by past prisoners. The adjacent 13th-century former church has a remarkable fresco cycle completed in 1466–7 by

The view around San Gimignano from the top of the Torre Grossa, beside the Palazzo del Popolo

Benozzo Gozzoli and other painters for the *Tabernacolo dei Giustiziati*. A bust dating from 1503 marks the tomb of Giovanni Boccaccio, author of the *Decameron*. Originally from Certaldo, his family moved to Florence in the late 13th century; Boccaccio is thought to have been born in 1313 on the banks of the Arno, and is known to have returned in or around 1361 to live in the ancestral

home until his death on 21 December, 1375. The house still stands: restored after the war, it contains an interesting research library.

ℹ️ *Piazza Masini*

▶ *Cross the Elsa again and follow the signs for San Gimignano to the left.*

8 San Gimignano

The first sight of San Gimignano takes your breath away. Its perfectly preserved medieval towers and streets seem to take you back to another age. Orginally there were no fewer than 72 towers (15 survive). They were built thanks to the immense wealth of this free *comune's* merchant and financial classes, gleaned from their principal trades of saffron and usury (as 13th-century canonical law defined financial speculation).

San Gimignano fell into decline in the 14th century, when its population was decimated by wars, civil strife, famine and plagues. In 1351 the town relinquished its independence and surrendered itself to Florence. In the meantime, an abundance of houses, towers and tower-houses, springs and reservoirs, churches, warehouses, hospices, convents and elegant mansions had grown up along the urban stretch of the Via Francigena. Protected by strict monument restrictions since 1929, San Gimignano is an extraordinary living museum. Perhaps it does have a few too many souvenir shops and tourists but come in the low season, on weekdays or at quiet times for an unforgettable visit.

[i] *Piazza del Duomo 1*

Above: rafting in Val d'Elsa
Right: Monteriggioni's ring of walls

▶ *After driving 5km (3 miles) towards Poggibonsi, turn right for the **SS68** which, to the left, leads to Colle di Val d'Elsa.*

🄅 Colle di Val d'Elsa
Three areas make up Colle di Val d'Elsa, developed between the 10th and the 13th century. The lower section, known as Piano, specialised in the manufacture of paper in the Middle Ages, using energy from the waters of the Elsa river. Today Colle Bassa is a major producer of glass and crystal. The other two sections, Castello and Borgo, together form Colle Alta, and feature splendid architecture of medieval origin with Renaissance additions. Via del Castello is the site of the centres of secular power, old tower-houses (one is said to have been the birthplace in 1245 of the architect and sculptor Arnolfo di Cambio) and fine 15th- to 16th-century mansions.

[i] *Via Campana 43*

▶ *Proceed towards Siena to the **SS429**, which to the right soon*

takes you to the turning on the left for Monteriggioni.

🔟 Monteriggioni

Dante was profoundly impressed by Monteriggioni's superb 'round circle' of towers, which he likened to the abyss guarded by 14 giants described in his *Inferno*. The citadel was erected by the Sienese, who founded this outpost against Florence in 1203. It took 70 years to complete the ring, which is 570m (1,870 feet) long and incorporates 14 towers. The village's medieval atmosphere and intact fortifications, arranged along an axis running from the gate facing Florence to that facing Siena, make it the most significant example of a 'walled land' on Sienese territory.

ℹ️ *Piazza Roma 23*

▶ *Take the Siena–Florence motorway northbound and exit at Firenze Certosa, then follow the signs to the Certosa del Galluzzo.*

🔟 Certosa del Galluzzo

Founded in 1342 by the Florentine Niccolò Acciaioli, the Certosa (Charterhouse) is surrounded by high walls and looks like an inaccessible fortress. Once inside, though, this impression is soon dispelled. Large cloisters and slender porticoes – mainly 15th-century – open on to the light and landscape. Initially the rich benefactor had intended to reserve a normal cell for himself (actually, they are two-storey mini-apartments). Then, ignoring the monks' objections, he started to build himself a mansion beside the monastery,

but died before its completion. Today, a picture gallery contains the frescoes removed from the grand cloister, where Jacopo Pontormo created them in 1522–4.

During the Napoleonic occupation, the Charterhouse was stripped of most of its treasures. In 1958, the Carthusians were replaced by Cistercian Benedictines who now organise guided visits to the complex.

▶ *Continue northwards to return to Florence.*

SPECIAL TO...

In San Gimignano look out for the delicious ice-cream flavoured with saffron pistils, a traditional local crop.

WINE & OIL

Wine-making has a long and respected history in Tuscany, kept alive by local skills and the initiatives of some of its oldest aristocratic families. A great way of learning more about its traditions is to follow the wine route, visiting museums, restaurants and wine cellars. The Tuscan regional authorities have approved 14 such routes – Carmignano, Chianti Colli Fiorentini, Chianti Rufina e Pomino, Colli di Candaie Lunigiana, Vino Colli di Maremma, Colline Lucchiese e Montecarlo, Delle Colline Pisane, Costa degli Etruschi, Monteregione di Massa Marìttima, Montespertoli, Terre di Arezzo, Vernaccia di San Gimignano, Vino di Montecucco and Vino Nobile di Montepulciano. Details are found in local town halls.

Carrara), Candia dei Colli Apuani (Massa-Carrara), Colline Lucchesi, Montecarlo (Lucca), Bianco Pisano di San Torpè (Pisa, Livorno), Bianco della Valdinièvole (Pistoia), DOCG Carmignano, Barco Reale di Carmignano and Carmignano (Carmignano and Poggio a Caiano, Prato), Bianco dell'Empolese (Empoli).

Maremma Montescudaio (Pisa), Bòlgheri (Castagneto Carducci, Livorno), Val di Cornia (Livorno, Pisa), Elba (Isle of Elba), Monteregio di Massa Marìttima, Morellino di Scansano, Bianco di Pitigliano (Grosseto), Ansonica Costa Argentario (Grosseto and Isle of Giglio) and Parrina (Orbetello, Grosseto), Sovana (Pitigliano, Sorano).

Chianti and much more

By far the most popular grape in the region is Sangiovese. This is followed by Trebbiano Toscano (11 per cent), Brunello (2 per cent – a local variety of Sangiovese) and Ciliegiolo (1.2 per cent). The undisputed champion wines are Chianti and the renowned Brunello di Montalcino (Chianti and Chianti Classico constitute a 'regional' wine that extends

Chianti country grape harvest

beyond the mountains from which it takes its name to more than 100 *comuni* in six different provinces). The other DOCG (origin controlled and guaranteed) wines are Carmignano (Prato), Vernaccia (San Gimignano) – the region's only white wine – and Vino Nobile di Montepulciano. There are also 29 DOC (origin controlled) wines. Below is a list of DOC and DOCG wines.

Northwest Tuscany Colli di Luni (La Spezia, Massa-

Northeast Tuscany DOCG Vernaccia di San Gimignano

(San Gimignano, Siena),
Pomino (Rùfina, Florence),
Colli dell'Etruria Centrale
(Arezzo, Florence, Pisa, Pistoia,
Siena), Bianco Vergine della
Valdichiana (Siena, Arezzo),
Cortona (Cortona), Montecucco
(Grosseto, Montecucco).

Inland Tuscany Val d'Arbia
(Siena including its capital
town), DOCG Chianti Classico
(Florence and Siena), Vin Santo
del Chianti (Siena, Florence,
Pistoia, Arezzo, Pisa, Prato),
Vin Santo del Chianti Classico
(Siena, Florence), DOCG
Chianti (Florence, Siena,
Arezzo, Pistoia, Pisa, Prato),
DOCG Brunello di Montalcino,
Moscadello di Montalcino,
Rosso di Montalcino,
San'Antimo (Montalcino,
Siena), DOCG Vino Nobile di
Montepulciano, Rosso di
Montepulciano, Vin Santo di
Montepulciano
(Montepulciano, Siena), Orchia
(Montaclcino, Montepulciano).

Umbrian wines
The DOC wine-producing areas
of Umbria are concentrated in
and near the Umbra Valley, the
upper Tiber Valley to the north,
the central Orvieto area and
Ternano to the south. Umbrian
vines are influenced by their
proximity to Tuscany; three-
quarters of the region's production comes from the Trebbiano
and Sangiovese vines, although
Umbrians tend to prefer white
to red; two indigenous grapes,
Sagrantino and Grechetto,
produce prized wines. There are
also two DOCG wines –
Montefalco Sagrantino and
Torgiano Rosso Riserva. DOC
wines are dominated by
Orvieto, which alone constitutes
two-thirds of the total. Other
DOC-producing zones are the
Altotiberini hills, the Trasimeno
hills, the Perugia hills, Assisi,
Torgiano, Montefalco, the
Martani hills and the Amerini
hills (in the province of Terni).

Oil, from Lucca to Trasimeno
Tuscan olive oil is the best-
known extra virgin oil in Europe.
It has a fruity smell with a touch

Above: harvesting olives
Right: producing olive oil

of almond, and quite a tangy
flavour. Its quality varies according to the type of olive, microcli-
mate and soil (or *cru*). Elegant,
delicate, golden oils with a hint of
green are produced in the Lucca
area, and more robust versions in
Maremma. The oils of Chianti
and the Sienese hills are tangy
and bitter, with a herbal after-
taste.

In the Florentine hills the
oils have a pleasant almondy
smell; Pratomagno's is tangy, and
Rùfina's (north of Florence) has
body. A light, fruity taste distinguishes the oil produced in the
Pisan mountains, an intensely
sweet product not unlike oils
from the province of Livorno.

Umbrian olive oil is one of
the most refined in Italy, with an
amber colour, very slight acidity
and high oleic content. Around
Trasimeno and Perugia, on

the calcareous slopes of the
mountains that extend between
Assisi and Spoleto, the olive
trees form a dense and continu-
ous band between 250 and 550m
(820 and 1,804 feet) above sea
level. Particularly fine is the oil
of Spoleto, a town that boasts the
most efficient oil industry in the
region, although those of Foligno
and Terni are also excellent.

Mugello
& Fièsole

2 DAYS • 148KM • 92 MILES

Etruscan tombs and sweeping views, Medici villas and old parish churches, romantic cypresses and symmetrical Italian gardens, the birthplaces of Giotto and Fra' Angelico, artistic ceramics and even knives – this tour, winding through the beautiful hills to the north of Florence, reveals a host of surprises to visitors.

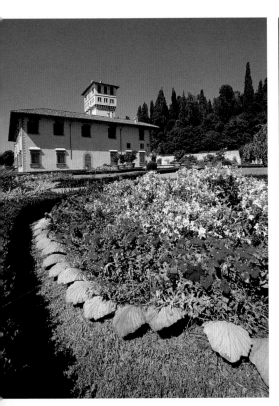

A view from the garden of the Medici Villa della Petraia, originally owned by the Brunelleschi family

i Via Cavour 1r; Piazza della Stazione 4a, Florence

▶ *After reaching Piazza Dalmazia at Rifredi take Viale Morgagni and Viale Pieraccini to the Careggi hospital (responsible for the Medici villa).*

1 Villa di Careggi

The Medici family bought a building on this hill in the early 15th century and had it restructured by Michelozzo. It then became the seat of the Accademia Platonica Fiorentina and was, from the middle of the century, patronised by the best-known scholars, philosophers and artists of the Medici circles, including Marsilio Ficino, Pico della Mirandola and Michelangelo.

▶ *Back in Piazza Dalmazia, proceed along Via Giuliani, Via delle Panche and then, following the signs, Via della Querciola, Via di Castello and Via della Petraia to Villa della Petraia.*

2 Villa della Petraia

This villa, originally a castle, was built in the 14th century and came into the hands of the Medici family after 1530. Bernardo Buontalenti (1536–1608) redesigned it in the last decades of that century. There is a beautiful three-tiered garden and a courtyard which was covered with iron and glass by the Savoy family after 1865 to create a ballroom. Frescoes inside created in the 17th century celebrate the splendours of the Medici house.

▶ *Return along Via della Petraia and take Via del Castello to Villa di Castello.*

3 Villa di Castello

Obtained by the Medici family in 1477, the villa was converted for Cosimo when he became Duke (1537), with subsequent additions by Bernardo Buontalenti (1536–1608). It is now closed to visitors – but you can see the magnificent gardens, laid out to symbolise the territory of the Duchy. Since 1974, the building has been the base of the Accademia della Crusca, an institution created in 1583 to publish the famous *Vocabolario* that established the conventions of the Italian language.

▶ *Return to Via delle Panche and follow this before taking Via Gramsci to Sesto Fiorentino.*

4 Sesto Fiorentino

Today, this is a major industrial town, having seen substantial urbanisation in recent decades.

Villa di Cafaggiolo, where Lorenzo the Magnificent came to relax

Its name indicates its position at the sixth Roman mile (approximately 9km/6 miles) from the centre of Florence. Two notable legacies of the town's ancient past still survive – 7th-century BC Etruscan tombs with false domes. One, called the *Montagnola*, is in the gardens of Villa Manfredi (Via Fratelli Rosselli) and the other, known as *Mula*, is situated in the grounds of the villa of the same name (Via della Mula).

i Palazzo Vittorio Veneto 1

▶ *In Via Gramsci turn right into Via Matteoti and take Via dei Colli Alti to Pratolino and the Demidoff Park.*

5 Parco Demidoff
The Villa Medici-Demidoff park lies close to Pratolino. Bernardo Buontalenti was commissioned to create the sumptuous residence in 1569 for the Venetian Bianca Cappello, unscrupulous lover and later wife of the Grand Duke Francesco I de' Medici. It fell into disrepair under the Lorraine family and was demolished in 1824. The park,

formerly full of 'wonders' (fountains, grottoes, statues enlivened with flowing water and even an automatic organ), was redesigned to suit romantic tastes. The Appennino fountain, created by Giambologna (1579–89, depicts a colossal crouching old man 11m (36 feet) high, which incorporates a number of spaces inside. From here you can see the garden and the little temple.

▶ *Return to Pratolino and follow the signs northeast to the Convent of Monte Senario.*

6 Convento di Monte Senario
At 815m (2,674 feet) above sea level, this convent was founded in 1233 by seven Florentine noblemen who had formed the Servite Order. Of the original structure, only the chapel, where the Virgin Mary is said to have appeared in 1240, remains. The church, with its rich baroque interior, the bell tower and the convent were repeatedly altered during the 17th and 18th centuries. The terrace surrounding the complex overlooks the Mugello Valley.

▶ *After reaching Vaglia and the SS65 (Futa), take this road*

northbound past the Nòvoli turning (left for the castle of Trebbio) to Cafaggiolo.

7 Villa di Cafaggiolo
Architect Michelozzo Michelozzi (1396–1472), who built the castle of Trebbio (visits by request) on a hillock between 1427 and 1436 for Cosimo the Elder, was commissioned by Lorenzo de' Medici in 1454 to create Villa di Cafaggiolo. Crowned with crenellations and corbels and featuring a large tower with a monumental gate, it was a favourite bolt-hole for Lorenzo the Magnificent.

SPECIAL TO...

The Medici villas were places of amusement and delight – as described in the *Nencia da Barberino*, a poem composed by Lorenzo de' Medici at Cafaggiolo, around 1473–6. In it, the magnificent lord of Florence, disguised as a peasant, does his utmost to seduce a local peasant girl. He imagines her accompanying him to the pastures, where 'I would put my beasts among yours / and we would seem one, although we were two'.

▶ Continue north towards Barberino di Mugello, turning right for Galliano and right again for Bosco ai Frati.

8 Bosco ai Frati

The same Medici client and the same architect reappear in the convent of Bosco ai Frati. Occupied first by Basilian and then by Franciscan monks in the 13th century, it was almost entirely rebuilt in the 15th century. This small complex created for Cosimo the Elder is admired more for its enchanting position, amid hills and Adriatic oak woods, and a dramatic wooden crucifix attributed to Donatello, than for the work of Michelozzo (visible in the choir and ribbed cross vaults).

Scarperia's 14th-century Palazzo dei Vicari with crenellated tower

▶ Go back and continue northwards to Galliano, where you turn right for Sant'Àgata.

9 Sant'Àgata

Ashlar stone alternates with serpentine green in this typical example of Tuscan Romanesque style. The parish church of Sant'Àgata – nave and two aisles divided by monumental columns – is the most important and one of the oldest holy buildings in Mugello, dating from 984. An enterprising 17th-century parish priest made the baptistery using the panels of a 12th-century pulpit. He was also responsible for the striking painting of the martyrdom of Sant'Àgata, on a gold background, which hangs above the reliquary of the saint, at the centre of an incredible collage of saints painted on fragments

of old panels. The date and provenance of the pieces have proved baffling.

▶ Take the southbound road to Scarperìa.

10 Scarperìa

Scarperìa is a 'new land' founded in 1306 by the Florentines against the Ubaldini, vassals of Mugello, and has preserved much of its medieval past. It still retains its grid plan, a section of medieval walls, and the imposing Palazzo dei Vicari, bearing the coats-of-arms in stone and majolica of successive governors of the village. It has also kept alive the trade that made its knife-makers famous all over Tuscany. Their history is recorded in the Knife Museum in Palazzo dei Vicari; an old knife shop survives near by. To the southeast is the Mugello racing circuit, opened in 1974, which hosts races. mainly for motor bikes.

ⓘ *Palazzo dei Vicari*

▶ Take the **SS503** southbound and, before reaching San Piero a Sieve, turn left for Borgo San Lorenzo.

11 Borgo San Lorenzo

Lying in a large hollow formed by the Sieve river, the most important and industrialised town in Mugello is visited for the Romanesque parish church of San Lorenzo (1263), which has a hexagonal bell tower. Inside, a Madonna's head painted on a panel by Giotto in the 1300s is the only work by the painter preserved in the province where he was born.

The view of Florence from San Francesco in Fièsole

ℹ️ *Via Togliatti 45*

▶ *Take the SS551 eastwards and go left at the turning for Vespignano-Casa di Giotto.*

12 Vespignano

Painter, architect and sculptor Giotto di Bondone was born here, probably in 1267. The story of his life is told in various documents, records and reproductions of his works at the house where he is said to have been born, now restored.

▶ *Back on the SS551 continue to Vicchio.*

13 Vicchio

Set on the border between Mugello and Val di Sieve, Vicchio, like Scarperìa, was founded by the Florentine Republic in the early decades of the 14th century as a strategic base and to control the roads to Romagna. The old centre, enclosed within pentagonal walls in 1324, was the birthplace of Fra' Angelico (c1400–55). The museum named after him shows holy works from the Mugello area – but none by his own hand.

ℹ️ *Via Garibaldi 1*

▶ *Continue towards Florence via Dicomano and Pontassieve to Sieci.*

14 Sieci

Standing in the centre of the village is the Romanesque parish church of San Giovanni Battista a Rèmole, dating from the first half of the 12th century. On the opposite side of the Arno, two massive, crenellated towers mark the Rèmole fulling mills, recorded since 1425 but certainly much older.

▶ *Continue towards Florence to Compiobbi, where you turn right and follow the signs for Fièsole via Montebeni.*

SPECIAL TO...

The Rèmole fulling mills are virtually all that survive of the numerous works that used to full woollen cloth. Heavy hydraulic hammers would beat the fabrics day and night to soften and strengthen them with the aid of solutions containing soda, soap and urine.

The mills were initially installed on rafts anchored in the centre of Florence, but after the disastrous Arno flood of 1333 they transferred their evil-smelling industry up- and downstream of the city.

SPECIAL TO...

Michelangelo's wet-nurse was the wife of a stone-cutter from Settignano; he later claimed that he had absorbed his love of the art with her milk. The people of Fièsole were said by Dante to have a character 'of mountain and stone', and the colour of the rock (*bigia* or *serena*) cut from the Monte Cèceri quarries still dominates Fièsole, Maiano and Settignano. Here, the stone-cutting trade created great sculptors such as Desiderio da Settignano (1428–64), Mino da Fièsole (1430–84), Giuliano (1432–90) and Benedetto da Maiano (1442–97).

15 Fièsole

A beautiful archaeological site reveals the origins of Fièsole. At the end of the 4th century BC Fièsole was already an important Etruscan town with megalithic walls – thought in the Middle Ages to be the work of giants – temple and necropolis. Having become a Roman colony in 90 BC, it acquired a forum, temples, spas and, in Augustan times, a theatre for 3,000 spectators. It fell into decline under the Lombards, but was brought back to prominence when Florence came to ascendancy in 1125. During the 18th and 19th centuries, the town was embellished with villas and gardens, and became a favourite destination of foreigners visiting Florence. The wealth of art and history, the historic Borgunto

The Roman theatre on the Fièsole archaeological site

quarter and the magical view from a clearing on the road up to the Gothic church of San Francesco add to its attraction.

Along the road to Florence stands the monastery of San Domenico, to which Fra' Angelico belonged. The church, begun in 1406, contains a much-altered triptych by the young artist (1425). From San Domenico a short walk descends to the old Badia Fiesolana, residence of the bishops of Fièsole from the early Middle Ages until 1028. In 1456 Cosimo the Elder – who was so fond of the Badia that he spent the last years of his life here – decided to enlarge it, but on his death in 1464 the new façade, incorporating the elegant marble geometry of the 12th century, was still incomplete.

i *Via Portigiani 3/5*

▶ *Follow the signs to Florence.*

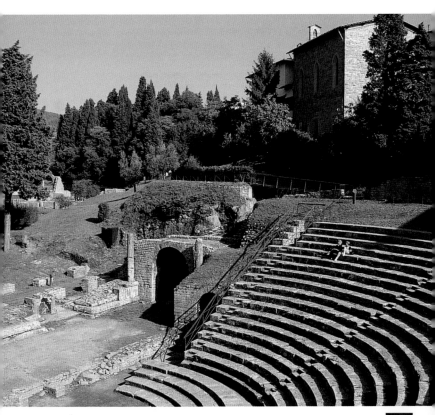

Casentino
& Pratomagno

The uncertain course of the Arno has few parallels among the great rivers. From the Monte Falterona springs, it flows south in the Casentino Valley, but within sight of Arezzo 'it takes a fright and turns back' (as the Florentines used to say), encircling the long Pratomagno ridge to the north. Not until Pontassieve does it finally choose its route – west to the sea.

ITINERARY		
AREZZO	►	Eremo della Verna (47km-29m)
EREMO DELLA VERNA	►	Poppi (33km-20½m)
POPPI	►	Camàldoli (15km-9½m)
CAMÀLDOLI	►	Eremo di Camàldoli (3km-2m)
EREMO DI CAMÀLDOLI	►	Castello di Romena (17km-10½m)
CASTELLO DI ROMENA	►	Pieve di Romena (4km-2½m)
PIEVE DI ROMENA	►	Vallombrosa (24km-15m)
VALLOMBROSA	►	Cascia (14km-9m)
CASCIA	►	San Giovanni Valdarno (21km-13m)
SAN GIOVANNI VALDARNO	►	Loro Ciuffenna (13km-8m)
LORO CIUFFENNA	►	Arezzo (29km-18m)

2 DAYS • 220KM • 137 MILES

Image of Dante Alighieri before the mansion of the Guidi counts at Poppi

ℹ Piazza della Repubblica 28, Arezzo

▶ *Take the SS71 to Ràssina, then turn right on to the SS208 and drive via Chitignano, following the signs for Chiusi della Verna and the Eremo della Verna.*

❶ Eremo della Verna

The wooded calcareous peak of Monte Verna is visible all over Casentino and from the upper Val Tiberina. In 1213, Count Orlando Cattani made a gift of it to Francis of Assisi, who embedded the little church of Santa Maria degli Angeli (1216–18) on its slope. Today the church itself is set in the side of a larger church, Chiesa Maggiore, which dates from the 14th to 15th century. Splendid glazed terracottas by Andrea della Robbia (1435–1528) adorn the interior of both buildings. Corridors, cells and grottoes lead to the Chapel of the Stigmata, built where the saint is said, in 1224, to have received the divine stigmata

from an angel with six blazing wings. The sanctuary, home of the Franciscan Minorites and visited by many pilgrims, is surrounded by a beautiful forest of fir, beech, maple and ash trees. The forest has been tended by the monks since the 14th century, and some trees are more than 400 years old.

▶ *After descending to the SS208 once more, proceed westwards to Bibbiena and then take the SS70 to Poppi.*

❷ Poppi

The soaring tower at the centre of the crenellated mansion of the Guidi counts, built in the second half of the 13th century

> **BACK TO NATURE**
>
> Wolves, bears, fallow deer, roe deer, water lynx, day and nocturnal birds of prey and even a colony of white Asinara donkeys (a species at risk of extinction) await visitors to Poppi's small zoo of European fauna, on the edge of the Foreste Casentinesi-Monte Falterona-Campigna National Park.

> **FOR HISTORY BUFFS**
>
> 'Those of Arezzo attacked the field so vigorously…that the ranks of Florentines recoiled sharply. The battle was bitter and harsh…The daggers rained down…the air was covered with clouds, the dust was great. Those on foot…crouched under the bellies of the horses with knives in hand and ran them through…those of Arezzo were broken not for being faint-hearted or for lack of courage, but for the excess of foes, and were driven away and killed; the Florentine soldiers, accustomed to defeat, slayed them; the scoundrels had no mercy.'
> Thus the chronicler Dino Compagni described the battle of Campaldino on 11 June, 1289.

by Jacopo di Cambio, is the distinguishing feature of Poppi, isolated on a green hill in the Arno Valley. Jacopo's son Arnolfo is said to have copied his father's masterpiece when designing the Palazzo Vecchio in Florence.

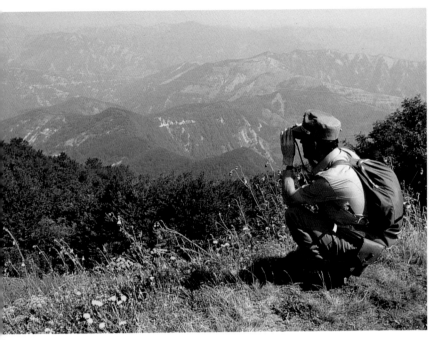

A forester in the Foreste
Casentinesi National Park

North of the town, at the
junction for Stia (SS310) and
the Consuma Pass (SS70), a
20th-century column marks the
Campaldino plain where, in
1289, 1,300 horsemen and
10,000 foot-soldiers of Guelph
Florence routed the 800 horsemen and 8,000 foot-soldiers of
Arezzo (see panel on page 81).
Even Dante was there, as a
'lightly-armed knight' in the
vanguard. Arezzo suffered
1,700 casualties, with another
2,000 or more taken prisoner.
This heavy defeat marked the
beginning of the decline of
Ghibelline fortunes in Tuscany.

☐ *Via Cavour 11*

▶ *Follow the signs north for
Camàldoli.*

🔳 Camàldoli
Count Maldolo d'Arezzo is
said to have donated the land
on which San Romualdo
constructed the original
hermitage in 1012. A few

years later, 3km (2 miles)
further south, the pilgrims'
hospitium (now the guests'
quarters) was built, followed by
the monastery of Fontebuona.
The monastic community
flourished here, especially
between the 12th and 15th
centuries, extending its
influence all over Casentino.

Camàldoli was an important
cultural centre. From the
presses of its printing works
came the *Costituzioni
Camaldolesi*, a tract that
included the planting and care
of the surrounding fir woods
designated among the duties of
religious practice.

▶ *Continue northwards to the
Eremo of Camàldoli.*

🔳 Eremo di Camàldoli
The hermitage, standing solitary 1,104m (3,622 feet) above
sea level, is reached through a
monumental forest of soaring fir
trees. You can visit the church,
renewed in the 17th and 18th
centuries (including that of the
founder's cell). Other cells are
clustered to form a sort of village

based on the model of eastern
monasticism, with about 20
one-storey houses arranged in
five rows, divided by right-
angled paths. Each has a small
portico, vestibule, bedroom,
latrine, study, oratory, wood
store and vegetable garden.
Francis of Assisi himself stayed
in one of them.

▶ *Take the road to the west
(bear right at the next two
main junctions) that leads via
Lonnano to Pratovecchio; here
cross the SS310 and follow
the signs for Castello di
Romena.*

🔳 Castello di Romena
Built around the year 1000 on a
scenic site already inhabited in
Etruscan and Roman times, the
castle came under Florentine
occupation, and from the 12th to
the mid-14th century it was one
of the major fortified bases of
the Guidi counts. Although
closed to the public, you can see
the remains of the mighty ring
of walls, the castle keep and
three of the original 14 towers
(donjon, postern and prison).

Above: Vallombrosa Abbey in its
present 17th-century guise
Below: San Romualdo, Camàldoli

▶ *Return to the junction signposted for the Pieve di
Romena.*

6 Pieve di Romena

Isolated in the most beautiful
countryside, the parish church
of San Pietro di Romena (12th
century) is one of the most
interesting Romanesque buildings in the Casentino – despite
having been mutilated over the
centuries by landslides and
earthquakes. Particularly
attractive is the exterior of the
apse, adorned with two rows of
arches featuring a pair of two-
mullioned windows and a
three-mullioned one. All works
of art have been removed from
the interior for safety (if closed,
knock at the country house
near by).

▶ *Continue to the SS70, which
to the right goes over the
Consuma Pass (1,060m/
3,478 feet) amid mountain
scenery. After passing the*

*village of Consuma turn left
for Vallombrosa.*

7 Vallombrosa

The road that climbs the northern tip of Pratomagno passes
through boundless woods of

silver fir trees (planted over the
centuries by monks), mixed
with beech, chestnut and
Corsican pine trees. Florentine
San Giovanni Gualberto,
disappointed by the lack of
rigour at Camàldoli, founded
the abbey for a Vallombrosian

SPECIAL TO...

Born in Ravenna to an aristocratic family around 952, the
restless Romualdo was always
torn between the importance
of community life and his
fascination with the
hermit's solitude.
Every monk in the
community can ask to be
transferred to the hermitage;
the theory runs that only
those who have developed
their own spirituality through
contact with the world have
the strength to cope with the
solitude that leads to
perfection. However, the
hermit can also ask to
return to the Benedictine
'communal house', a hive of
monastic industry.

congregation in 1055. Driven by the desire for poverty and the eradication of hierarchy, the Vallombrosian Benedictines distinguished themselves for their opposition to the corrupt Florentine bishopric. The grandiose complex today presents an almost military appearance, a result of its restoration in the 17th century. The English poet John Milton visited the abbey in 1638 and was inspired to refer to Vallombrosa in his famous work, *Paradise Lost*.

i *Via San Giovanni Gualberto 40, Saltino (seasonal)*

▶ *Travel via Saltino and Pietrapanna, following the signs for Reggello and Cascia.*

8 Cascia

The treasure of tiny Cascia is the parish church of San Pietro, a well-preserved Romanesque structure in ashlar sandstone (12th–13th century). At the end of the left-hand aisle, a triptych dated 1422 is said to be the first work by Masaccio, who painted it at just 21 years of age, already showing his innovatory sense of volume and mass.

i *See above*

▶ *Turn around and take the first road on the right that leads via Pian di Scò to Castelfranco di Sopra; after*

passing through the village, follow the signs for San Giovanni Valdarno.

9 San Giovanni Valdarno

A square gridplan, enclosed within rectangular walls broken by four gates, is a clue to this town's origins as a 'new land', founded by the Florentines on the left bank of the Arno in 1299. Like the nearby Terranuova Bracciolini and Castelfranco di Sopra, it was designed by Arnolfo di Cambio (1245–1310); he was also responsible for the Palazzo d'Arnolfo, altered from the 15th century on. In 1401, San Giovanni Valdarno was the birthplace of Tommaso di Ser Giovanni Cassai, better known as Masaccio and destined to revolutionise Florentine

RECOMMENDED WALK

For a fine view of Vallombrosa (958m/3,143 feet) climb to the left of the monastery up a lovely path past small shrines and shelters – the scene in the past of miracles and harsh hermit asceticism – to the so-called Paradisino terrace (1,032m/3,386 feet). The views of the woodlands surrounding the abbey, built on the east bank of the Arno, are superb.

SPECIAL TO...

On the outskirts of Castelfranco di Sopra stands the former abbey (Badia) of Soffena, built in the 14th century by the Vallombrosian monks, abandoned in the 18th century and today restored and designated a national monument. Frescoes by 15th-century Tuscan artists decorate the walls of the Greek cruciform interior.

painting during his brief, intense life (he died at the age of 27). Recently reappraised works by his brother Giovanni are kept in the 14th-century church of San Lorenzo. The Museum of the Basilica of Santa Maria delle Grazie houses an *Annunciation* painted by a young Fra' Angelico.

i *Piazza Cavour 3*

▶ *Proceed southeast along the SS69 for Arezzo, turning left at the junction signposted for Terranuova Bracciolini and Loro Ciuffenna.*

10 Loro Ciuffenna

As you leave Loro Ciuffenna, a medieval village situated on a chasm cut by the Ciuffenna river, an asphalt road to the left leads to the Romanesque parish church of San Pietro di Gròpina, built around 1000 on an existing religious site. Of note inside is the pulpit, sculpted with a lion, a deacon, and an eagle that serves as a lectern. It's now time to return to Arezzo but, just before you cross the Arno at Ponte a Buriano, the grassy bank of a bend in the river on the right is an enchanting spot for a little relaxation.

▶ *Follow the signs for Arezzo to the southeast.*

Above: view of Loro Ciuffenna
Right: the central panel in the triptych of San Pietro, at Cascia, attributed to Masaccio

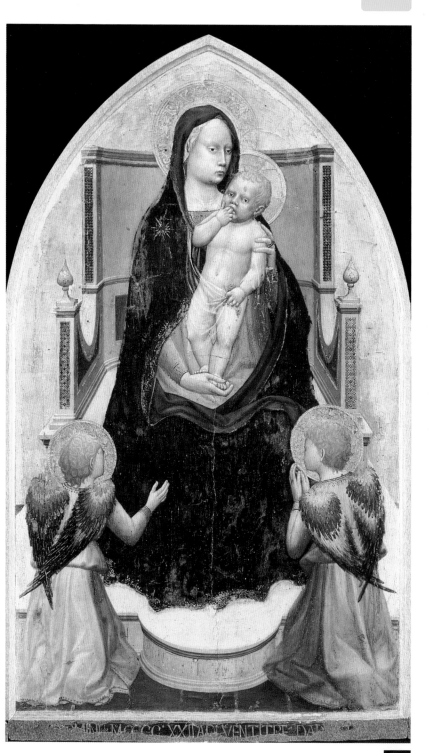

Upper Val Tiberina
& Valdichiana

Before embarking on this tour visiting locations associated with
Piero della Francesca, enjoy an introduction to his art by viewing
the *Legend of the True Cross*, his fresco cycle in the Gothic church
of San Francesco in Arezzo, created between 1453 and 1466.

The old village of Anghiari, within
its walls

i *Piazza della Repubblica 28,
Arezzo*

▶ *Take the* **SS73** *towards
Sansepolcro-Città di Castello,
turn right on to the* **SS221** *for
Città di Castello and continue
to the turning signposted on
the right for Monterchi.*

❶ Monterchi
From the pretty walled village
on a hillock, descend to the
former school to see the fresco
Madonna del Parto, one of Piero
della Francesca's masterpieces.
An excellent exhibition illus-
trates the phases of its recent
restoration. It was completed
around 1455 for a chapel in what
is now the cemetery; at some
point the fresco will be returned
to its original location.

i *Piazza Umberto I*

▶ *Return along the* **SS221**
to the junction with the
SS73 *and follow the latter
to the turning on the left
for Anghiari.*

❷ Anghiari
The Tarlati family, 14th-century
lords of Arezzo, built the long
straight stretch of road to
Sansepolcro, and Anghiari developed in its wake, becoming a
Florentine domain after a
famous battle fought in 1440. It
has steep, narrow streets, charming little squares and the
wonderful atmosphere of the
Renaissance Palazzo Taglieschi
(home of the State Museum),
combined with several old tower-
houses. An unusual collection of

SPECIAL TO...

Several places on this tour
have associations with the
artist Piero della Francesca.
He was born in Sansepolcro
around 1420, and the Civic
Museum there contains two of
his works. Arezzo is home to
one of his most famous pieces,
Legend of the True Cross, in the
church of San Francesco, while
the *Madonna del Parto* can be
seen in Monterchi. Further
afield, more of his work can be
seen in Perugia (see page 121).

---

stretchers is on display in the
16th-century rooms of the
Confraternità di Misericordia,
not far from the old Camaldolese
church of Badìa.

About 17km (11 miles)
to the north of Anghiari is
Caprese Michelangelo, where
Michelangelo's home has been
turned into a small museum
which, unfortunately, does not
contain any of his works.

i *Corso Matteotti 103*

▶ *Follow the signs northeast for
Sansepolcro.*

❸ Sansepolcro
Borgo Sansepolcro (as it was
once called) is said to have
developed after two 10th-
century monks returning from
the Holy Land founded an
oratory here to house the relics
of St Sepolcro. This lovely little
town, packed with houses and
mansions in pure Renaissance
style, is renowned for its crafts
(embroidery, wrought iron,
gold-work), for the Palio della
Balestra (crossbow shooting
competition) in 15th-century
dress and, above all, as the

birthplace of Piero della Francesca (1415/20–92). Some of his works – all sublime – can be admired in the Civic Museum (from the outside, you can see the detached fresco of the *Resurrection* through a window). The Renaissance church of San Lorenzo contains a *Deposition* painted by Rosso Fiorentino (1528–30).

[i] *Piazza Garibaldi 2*

▶ *Follow the old Tiberina state road southeast to San Giustino.*

◪ San Giustino
Make sure you visit the Bufalini castle, now owned by the state. Built in 1480–92 as a fortress with corner towers, drawbridge and moat, it was converted in the 16th century by the Bufalini

family, who turned it into a stately residence. Paintings, furniture, majolicas, marble busts and furnishings (accumulated between the 16th and 19th centuries) reflect the tastes of the former owners.

▶ *Continue southeast along the old Tiberina road to Città di Castello.*

◩ Città di Castello
This rarity among the towns of medieval Umbria is essentially Renaissance in style – flat, with wide, straight streets. All this is revealed when you take the SS257 Apecchiese road to the sanctuary of the Madonna del Belvedere (17th century). In the 1st to 2nd century AD Pliny the Younger owned a villa and vast estates here; the modern urban layout was developed

during the rule of the Vitelli family, from the middle of the 15th to the 16th century. Their power was symbolised in four grandiose mansions, each dominating a district, and the face of the town was changed by their redesigning, demolition and restructuring work. The Vitelli family called on outstanding artists such as Luca Signorelli from Cortona, Raffaello Sanzio (Raphael) from Urbino (who painted four of his masterpieces here), Giorgio Vasari from Arezzo and Rosso Fiorentino to embellish their residences and churches. Some of these works, now mainly scattered, remain in the town's Picture Gallery, arranged in Palazzo Vitelli alla Cannoniera, whose elegant façade overlooking the garden was designed by Vasari. In the museum of the Duomo

The round bell tower of Città di Castello's Duomo

(beneath which lies a 'lower' church with sunken vaults on stocky pillars) you can admire a *Transfiguration* painted by Rosso Fiorentino. Lovers of contemporary art can enjoy numerous works by Alberto Burri (1915–95) donated by the artist to his fellow citizens from 1978 onwards. These are displayed in the 15th-century Palazzo Albizzini and, outside the town, in the disused Seccatoi Tabacchi sheds. Also outside the town, at Galazzo, is a fascinating Centre of Popular Traditions.

[i] *Piazza Matteotti, Logge Bufalini*

▶ *Continue along the old Tiberina road to the*

turning signposted on the left for Montone.

6 Montone

At the end of the 13th century the Fortebracci family of Perugia took possession of the fortress of Montone, founded in the early Middle Ages on the road between Città di Castello and Gubbio. Their rule is recalled in a costume ceremony that re-enacts the 'donation of the Holy Thorn', a relic which the son of the famous Braccio da Montone (see box) gave Montone in 1473. It is displayed on Easter Monday beneath the gilded baroque coffered ceiling of the collegiate of Santa Maria. At the top of the village stand the ruins of the Rocca di Braccio, destroyed in 1478. On another rise, the Gothic San Francesco (14th century with important votive frescoes) is today used as the town museum. Holiday flats have been created in the adjacent cloister.

[i] *Via San Francesco 1*

The Tuscan countryside surrounding Arezzo

▶ *After a short stretch to the northeast, turn right on to the road for Umbèrtide.*

7 Umbèrtide

Devastated by bombing in 1944, Umbèrtide was rebuilt as a

FOR HISTORY BUFFS

Many Umbrian adventurers roamed Italy during the restless period of transition from city-state communal government to the feudal Signoria. The ambitious Braccio da Montone (born Andrea Foretebracci in 1368) was one notorious example. Having served as a mercenary under Alberico da Barbiano, he worked his way into high society, becoming lord of Bologna and later of Perugia (1416) and Città di Castello (1422). Veering between alliance and enmity with the papacy, he is said to have cast his sights on the throne of Italy. In 1424, however, he was wounded beneath the walls of L'Aquila and lay there for three days, refusing food and medicine before dying without a word.

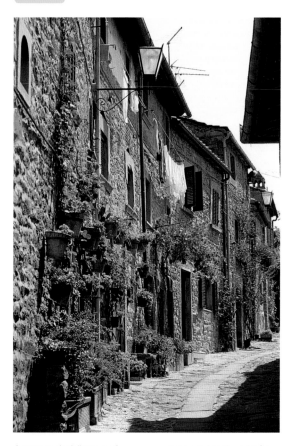

A street in the hilly town of Cortona

thoroughly modern town, but it has ancient origins. It was the site of the 14th-century Rocca (feudal stronghold) of Fratta, in whose dungeon the young condottiere Braccio da Montone was incarcerated in 1393 for causing the family financial difficulties. The nearby octagonal collegiate, surmounted by a large dome, dates from the 16th century. A few steps away, across the Tiber, is the secluded Piazza San Francesco with its picturesque row of three old churches. Umbèrtide gained its current name in 1863, in honour of the then Crown Prince and future King Umberto.

▶ *Follow the old Tiberina road southeast to the turning*

signposted on the right for the Badia di Monte Corona.

8 Badia di Monte Corona

Founded by San Romualdo in 1008 as the headquarters of the Camaldolesi Coronesi order, this grew to be the centre of a vast estate that still survives, and is the base of one of the region's largest farming companies. Beneath the Romanesque church is a half-lit crypt with three apses and five aisles. Inside the church is a fine 8th-century sculpted ciborium. From the abbey, a sandstone block path known as the *mattonata* (there is also an 8km/5-mile unsurfaced road) climbs through beech and chestnut trees to the Monte Corona hermitage. The present occupants belong to the Carthusian Order, which forbids visits by members of the public.

▶ *Return to Umbèrtide on the old Tiberina road, turn left on to the SS416 to Mercatale, then turn right for Cortona and stop at Pierle.*

9 Pierle

As you climb the slopes of Monte Maestrino, the white castle of Pierle with its few surrounding houses stands out against the greenery. According to tradition this was, in the 5th century, the birthplace of Pope St Leo I the Great. In the 12th century it belonged to the Del Monte marquises, from whom it was taken by the Milanese Bernabò Visconti around the middle of the 14th century. Rebuilt in 1371 and then abandoned, it became a den of bandits until 1574, when Duke Ferdinando I de' Medici ordered its destruction. The imposing ruins are not open to visitors but the location is one of unquestionable charm.

▶ *Proceed to Cortona.*

10 Cortona

Cortona stands on a series of man-made hills known as 'the melons'. The Camucia tumulus, never fully explored, measures 200m (656 feet) in diameter and 14m (46 feet) high, and the Sodo hills are both around 60m (197 feet) across. Opening out of the hills are Etruscan tombs dating

---

SPECIAL TO...

Tanella di Pitagora (Pythagoras' Den) is the name given to a small Etruscan tomb of the Hellenistic period (2nd century BC), built with a barrel vault on a round stone tambour on the lower slopes of the Cortona hill. What was the Greek philosopher (570–490 BC) doing in Valdichiana? Nothing: he was never there. Scholars of the 16th and 17th centuries wrongly interpreted a source that spoke of the foundation of the Pythagorean school, mistaking Crotone for Cortona.

RECOMMENDED WALK

At Cortona, a shady avenue known as the 'flat stroll' extends for more than 1km (0.6 mile) after the scenic Piazza Garibaldi. Only the fit should attempt the ascent up steep Via Berrettini and Via Santa Croce to the imposing Medici fortress (open to visitors; contact the tourist office for details) of Girifalco (651m/2,136 feet) built in 1556. There is an exceptional view from the clearing in front of it. Near Via Berrettini, in a magical courtyard lined with cypresses, the 15th-century church of San Nicolò houses an altar flanked by paintings by Signorelli.

from the 6th to the 4th century BC. Do not miss the step-altar, unique in Etruria. It could be said that modern Etruscology was born here in 1727, when the Accademia Etrusca was founded. Surprising finds in its museum include the famous Etruscan bronze oil chandelier of the 5th to 4th century BC.

The Etruscan town of Curtum was a powerful centre in

A detail of a capital in the old centre of Cortona

Valdichiana, and the late medieval and Renaissance Cortona was equally prosperous. The cobblers' guild commissioned Francesco di Giorgio Martini to build the majestic church of the Madonna del Calcinaio in 1485, to honour a picture painted outside the walls near a vat used to tan hides. Completed in 1513, the church and its harmonious lines evoke the clarity of Brunelleschi's architecture. A wealth of monuments and haunting views can be found throughout the town. The Diocesan Museum in front of the cathedral contains a sculpted sarcophagus of the 2nd century AD, a masterpiece by Fra' Angelico and a magnificent collection of works by Luca Signorelli and his school.

i *Via Nazionale 42*

▶ *After reaching the SS71 proceed towards Arezzo to the turning on the right for Castiglion Fiorentino.*

⓫ Castiglion Fiorentino

The well-preserved medieval structure of this village reaches a Renaissance peak in the square that overlooks the countryside through the stone arches of the 16th-century Vasari loggias. A

few steps away, a narrow street descends steeply to a solitary little square surrounded by three churches. Luca Signorelli painted a fresco, *Deposition*, in the oldest – the Pieve Vecchia, dating from 1451.

i *Piazza del Municipio 12*

▶ *Return to the SS71 and follow it to Arezzo.*

RECOMMENDED EXCURSION

Isolated in a hillside meadow to the right of the SS71, between Cortona and Castiglion Fiorentino, is the Castello di Montecchio Vesponi (owned by the Arezzo family in the 11th century). The castle was passed to Florence after the battle of Campaldino (1289), and later entrusted to Englishman John Hawkwood (1325–94), forerunner of the Italian mercenaries who led the Florentines to victory at Càscina in 1364. In honour of Giovanni Acuto, as the Tuscans called him, Paolo Uccello created an equestrian portrait fresco at Santa Maria del Fiore in Florence, in 1436.

INLAND TUSCANY

Central inland Tuscany more or less corresponds to the province of Siena, one of the Tuscan areas most given over to tourism and yet still for the most part uncrowded and full of surprises. You start with the hills of the Chianti region, between Siena and Florence. This is a magical landscape of olive groves, vineyards blanketing exposed slopes, fields and wooded *maquis* and rows of cypresses climbing towards hilltop farmhouses, turreted castles and villages.

The Crete represents another typical Tuscan landscape – undulating clay hills extending as far as the eye can see between Siena and Asciano, irrigated by the Arbia river and forming a patchwork of erosion furrows, barren clay and a multitude of colours. The same can be said of the whole Sienese hill landscape – from Val d'Orcia, cut in two by the ancient (and modern) Via Cassia, on the edge of the metal-producing hills, to the slopes of Monte Amiata, the extinct volcano that dominates the southern Tuscan landscape with its belt of woods and villages.

Between these hills, the area is bisected by the River Ombrone, from the lofty Chianti mountains in the east to the Uccellina mountains in the west.

Apart from the visit to Siena, a medieval and Gothic delight established in the few brief decades straddling the 13th and 14th centuries, the key to this region's charm is its humanised landscape – Chianti, with its villages and wines, and the fascinating towns of the Siena hills, each marked by unique episodes of history and art, with the high points of Pienza, Montepulciano, Sant'Antimo and San Galgano.

Celebration in Siena

Roads and cypress trees trace an 'S' in the Tuscan countryside

Tour 15

No fixed itinerary is needed to tour Siena. The whole city has such appeal, and its areas are so uniformly medieval, that the whim of the moment is as useful a guide as any other. What you will need, though, to appreciate its charms to the full, is information. Behind every stone, every piece of iron or wood and every patch of colour is a history of centuries of a city's development and of enthusiastic participation in its traditions, as well as a background of devotion to Sienese culture.

Tour 16

The prime reason for Chianti's worldwide fame, and the principal feature of its farming landscape, are the slopes covered with row upon row of grapevines. Alternating with the wine-growing area is the extensive wooded *maquis* of oaks, chestnuts and ilex. This tour visits the most interesting Chianti centres, historically divided between Siena and Florence but all telling the story of a battle to grow crops in a predominantly mountainous and stony terrain. Modern viticulture has absorbed most of the sharecroppers' farms, after centuries of settlement by the urban bourgeoisie. Chianti-lovers can choose from a range of different kinds of hospitality, including elegant and relaxing *agriturismos* and many opportunities to taste and buy local food and drinks.

Tour 17

The Crete is an area of barren hills, making up a strange, rolling landscape southeast of Siena. The Montalcino plateau, closed on three sides by the Ombrone and Orcia rivers, features one of the finest, and perhaps the most fascinating, Romanesque monuments in all Tuscany – Sant'Antimo. Other highlights include a spa town with a pool set in its square, a miniature Renaissance town and the Palazzo Comunale, built as a copy of the Palazzo della Signoria in Florence. Between visits you can relax in the picturesque surroundings with a glass or two of the great wine produced on the local hills.

Tour 18

This tour takes you around the territories once ruled by Siena, before it was taken by the Spaniards in 1555. In parts, this surprisingly varied scenery has a northern European feel – especially the countryside around remote San Galgano. After taking in views of inland Maremma, the route climbs the great wooded pyramid of Monte Amiata. Dark volcanic stone is used in the buildings of the towns that encircle it, seen at a distance from the bare peak of Monte Labbro and the towering Rocca di Radicòfani. There's a gentler feel to the scenery around San Casciano and the Etruscan Chiusi, the only major urban centre along a mainly rural route.

Siena

Siena is a medieval city *par excellence*, crammed with rich treasures, and for many people it is infinitely more appealing than Florence, the Tuscan capital. All over the city, statues of Romulus and Remus being suckled by a she-wolf serve as a reminder that, according to legend, it was founded by Senius, the son of Remus.

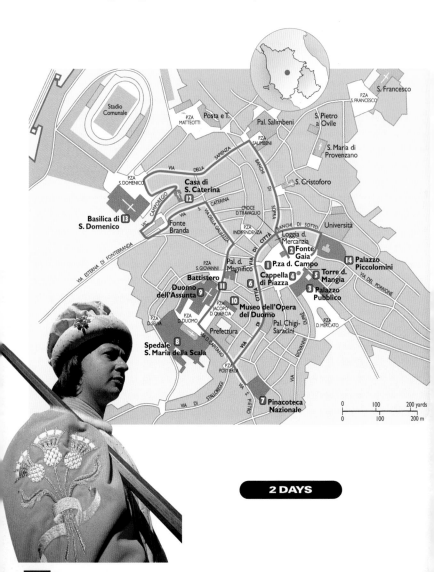

2 DAYS

ℹ️ *Piazza del Campo 56*

▶ *Leave your car in one of the outlying car parks and take the shuttle service to the old centre and Piazza del Campo.*

❶ Piazza del Campo

Sloping to the south, this square has been likened to the valve of a shell, divided into nine sections by lighter strips. It could also be compared to a theatre, with the imposing Gothic Palazzo Pubblico (the Town Hall) as the stage. In the 12th century, livestock, chickens and wheat were traded here; during the first half of the 14th century the inner section was paved with bricks and the outer ring flagged. The latter measures 333m (1,092 feet) and provides the track for the Palio (see panel), a horse-race between the city's *contrade*, or districts. During this time, the ring is covered with a thick layer of soil to provide better grip for the horses' hooves.

❷ Fonte Gaia

The popular jubilation that greeted the first gushes of water conveyed to the city by the *bottini* (approximately 30km/19 miles of underground passages

and cisterns) in 1346 prompted the name of this 'fountain of joy'. In 1868, the rectangular marble basin sculpted by Jacopo della Quercia (1374–1438) between 1409 and 1419 (the lovely original panels are being restored in Santa Maria della Scala) was moved to the centre of the square from its original position, further back.

❸ Palazzo Pubblico

In the last decade of the 13th century, the merchant oligarchy,

represented by the Council of Nine (1287–1355), started this Gothic masterpiece. Its design marks the transition from a fortress, built purely for defence, to the city mansion, a domestic residence with space for guests. When the building was completed in 1310 the Nine called in major artists to paint frescoes for its rooms (now housing the Civic Museum).

Above: the Palazzo Pubblico
Below: Piazza del Campo during the biannual Palio

4 Cappella di Piazza

The chapel loggia, constructed in front of the Torre del Mangia (see below), is the result of a vow made during the catastrophic Black Death, which carried off three-quarters of the city's inhabitants between 1328 and 1348. It proved to be an extravagant way of fulfilling a promise, making a deep hole in the Sienese economy.

5 Torre del Mangia

The 88m (289-foot) high brick tower, the second tallest medieval campanile in Italy after Cremona, was built between 1338 and 1348. In 1666 the great bell known as 'Sunto' (an abbreviation of its dedication to Our Lady of the Assumption) was cast. Its majestic peals still mark special events, such as the Palio. The view from the top is breathtaking, as are the 400 steps that lead up to it.

▶ *From the square, Passaggio San Pietro leads to the Croce del Travaglio where the main thoroughfares of the terzieri (Siena's three wards) cross – Via di Città (Terzo di Città), Banchi di Sotto (Terzo di San Martino) and Banchi di Sopra (Terzo di Camollìa).*

6 Via di Città

Dominating the Croce del Travaglio (which in the event of war was barricaded with beams to prevent incursions by enemy cavalry) is the Loggia della Mercanzia (1417–44), built for the merchants' tribunal. During the 17th century it became the meeting place of the city's nobility. Of note among the aristocratic mansions that line Via di Città is Palazzo Patrizi (14th century), now housing the Accademia degli Intronati, founded in 1525 by a group of scholars who declared themselves deafened (*intronati*) by the noise of the world. Also dating from the 14th century is the curvilinear Palazzo Chigi-Saracini; this houses the prestigious Accademia Musicale Chigiana (1932), which organises concerts for Siena's Music Week in July.

▶ *From Piazza della Posteria, turn left into Via San Pietro.*

7 Pinacoteca Nazionale

Arranged in two stately 14th- to 15th-century mansions, the Picture Gallery offers an exhaustive review of the Sienese school of painting between the late 12th century and the first half of the 17th century, exemplified by artists such as Guido da Siena, Duccio di Buoninsegna, Simone Martini and brothers Pietro and Ambrogio Lorenzetti (both victims of the Black Death), as well as Sassetta, Sano di Pietro, Sodoma and Domenico Beccafumi.

▶ *Return along Via San Pietro, Piazza della Postierla and Via del Capitano to Piazza del Duomo.*

8 Spedale Santa Maria della Scala

This hospital, according to tradition, was founded by a cobbler in 898 to tend to pilgrims, the poor and foundlings. Thanks to alms, bequests and public contributions, by the 14th and 15th centuries it had become a formidable economic and political influence; its emblem, a staircase surmounted by a cross, is seen on numerous fortified farms in the Sienese area. Indeed, such was its power that the *comune* decided to take control of it in the late 14th century. Inside the building, don't miss the Pellegrinaio Hall,

Spedale di Santa Maria della Scala

with frescoes illustrating life in a 15th-century hospital.

⑨ Duomo dell'Assunta (cathedral)

The construction of this splendid Romanesque-Gothic cathedral took 200 years (13th–14th century). The Pisano family embellished it; the father, Nicola, created the famous octagonal pulpit (1266–8) and his son, Giovanni, worked on the bottom of the façade (1285–96). Inside is the Piccolomini library, built by Cardinal Francesco for books inherited from his uncle, Pope Pius II. Its frescoes were created by Pinturicchio in 1502–9. The most extraordinary masterpiece in the cathedral is beneath your feet – the floor, all marble inlay and graffiti, divided into 56 panels designed between 1369 and 1547 by skilful Sienese

artists. Domenico Beccafumi, the most prolific, completed 35 between 1517 and 1547. Sadly, the floor is covered all year, except during the Palio.

▶ To the right of the cathedral, pass into Piazza Jacopo della Quercia.

⑩ Museo dell'Opera del Duomo

The cathedral's Museum of Works is really an artistic extension of the cathedral. Among its treasures are: the *Madonna dagli occhi grossi* (*Madonna of the Large Eyes*), before which, on the eve of the battle of Montaperti in 1260, the Sienese dedicated the city to the Virgin Mary; the enormous *Majesty* by Duccio which replaced it in 1311, on the main altar of the cathedral; the statues made by Giovanni Pisano for the façade; and works by Donatello, Jacopo

An aerial view of the Duomo

della Quercia and Pietro Lorenzetti. The building stands in the bays of the right aisle of the 'new cathedral' of 1339, which involved erecting the largest church in Christianity (and turning the hated Florence green with envy). A central axis 55m (180 feet) long was added to the side of the already completed 89m (292-foot) cathedral, turning it into the transept of a church 110m (361 feet) long. The great façade was built, but errors, lack of funds and the Black Death all intervened. Reluctantly, in 1355, the Sienese relinquished their dream. Enormous walls and arches remain, better appreciated from the top of the great façade, reached via the museum.

Duccio di Boninsegna's Majesty *in the Museo dell'Opera del Duomo*

SPECIAL TO…

The elegant Piazza Salimbeni, enclosed by three medieval and Renaissance mansions 'reassembled' in period style at the end of the 19th century, has, since 1866, been home to the still extremely powerful Monte dei Paschi. Founded in 1624 as a lending bank, its operations were guaranteed by revenue from the pastures of the Sienese Maremma.

▶ *Pass beneath the lovely side
doorway (1345) of the 'new
cathedral' and descend the
marble staircase leading to
Piazza San Giovanni.*

❶ Battistero

Perhaps as consolation after the
aborted 'new cathedral', the
entrance to the baptistery at the
rear of the cathedral was transformed into a second façade
between 1355 and 1382, incomplete, yet almost as imposing as
the main façade, and totally
hiding the apse. Inside is the
great baptismal font (1417–30)
by Jacopo della Quercia, with
additions by Lorenzo Ghiberti
and Donatello. Standing on
the square is Palazzo del

The Santa Barbara fortress

Magnifico, dedicated to
Pandolfo Petrucci, lord of Siena
between 1487 and 1512.

▶ *From Via dei Pellegrini (the
main street between the
cathedral and Piazza del
Campo, reached along the
Costerella dei Barbieri), turn
into Via di Diacceto, Via della
Galluzza and Via Santa
Caterina, all on the left.*

❷ Casa di Santa Caterina

Caterina Benincasa (1347–80)
was the daughter of a dyer,
whose eloquence enabled her to
convince Gregory XI to return to
Rome after the popes' long exile
in Avignon (1308–77). The
kitchen, bedroom, cell and
indeed the saint's whole house
were turned into a sanctuary by
the *comune* of Siena in 1464.
Slightly further on are the arches
of the fine Fonte Branda spring,
rebuilt in 1245.

▶ *After the Fonte Branda, take
the steps of Vicolo di
Camporegio to the right then
Via di Camporegio, to climb to
Piazza San Domenico.*

❸ Basilica di San Domenico

This massive church, founded
by the Dominicans (1226–1465),
looms up like a fortress from the
Camporegio hill; mendicant

orders often chose outlying locations suited to mass preaching. It
deserves a visit for Sodoma's
masterpieces of St Catherine in
Ecstasy and *Swooning* (1526).

▶ *Walk eastwards along Via
della Sapienza to Piazza
Salimbeni, then turn right into
Via Banchi di Sopra and left
into Via Banchi di Sotto to
come to Palazzo Piccolomini.*

❹ Palazzo Piccolomini

The name of Piccolomini
was synonymous during the
Renaissance with money-
changing and high finance.
Their mansion (1469) was
inspired by the styles prevalent
in Florence, where this very
wealthy family lived. Today, visitors come to see the *biccherne* of
the State Archives. These are
wooden covers used to bind the
books of the Biccherna adminis-
tration (the Treasury of Siena).
Every six months the outgoing
magistrate would have the regis-
ters of his half-year period
bound, and the covers painted
by leading Sienese artists. They
now provide an archive of
exceptional documentary and
artistic value; more than 100
survive from the period between
1258 and 1682.

▶ *Via Rinaldini leads back to
Piazza del Campo.*

The Chianti
Hills

Woods, wheat fields, olive trees, vines on hillside slopes, black cypresses beneath farmhouses and villas, walled villages, castles, parish churches and abbeys – all add to the charm of the Chianti hills.

1/2 DAYS • 175KM • 109 MILES

Brolio Castle dominates the
Chianti landscape

i *Piazza del Campo 56, Siena*

▶ *Take the **SS73** for Arezzo-
Perugia and turn left after
14.5km (9 miles) for
Castelnuovo Berardenga.*

❶ Castelnuovo Berardenga
In the 10th century, the area on
the border with Sienese territory, was subject to the author-
ity of Berardo, a nobleman of
Frankish descent. Little more
than a tower remains of the late
14th-century castle. Taken
repeatedly by the Florentines
and recaptured by the Sienese,
it finally fell into disuse after
Siena's collapse in 1555. The
Landscape Museum provides
an excellent interpretation of
the Sienese area. Local industries include wine production
and wrought ironwork.

i *Via del Chianti 61*

▶ *Proceed north on the **SS484**
towards Radda to the turning
on the left for the Castello
di Brolio.*

❷ Castello di Brolio
Brolio stands on a solitary
hillock, within the mighty 15th-
century ramparts erected by
Florence and at the centre of
the territory that belonged for
centuries to the family of Baron
Bettino Ricasoli, prime minister
of the Kingdom of Italy (1861–2
and 1866–7). In 1860 he built a
crenellated mansion in the
romantic style, where he died
20 years later. The baron – an
expert in wines – devoted
himself to wine production in
the estate cellars from 1838.

▶ *Return to the **SS484**
towards Radda then turn
right on to the **SS408** for
Gaiole.*

❸ Gaiole in Chianti
Lying on the valley floor, framed
by vineyards, this market town
developed in the mid-13th
century. A hundred years later it
joined the Chianti league and its
emblem was the black cockerel,
still found on DOC bottle
labels. Above the town of
Gaiole, you can pay a visit to
Spaltenna and the 12th-century
Romanesque parish church of

Santa Maria, as well as to the
walled town of Vèrtine, which
developed in the 12th and 13th
centuries and belonged to the
Ricasoli family.

i *Via Galilei 11*

▶ *Continue along the **SS408**
northbound to the turning off
for the Badia a Coltibuono.*

❹ Badia a Coltibuono
The Romanesque church of
San Lorenzo is all that remains
of the abbey that, from 1095
to 1810, belonged to the
Vallombrosian Benedictines.

SPECIAL TO...

Northwest of Castelnuovo
Berardenga, at Pievasciata, is
the Chianti Sculpture Park,
which has a collection of modern installations and sculptures
by artists from all over the
world. These sculptures are
arranged in over 13 hectares
(32 acres) of woodland. The
original pottery building has
also been transformed into an
imaginative art gallery.

The monastery complex, surrounded by green age-old fir trees, now houses a wine-producing estate along with a restaurant.

▶ *Follow the signs for Radda.*

5 Radda in Chianti
High on the hill that separates the Pesa Valley from that of the Arbia, Radda (530m/1,739 feet above sea level) was an important castle controlled by Siena until 1176. Under Florence it was fortified and made the capital of the Chianti league (1384). Fine 15th- and 16th-century buildings stand out in the medieval centre, which has an elliptical plan. Radda combines traditional production of wine and oil with its role as a resort and *agriturismo* holiday centre. A lovely detour north from the road to Greve leads to the small fortified village of Volpaia and its castle.

[i] *Piazza del Castello*

▶ *Drive a little way back and turn left, following the signs for Greve.*

6 Greve in Chianti
Now named after the navigator Giovanni da Verrazzano (1480–1528, family castle slightly further north), Greve's large square was once the venue for a major market. Goods were

displayed and business was conducted beneath the two wings of terraced porticoes that converge like a funnel towards the church of Santa Croce. Today, it makes a delightful place to rest.

In the Middle Ages the town was controlled by the ancient castle of Montefioralle, just west of Greve. The lovely stone village with streets cobbled in a circular pattern and picturesque closed passages is a great place to wander around.

[i] *Piazza Matteotti 11*

▶ *Continue along the SS222, turn left after 3.8km (2 miles) and drive north following the signs for Impruneta.*

7 Impruneta
In the event of human or bovine plagues, drought, wars and persistent rainfall, the devout Florentines would rush to the miraculous picture of the Madonna dell'Impruneta and accompany it in procession to Florence. Built on a site that had been a place of worship since Etruscan times (6th century BC), the sanctuary was consecrated as a parish church in 1060, then rebuilt and enlarged several times, until its final restructuring in the mid-15th century. The

The market in the lovely Piazza di Greve in Chianti

entrance portico and loggias date from the 16th century. The streets of this large village radiate from the square, where the ancient agricultural fair of San Luca, a major event, is held in mid-October. The parade of floats for the grape festival held here at the end of September is only about 70 years old. Impruneta is the centre of the local terracotta industry.

[i] *Piazza Buondelmonti 30*

▶ *Follow the signs for the A1 northwest to Firenze-Certosa and here take the motorway for Siena leaving it at Poggibonsi Nord; the SS429 for Radda leads to Castellina.*

8 Castellina in Chianti
From Val d'Elsa, you pass the ilex and cypress trees of lovely

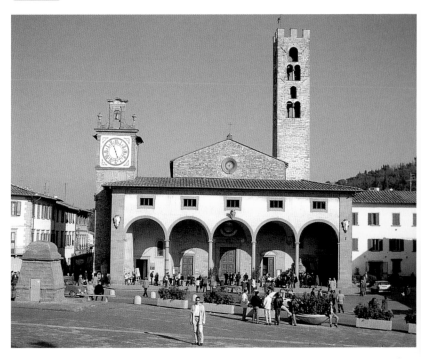

Sant'Agnese wood (nature reserve) to return to the domains of the Chianti league, of which Castellina was an important centre. Magnificently positioned in beautiful country-side scattered with buildings from the era of the grand dukes (many now converted into holiday homes), the town has a medieval square plan and 15th- to 16th-century houses, domi-nated by the crenellated tower and castle-keep (14th–15th century). Picturesque views can be enjoyed from the medieval Via delle Volte. On the road to Siena, five Etruscan tombs dating back to the 6th century BC have been excavated from the necropolis at Poggino.

i *Piazza del Comune 1*

▶ *Return to Siena on the SS222.*

Above: Impruneta's Sanctuary
Below: celebrating the wine festival in Impruneta

SPECIAL TO...

Weary of armed conflict, rivals Florence and Siena came up with an alternative means of dividing Chianti between them. At the first cock's crow, two horsemen were to set off at full speed from their respective cities; the point where they encountered each other was to mark the new border. The wily Florentine entrusted with the task skimped on the feed of his cockerel, which started to sing with hunger when it was still dark. The Florentine rider set off earlier, as a result, and this is why – so they say – Florentine Chianti is larger than that of Siena.

The Crete
to Val d'Orcia

2 DAYS • 187KM • 116 MILES As well as the harsh and gently undulating Sienese Crete, meaning 'craters' – one of Tuscany's great landscapes – this tour winds past fortified towns, castles, abbeys, country churches, farms, storehouses, magnificent Renaissance cities of art and delightful spas, offering a journey through the Sienese Middle Ages.

ITINERARY		
SIENA	▶	**Asciano (26km-16m)**
ASCIANO	▶	**Abbazia di Monte Oliveto Maggiore (9km-5½m)**
ABBAZIA DI MONTE OLIVETO MAGGIORE	▶	**Montalcino (23km-14m)**
MONTALCINO	▶	**S.ant'Àntimo (10km-6m)**
SANT'ÀNTIMO	▶	**Rocca d'Orcia (19km-12m)**
ROCCA D'ORCIA	▶	**Bagno Vignoni (5km-3m)**
BAGNO VIGNONI	▶	**San Quirico d'Orcia (6km-4m)**
SAN QUIRICO D'ORCIA	▶	**Pienza (10km-6m)**
PIENZA	▶	**Montepulciano (14km-9m)**
MONTEPULCIANO	▶	**Serre di Rapolano (33km-20½mm)**
SERRE DI RAPOLANO	▶	**Siena (32km-20m)**

[i] *Piazza del Campo 56, Siena*

▶ *Take the SS326 for Perugia and turn right on to the SS438 to Asciano.*

1 Asciano

An extraordinary landscape known as the Crete – an expanse of rounded hills largely devoid of trees – awaits visitors who venture south of Siena. Often used just for pasture, they're made bizarrely uneven by erosion furrows and outcrops of greyish clay (known as *biancane*). The sunshine and the shadows colour them a thousand unusual shades, depending on the season and the time of day. The shapes

SCENIC ROUTES

The loveliest part of this tour is the road between Siena and Asciano, used on both the outward and return journeys, and therefore caught in changing light at different times of the day. The rolling hills that disappear on the horizon are green with wheat and sweet-smelling meadows in spring but bare and arid in summer. Spectacular views of the Crete can be enjoyed both before and after the Abbey of Monte Oliveto.

A summer scene in the Crete near Asciano

and colours of the Crete appear in the pictures of the Sienese school, and interesting works by its 15th-century artists (such as Matteo di Giovanni and the Master of the Osservanza) can be admired in the Civic Museum of Casa Corboli, in Asciano. At the other end of this fortified Sienese town stands the fine collegiate of Sant'Agata (11th-century).

[i] *Via delle Fonti (seasonal)*

▶ *Return along the SS438 and turn left on to the SS451, then follow the signs for the Abbazia di Monte Oliveto Maggiore.*

2 Abbazia di Monte Oliveto Maggiore

Founded in 1319 by the Blessed Bernardo, this Olivetan Benedictine monastery stands in a wooded park on a scenic rise, protected on three sides by the steep Crete and barred on the fourth by a crenellated tower. Most visitors come to Monte Oliveto to see the frescoes in the abbey's main cloister. These form one of the most important Renaissance cycles, painted between 1495 and 1505

by Luca Signorelli and by Sodoma (whose real name was Giovan Antonio Bazzi; the nickname is a reference to the artist's supposed homosexuality). The 36 scenes depict episodes from the life of St Benedict. In the adjacent church, a magnificently inlaid wooden choir portrays 16th-century scenes of Siena. It's also worth visiting the abbey library, which has a basilica plan and three aisles and is rich in 14th- and 15th-century illuminated choir-books.

▶ *Follow the SS451 to Buonconvento, then take the SS2 (Via Cassia) south before turning right for Montalcino.*

3 Montalcino

The bastions of the pentagonal Rocca (stronghold) that crowns the Montalcino hill (the Roman

SPECIAL TO...

The fish farmed in the large brick pool in the Abbey of Monte Oliveto's park allowed the monks to respect the rules prohibiting the consumption of meat at certain periods. This traditional dietary expedient was adopted to alleviate the rigours of the Christian lifestyle.

Mons Ilicinus or Hill of Ilex Trees) offer splendid views of the village and vineyards, spread across the uneven plateau between the Ombrone and Asso valleys. Inside it reveals evidence of the past and present importance of the village. A wine cellar on the ground floor of the keep invites visitors to taste famous local wines such as Brunello and Rosso di Montalcino. In a hall above, a threadbare standard is a reminder that this fortress, built in 1361, was the last bastion of Sienese independence. When the city fell into the hands of Florence in 1555, the steadfast defenders of the republic barricaded themselves inside and for four years resisted the superior Medici forces. Of note in the square are the Palazzo dei Priori and the nearby Gothic loggia. All along the main street shops

housed in late-medieval buildings tempt wine-lovers with their merchandise.

ℹ️ *Costa Municipio 8*

▶ *Continue south, following the signs to Sant'Àntimo.*

⓭ Sant'Àntimo

Descend through the vineyards of the legendary Brunello wine to the splendid abbey church of Sant'Àntimo, standing solitary in a small valley near a stream. According to legend, it was founded by Charlemagne in 781; in the Middle Ages the abbey controlled another 38 churches besides Montalcino, scattered as far as Grosseto, Florence and Pistoia. The present church dates from the 12th century and has travertine stone walls, given a remarkable brilliance and golden reflections

by the onyx used as decoration. A fine sculpted doorway (bearing the name of the monk and architect Azzone dei Porcari) leads to the irregular interior, with a nave and two aisles divided by round arches, on to which open the elegant, double-lit apertures of the women's gallery. Of note among the capitals, all covered with symbols and fantastic creatures, is that portraying *Daniel in the Lion's Den*. There is an attractive semi-circular apse with radiating

**Above: the abbey of Sant'Àntimo
Left: the Montalcino stronghold**

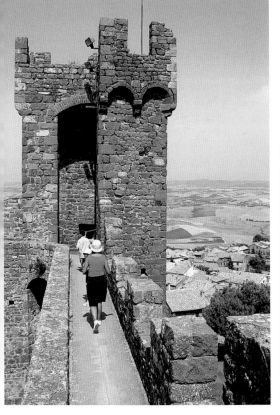

FOR HISTORY BUFFS

Around the middle of the 19th century, a local vinedresser, Ferruccio Biondi Santi, decided not to blend Sangiovese grapes but to leave them instead to mellow in oak or chestnut barrels. Thanks to its strictly circumscribed production area – officially limited to 800 hectares (1,977 acres) – and refined ageing process (at least three years, on average seven), Brunello became, in 1980, the first wine in Italy to be labelled DOCG (Origin Controlled and Guaranteed).

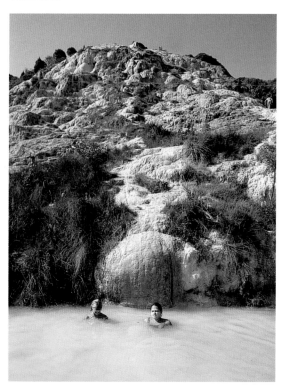

Spa delights in the waters of
Bagno Vignoni

chapels – a design of French
inspiration rarely found in
Italian churches.

▶ *Continue southeast and turn
left on to the SS323, which
climbs north to Castiglione
d'Orcia and Rocca d'Orcia.*

5 Rocca d'Orcia

Nestling at the foot of the vertig-
inous remains of the Rocca di
Tentennano, whose windy
summit offers a breathtaking
view of Monte Amiata, the Orcia
Valley and the Rocca di
Radicòfani, this village retains its
medieval character in its little
stone houses. St Catherine of
Siena stayed in one of these
houses in 1377, while trying to
restore peace to two branches of
the Salimbeni family, powerful
lords of Val d'Orcia between
1274 and 1419. The small, irregular square features a wonderful

old polygonal water basin.
Those who climb towards the
overhanging Rocca can visit the
small church of San Simeone,
and the church of the company
of St Sebastian.

i *Viale San Giovanni, Castiglione
d'Orcia*

▶ *Follow the SS323 north, then
turn left on to the SS2 and,*

FOR CHILDREN

Today, use of the pool in the
square at Bagno Vignoni is
prohibited, but a hotel with a
fine swimming pool on the
outskirts of the village
commands beautiful views of
the Orcia Valley below. Open
summer and winter, it offers
relaxation to the weary
traveller even on the coldest
days, and has a splendid water
games area for tiny tots.

---

*shortly afterwards, left again
for Bagno Vignoni.*

6 Bagno Vignoni

Bagno Vignoni, a spa that developed in the Middle Ages, is a
true surprise to visitors. The
town square is surrounded by
old houses and occupied by an
enormous pool of steaming
sulphurous water. It has seen
illustrious guests – even the 13-
year-old Caterina da Benincasa,
the future St Catherine, came
here from Siena. The loggia
with a small shrine that closes off
one side of the square is named
after her. She was brought here
by her mother, who hoped to
distract her from her solemn religious vocation, but she apparently went so close to the hot
springs – the water flows out of
the pool at 51°C (124°F) – that
she turned even the pleasure of
the spa into religious penitence.
In 1490 the gout-ridden
Lorenzo de'Medici came here.
Not all visitors, however, were
satisfied in times past (in 1581
Michel de Montaigne considered the spa 'a hole') but in
recent times the unusual charm
of Bagno Vignoni has led several
directors to set their films here:
Andrej Tarkovskij filmed
Nostàlghia (1983) here, and
Carlo Verdone used it for part
of his *Al lupo, al lupo* (1992).

▶ *Rejoin the SS2 and continue
left to San Quìrico d'Orcia.*

7 San Quìrico d'Orcia

Situated along the ancient
pilgrims' way, Via Francigena,
San Quìrico was an important
stopping place between
Florence and Rome. Its walls,
broken at intervals by towers,
surround the shady park and
Italian garden of the Horti
Leonini family, created around
1540. The main attraction in
this village is a 14th-century
collegiate with three extraordinary carved doorways. The
main portal, dating from 1080,
features clustered columns,
tied with a loop at the centre,
resting on lionesses, with
mythical monsters grappling in

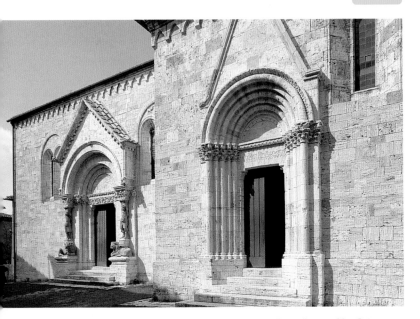

the bas-relief on the architrave. The first of the two, on the right side, presents powerful lions beneath caryatids, sculpted in the 13th century. Inside, there is a fine 16th-century wooden choir.

ℹ️ *Via Dante Alighieri 33*

▶ *Take the SS146 to Pienza.*

8 Pienza
Pienza was known as Corsignano until Pope Pius II ordered Bernardo Rossellino, a pupil of Leon Battista Alberti, to turn his native country village into a vision of rationalist beauty. In 1459 work began on the 'Utopian town' that was even named after its patron, Pienza. The planned architectural transformation – sadly interrupted by the deaths of both Pius II and Rossellino in 1464 – was accomplished in the square, paved in brick and strips of stone, on which stand a cathedral in travertine stone (the interior glitters with the gold of splendid Sienese altarpieces

Strolling through the castle at Pienza, with sweeping views of Val d'Orcia

ordered by the Pope) and Palazzo Piccolomini (similar in design to Alberti's Palazzo Rucellai in Florence). The loggia overlooking the mansion's hanging garden offers a splendid view of the Orcia Valley; all around are the residences that the erudite Pope forced the cardinals to build, to add lustre to his magnificent extension of the Roman court.

ℹ️ *Corso Rosselino 30*

The collegiate of San Quìrico

▶ *Continue along the SS146 to Montepulciano.*

9 Montepulciano
Montepulciano lies along the crest of a hill between the Orcia Valley and Valdichiana, When, in the 12th century, Valdichiana turned into marshland, traffic shifted towards Montepulciano, resulting in expansion of trade and manufacturing. The town started to accumulate great riches in the 14th century and over the next 200 years, under Florentine rule, spent lavishly on secular, religious and military constructions. An enviable art heritage was amassed and the creators of the town include names such as Michelozzo, Antonio da Sangallo, Baldassarre Peruzzi and Jacopo da Vignola. Stylish aristocratic homes line the two main streets, which culminate in the monumental Piazza Grande. Here, alongside Palazzo Comunale (a small-scale copy of Florence's Palazzo Vecchio), stand the Duomo (cathedral), Palazzo Tarugi, Palazzo Contucci and that of the Palazzo del Capitano del Popolo; facing this is the Pozzo

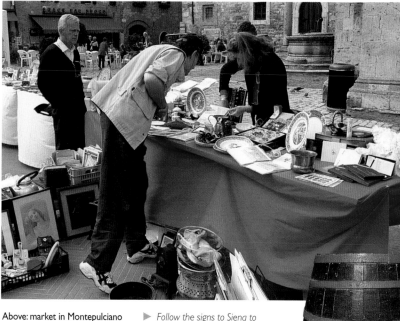

Above: market in Montepulciano
Right: an invitation to the town's famous Vino Nobile

dei Grifi e dei Leoni fountain. A short distance away is the 18th-century Regio Poliziano theatre, named after Agnolo Ambrogini, commonly known as Poliziano. This humanist poet and close friend of Lorenzo the Magnificent was born in Montepulciano in 1454. Lower down, on Via di Gracciano, is the tower surmounted by a metal-covered figure of Pulcinella, which strikes the hours. Montepulciano's most famous church, San Biagio, stands isolated outside the town on the side of a hill. This austere Renaissance masterpiece in travertine stone has, over the years, turned a mellow golden colour. Erected by Antonio da Sangallo the Elder between 1518 and 1545, it has a Greek cross plan and a high central dome; the exterior is decorated in recurring classic orders, seen also in the two bell towers (the right one unfinished) set in the intersections between the arms of the cross.

ℹ️ *Via Don Minzoni*

▶ *Follow the signs to Siena to the north via Torrita di Siena, Sinalunga and the SS326, to the second turning on the left for Serre di Rapolano.*

🔟 Serre di Rapolano

This was the site of a Byzantine fortress in the 6th century; at the time of Frederick Barbarossa it acquired an imperial palace, which, under 13th-century Sienese rule, was turned into a *grancia* – a fortified storehouse with barns, vat-rooms, olive-store and hayloft. The building is said to have been purchased from the Cacciaconti family by the Sienese merchant Giovanni de'Rossi as a home for the beautiful Ciambragina, a young girl he had married in Cambrai. Between the first two Sundays in May, the silent maze of streets and alleys that branch out around the *grancia* come alive with a medieval market filled with craftspeople, musicians, falconers, magicians, beggars, jugglers, genteel ladies and valiant cavaliers.

▶ *Take the SS438 and continue via Asciano to Siena.*

Visitate le
Antiche Cantine
Contucci

BACK TO NATURE

About 6km (4 miles) north of Serre di Rapolano, near the San Giovanni Battista spa pool, is an impressive *mofette* – a fissure in the earth, exhaling volcanic gas. Contained in an enclosed hollow, 80m (262 feet) wide and around 6m (20 feet) deep, stagnating toxic vapours of hydrogen sulphide and carbon dioxide prevent all vegetation growth. In the pleasant grove before the baths, surface springs rich in calcium (now piped) have produced a bizarre 'mountain' of white travertine stone, set amid broom bushes and oak woods – a wild but delightful spot.

Monte
Amiata

This tour takes in the majestic volcanic dome of Monte Amiata, an extinct volcano. The impermeable layer of sedimentary rocks that was covered with magma about 300,000 years ago has produced wonderful, gushing, hot springs in the area. Covered in snow for several months of the year, it is also a popular skiing centre.

2/3 DAYS • 323KM • 201 MILES

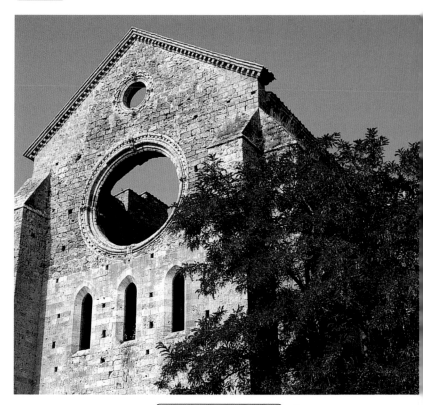

The Abbey of San Galgano stands open to the skies

ⓘ *Piazza del Campo 56, Siena*

▶ *Follow the SS73 to the south-west to Bivio del Madonnino, where you take the SS441 to the turning on the left for the Abbazia di San Galgano.*

❶ Abbazia di San Galgano
This abbey stands alone in the depths of the countryside, with the sky for a roof and a meadow for the floor. The Gothic vaults of this grandiose Cistercian monument (69m/226 feet long and 29m/95 feet wide) were erected between 1224 and 1288, but collapsed towards the end of the 18th century. Of particular beauty a few steps away, on the hilltop of Monte Siepi, is the dome of an unusual circular church. It covers the stone into which nobleman Galgano Guidotti is said to have thrust

---

SPECIAL TO...

A few miles north of Castel del Piano lies the village of Seggiano, and just to the east of that village, on the road to Pescina, is an amazing Sculpture Garden. Assembled by the Swiss artist Daniel Spoerri, it consists of almost 80 pieces of modern sculpture, arranged in a landscape setting.

---

his sword to make a cross in around 1180.

ⓘ *Abbazia di San Galgano*

▶ *Back at Bivio del Madonnino, turn right and continue to Monticiano, then go left via San Lorenzo a Merse to Ponte Macereto, right for a short way on the SS223 and then left, following the signs for Bagni di Petriolo.*

❷ Bagni di Petriolo
Hidden in the remote Farma gorge, the spa is still surrounded by sections of walls erected between 1404 and 1419. The cross vaults of a portico cover three baths, once filled with the hot sulphurous water that now flows through small natural pools on the riverbanks.

▶ *Continue and turn south-bound on to the SS223 Siena-Grosseto road, then, at the Pagànico exit, go east, following the signs for Castel del Piano; from here go via Prato delle Macinaie, skirting the northeastern slopes of Monte Amiata to the end of the road. The peak (1,738m/ 5,702 feet) is reached on foot in just a few minutes.*

❸ Monte Amiata
The peak of Monte Amiata is made up of a pile of bare reddish rocks, topped with a

large 1910 iron cross. It is one of the best skiing resorts in Tuscany.

▶ *Descend the south slope, following the signs for Arcidosso/Santa Fiora, to the turning on the left (to the right you go to Arcidosso, continuing southwards to Monte Labbro) for Santa Fiora.*

❹ Santa Fiora

This village, built with the dark grey volcanic stone that distinguishes all the centres on Monte Amiata, extends from the foot of the Aldobrandeschi's castle. Between the 11th and 15th centuries this family chose Santa Fiora as its county seat. After passing to the Sforza family in 1439, it was the only mountain village to escape Sienese rule. Grand Duke Pietro Leopoldo I did not abolish the fiefdom until 1789. From the castle, after passing the Romanesque parish church of SS Fiora e Lucilla, with its splendid polychrome altar frontals by Andrea della Robbia (1435–1525/8), you descend to the crystal-clear Peschiera (fish pond) built in the 18th century on the Fiora Springs. Its cool

Monte Amiata, a peak in Tuscany south of the Arno river

surrounding park offers an inviting and pleasant interlude.

ⓘ *Piazza Garibaldi 39*

▶ *Follow the signs eastwards for Piancastagnaio.*

❺ Piancastagnaio

Piancastagnaio also culminates in an Aldobrandeschi stronghold (13th–14th century), which, from the edge of a scenic plateau, dominates the old centre, with its compact arrangement of streets sandwiched between austere buildings built in volcanic trachyte. As you leave the village, on the right is the church of the Franciscan convent of San Bartolomeo, founded

in 1278. Facing it is a huge chestnut tree hollowed out by lightning.

▶ *Take the road north for Abbadia San Salvatore.*

❻ Abbadia San Salvatore

The new residential districts of Abbadia San Salvatore reveal its present role as the largest summer holiday and winter sports resort on Amiata. Its recent past, however, is illustrated in the museum opened in the cinnabar mines. These were worked between 1897 and 1977, during which time they produced the world's second largest output of mercury. The past is represented not only by the vast medieval centre full of Gothic and Renaissance buildings, blackened by time, but also by the Benedictine abbey of San Salvatore, whose territories extended from the Tyrrhenian Sea to Valdichiana between the late 8th century and the 12th century. The façade of the Romanesque church was begun in 1036 and the interior altered in 1590. Its remarkable column-filled crypt dates from the Lombard foundation of the complex (traditionally attributed to King Ratchis, in 743).

i *Via Adua 25*

▶ *Continue northwards to the turning on the right which passes over a tunnel on the SS2 to Cassia to reach a road on the right climbing to Radicòfani.*

7 Radicòfani

Sienese exile Ghino di Tacco was notorious for levying heavy taxes. From 1297 to 1300 he was master of Radicòfani and anyone passing through the surrounding territory was likely to be set upon and robbed by his marauders. Immediately before the village is La Posta, a late 16th-century Medici hunting lodge, subsequently turned into a resting place for travellers on the Via Cassia; Charles Dickens was among those who stayed here. In the typically medieval centre, the Romanesque church of San Pietro (13th century) has fine terracottas by Andrea della Robbia. Radicòfani's greatest attraction, however, is the massive, looming Rocca (stronghold), founded by Pope Adrian IV in 1154, turned into a fortress in 1417 and rebuilt and strengthened by Cosimo I de' Medici after 1565 (today's version is a recent reconstruction).

i *Via R Magi 59*

▶ *Leave Radicòfani and drive east towards Sarteano/Chiusi to the turning on the right, which leads, via Celle sul Rigo, to San Casciano dei Bagni.*

8 San Casciano dei Bagni

A fine little town of medieval origin on the southern slopes of Monte Cetona, San Casciano stands on a plentiful spa basin,

The tower atop Monte Labbro

and is considered the third most productive spa in Europe after Karlovy Vary (Karlsbad) and Aix-les-Bains, with over 40 hot springs. South of the town, clustered around a 19th-century villa in the form of a castle, is the luxurious Bagno di Portico spa. The establishment's hot pool overlooks the undulating hills around the town.

i *Via San Cassiano 11*

▶ *Follow the Monte Cetona road north for Sarteano to the turning on the right sign-posted for the Grotte del Belverde and Cetona.*

9 Cetona

Above the hermitage of Santa Maria a Belverde (1367), arranged around three oratories entirely decorated with frescoes, are some gloomy refuges and caves used as a shelter during the Bronze Age (2nd millennium BC). Those wishing to visit the beautiful Belverde caves – St Francis stayed in one – must contact the Civic Museum in Cetona. This is found on the

Above: Radicòfani's stronghold
Below: the Palio at San Casciano

vast 16th-century square that acts as a spectacular introduction to the village, arranged in concentric circles to imitate the dual ring of walls erected by Siena in 1458.

i Piazza Garibaldi 63

▶ *Leave Cetona to the east on the secondary road that passes over the A1 to reach the SS146 for Chiusi.*

⑩ Chiusi

Chiusi was an important centre until around AD 1000, when Valdichiana succumbed to the marshes and malaria, and went into decline. To learn about this past you must go underground: the hydraulic network of intricate tunnels, reached from the cathedral museum and also from the Museo Civico, dates from the time of Etruscan *Chamars*, which in the 6th century BC saw the splendours of Lars Porsena's reign. The route, 120m (394 feet) long, leads out into a huge 1st century BC Roman reservoir, from which you climb to the top

of a 13th-century tower that acts as a bell tower, and gives fine views all around. The museum organises guided visits to the impressive catacombs of San Mustiola (3rd–4th century), outside the town. Contact the National Archaeological Museum for visits to the Etruscan tombs.

i Piazza del Duomo 1

▶ *Take the A1 towards Arezzo and leave it at Val di Chiana to take the SS326 Bettolle-Siena road westwards.*

RECOMMENDED EXCURSIONS

The Etruscans dug a mass of tombs and underground passages in the tufa of the steep Poggio Gaiella, north of Chiusi, between the 7th and 3rd centuries BC. This area was identified by 19th-century scholars as the labyrinthine mausoleum of Lars Porsena, the sovereign who managed to take control of Rome between 509 and 504 BC, as described in Latin sources. This theory has been discarded, but some swear they have heard, in the vicinity, the cheeping of the 5,000 golden chicks said to have accompanied the King of *Chamars* to his last resting place. In the absence of the chicks, consolation can be found in the exquisite *brustico* (barbecued) fish, prepared on the traditional reed fire by restaurants on the shores of the nearby lake.

TUSCANY'S HOT WATER SPAS

'For more than 600 years the Romans had no doctors other than their baths' wrote Pliny the Elder (AD 23–79). Actually it wasn't the Romans who discovered hot water spas in Tuscany. The Etruscans already knew a thing or two on the subject; they had special magistrates, called *aquilegi*, who were responsible for protecting the spas – whose sites often coincide with modern centres.

It can't be denied, though, that the ancient Romans were great lovers of water – hot water in particular. The wealthy made sure they had a constantly heated supply by installing household systems; and the therapeutic properties of water were widely accepted, with careful distinctions drawn between various types of mineralisation, each related to the treatment of a specific condition. Indeed, the Romans developed a whole lifestyle in which shared hot baths played an important role. Spas were believed to restore and purify the body and the spirit; they were places in which to relax and socialise. In imperial times, luxurious spa buildings became synonymous with well-being, and refined and cultured tastes.

In the Middle Ages, mineral water therapy went through a period of decline. The barbarian invasions destroyed aqueducts and springs, the bathhouses were stripped and abandoned. The Christian religion waged war on them as pagan sites and places of promiscuous licentiousness. At a local level, though, use of the Roman *balnae* (pools) continued; some were even restored in the early Middle Ages. What changed was the purpose and manner of mineral water therapy. It became purely a treatment – no longer recreation – and was carried out solemnly as a medical necessity, without luxury, marble or statues: just baths, mud and lots of sweat.

The practice of hygienic and curative baths came back into fashion during the *comune* period. Hydrology appeared as a subject of study at the newborn universities of medicine; in 1292 an *ordinamentum balneorum* issued by the Podestà of Siena regulated the use of spas, introducing partitions between the different sexes. In 1337, Siena renewed the Petriolo spa, sending guardians to maintain it and collect payment from users. Large communal pools, covered with roofs, canopies or branches, were the norm, although some spas had socially differentiated pools. Those of San Giovanni at Bagni di Lucca had one pool for each rung on the social ladder – knights, ladies, male citizens, female citizens, Jewish men, Jewish women and servants.

From past to future

The Renaissance saw a flurry of treatises on the curative virtues of Tuscan waters, by scholars such as Ugolino da Montecatini (1348–1429). The Medici family's involvement in spas was temporary (late 16th century to

The open-air Saturnia spa

amusement, and pleasure, as well as treatment.

Treatment and pleasure
There's no need to be suffering from an ailment to visit a spa. Just stop along the way and try immersing yourself in a lovely, steaming, open-air pool, perhaps after a day's driving and walking. Here's a very brief selection of baths (waters 30–40°C/ 86–104°F and 40°C+/104°F+ respectively), divided by province. Check opening times.

Massa Carrara: the Equi Terme pool, in the mountains north of Carrara (see Tour 1, only 24°C/75°F but pleasant).

Lucca: the pools of Villa Ada at Bagni di Lucca (see Tour 3) and the Lake Pra' di Lama, at Pieve Fosciana in Garfagnana (see Tour 3, cloudy but inviting).

Casciana Terme: southeast of Pisa is the Casciana Terme pool (36°C/97°F in a garden in the centre; see Tour 6).

Livorno: at Venturina (see Tour 6), the Terme di Caldana pool and the Calidario lake; on the isle of Elba is the San Giovanni Spa at Portoferraio (see Tour 7).

Siena: the pools of San Giovanni Battista and the Antica Querciolaia, at Rapolano (see Tour 17); the spa at Montepulciano (see Tour 17); Bagni di Petriolo (see Tour 18; not many 'pools' but a splendid environment); the very scenic hotel pool of Bagno Vignoni (see Tour 17) and that of Bagni San Filippo, between Abbadia San Salvatore and Radicòfani (see Tour 18); the elegant pool of San Casciano dei Bagni (see Tour 18).

Grosseto: Saturnia (see Tour 9; the best known spa).

Two ways of taking the waters

early 17th century), and restricted to those of San Giuliano, San Casciano and San Filippo. Although the 17th century brought a sharp drop in attendance at spas, there was a recovery in the second half of the 18th century. Inspired by European models, the Grand Dukes of Lorraine created splendid spa towns at San Giuliano and Montecatini. In the early 19th century, Napoleon's sister Elisa Baciocchi spent her time at Bagni di Lucca. In the 19th century, these three spa centres became renowned all over Europe for their society life and frivolous encounters between scholars, politicians, royal families and the grand bourgeoisie. The middle classes visited small spa towns scattered over the territory. Unpretentious rural establishments, often with multiple communal pools, satisfied the needs of the less well off.

The golden age of spas extended into the 20th century – Montecatini was renewed in the 1920s and the Chianciano spa also took off. After World War II, spas experienced a new popularity (fuelled partly by health service reimbursements), but by the mid-1970s they were in decline again, and have recovered considerably in recent years. The future lies, perhaps, in a return to the past, with spas being seen as places of

UMBRIA

Enclosed by Tuscany, Marche and Lazio, Umbria is the only Italian mainland region with no outlets to the sea. It extends over 8,456sq km (3,265 square miles) and has over 850,000 inhabitants (the fourth smallest region in terms of population). A predominantly hilly territory, few peaks rise above 1,500m (4,920 feet); the highest mountains are in the southeast, near the Sibillini and Terminillo ranges. Then there are the fluvial basins: the 'Umbrian Valley', in particular, between Perugia and Spoleto; the valley of the Tiber; and the plains of Gubbio, Norcia and Terni. But the landscape of hills, fields, high towns and villages and mountain settings has a magic beyond dry statistics – and a reputation for great wine, especially in the Orvieto area, and olives, grown in the Trasimeno region.

Umbria has been a unified region only since the mid-16th century, when it became part of the Church State. In ancient times the axis of the River Tiber divided it into a western Etruscan area (Perugia, Orvieto) and an eastern one, initially the land of the Umbrians and later of the Romans (from 295 BC). This division was reimposed in the 6th century, when it was shared between the Byzantines (who controlled a narrow corridor between Rome and Rimini, including Amelia, Narni, Perugia, Gubbio and, further west, Orte, Orvieto, Chiusi and Cortona) and the Lombards, who installed themselves from 576 in the Duchy of Spoleto (with Terni, Foligno, Spello and Assisi). Subsequently the temporal power of the popes waned, and in 1860 Umbria became a region with a single province – with Perugia as its capital. The province of Terni was created in 1927.

Small, lush, neat and civilised, Umbria has appealing locations with a fascinating medieval atmosphere. Assisi is bound to the life of St Francis but also to the work of major western artists, including Giotto, Cimabue, Simone Martini and Pietro Lorenzetti. Then there are Gubbio, Spoleto, Orvieto, Spello, Montefalco, Bevagna and Todi, each with its own particular charm. Museums are found all over the region, some housing tiny collections but all providing a testimony to the Umbrian people's love for their native land. The scenery here is gentle, verdant and largely unspoiled in the hill areas and, along with Lake Trasimeno, comprises one of Italy's most fragile and important wetlands.

Umbrian pottery – a tradition that lives on all over the region, from Orvieto to Gubbio

Hill scenery with olive trees, one of the symbols of Umbria

Tour 19
Founded by the mythical Etruscan Euliste (whose brother, Ocno, founded Bologna and Mantua), the ancient town of Perugia remains enclosed within the 3km (2-mile) perimeter of colossal walls that date from the 4th to the 3rd century BC. The route followed by this tour is similarly confined within those walls, taking advantage of the fact that most of Perugia is a pedestrian zone.

Tour 20
Retracing the steps of the young Francis of Assisi, this itinerary explores the monuments and surroundings of Gubbio, an ancient gem of a town, built in grey calcareous stone. It then ventures across the border with Marche to the breathtaking gorges of Monte Càtria and the abbey of Fonte Avellana. Smoother roads lead back into Umbria and a special destination: Nocera Umbra, which will not fail to move you.

Tour 21
Those who are curious to discover how many shades of green exist in nature can do so on the Lake Trasimeno tour (some have counted more than a hundred). Changing with the angle of observation, the scenery that inspired the Umbrian painter Perugino (c1450–1523) is dominated by the delicate light reflected from the waters on to the hills. With a little luck and some patience you may even see the spectacular dives of the ospreys.

Tour 22
The fertile plain of the Umbrian Valley, from Assisi to Spoleto, has changed considerably over the last 50 years. Industrialisation has almost erased all signs of history, and fields of tobacco, beetroot, maize and sunflowers abound. But the hillside has, none the less, managed to preserve its gentle beauty, and vines are now cultivated alongside the area's traditional olive trees.

Tour 23
The main objective of this journey into the heart of Umbria stands on red tufa walls that plunge down between the green vineyards and golden crops of the Paglia Valley. This is the unequalled spectacle of Orvieto, particularly lovely when viewed from the SS71 from Bolsena. The scenery and even the speech seem closer to the Etruria of Pitigliano and Sovana than to the region Orvieto has belonged to since 1860. The Tiber forms a winding boundary that once separated Etruria and the Umbrian territory. Todi, perched on its triangular hill, is a delightful sight, and on the return journey you can go shopping for ceramics and great wines.

Tour 24
This tour explores the area between the Tiber and its tributary, the Nera, and between Terni and Narni, where urbanisation and industrial development contrast with islands of unspoiled hill country. In the countryside you can still see small fiefs and villages dominated by the lord's mansion or castle, as in the cases of Alviano, Lugnano and Baschi.

Tour 25
Winding past rugged mountain backdrops, Valnerina – an ancient sheep-track once used to move flocks between the Tyrrhenian and the Adriatic seas – presents very different scenes from the gentle slopes and rounded peaks so typical of the Umbrian landscape. This tour climbs the valley and ventures on to the unspoilted 'little Tibet' of the Castelluccio plateau, on the Sibillini mountain range. Norcia and Cascia are old towns with long histories, and the sanctuary of Madonna della Stella is the last surprise planned on this tour.

Perugia

Perugia is a modern, cosmopolitan town with an ancient heart. Sharing the space within its walls is 1970s and 1980s architecture designed by Aldo Rossi for the Fontivegge district; flourishing food and textile industries; fine shops; and two universities (one reserved for foreigners). The town comes alive with regular music festivals – and a chocolate festival in October.

1 DAY

- **4** PALAZZO DEI PRIORI
- **5** Collegio della Mercanzia
- **6** Collegio del Cambio
- **7** Sala dei Notari
- **8** Galleria Nazionale dell'Umbria

The Fontana Maggiore, a 13th-century masterpiece by Nicola and Giovanni Pisano

i Loggia dei Lanari, Piazza Matteotti 18

▶ *Leave your car in the underground car-park in Piazza dei Partigiani and follow the so-called Via Bagliona which rises the 50m (164 feet) up to the centre on escalators.*

❶ Via Baglioni

Entering the remains of the Rocca Paolina and the medieval Baglioni quarter, this underground route recalls two crucial moments in Perugia's history. Churches, convents, 300 houses and 26 towers were demolished and partially buried to make room for the Rocca (fort), built in 1540 by Paolo III Farnese to confirm papal control of the town. Still visible are alleyways, wells, stores and squares, overlooked by furnaces and workshops. The truncated skeletons of tower-houses vanish in the shadows of the vaults. Little more than the embrasures remain today of the once formidable fortress, into the walls of which the architect Antonio da Sangallo the Younger managed to set the arch and loggia of the Marzia gate (3rd century BC). All the rest was demolished in 1860, during Italian Unification, by

Detail of the Marzia gate; point of access to Via Baglioni

the people of Perugia, who were protesting against massacres perpetrated the previous year by the papal Swiss guards.

▶ *Having come out on to Piazza Italia proceed along Corso Vannucci to Piazza IV Novembre.*

❷ Fontana Maggiore

This monumental fountain, the visual focus of the square, was created between 1275 and 1278 to mark the completion of the 20-year construction of the 3km (2-mile) aqueduct. Its design and decoration are by Nicola Pisano (c1225–84) and his son Giovanni (c1250–1320). Sculptures are set on two marble basins, surmounted by a bronze one. Below is an agricultural calendar, the signs of the zodiac and representations of the arts, above 24 statuettes celebrating the town's Etruscan foundation, and combining biblical characters and contemporary figures; at the top are three nymphs. The whole work embodies the ambitious political and cultural programme of the *comune*, in its portrayal of history and universal knowledge. Beside the fountain, a drain cover bearing the inscription 'medieval well' conceals an Etruscan-Roman well more than 47m (154 feet) deep. However, the Etruscan town's main water source is found to the right of the cathedral, in Piazza Danti (once known as 'Piazza della Paglia' because straw (*paglia*) and bread were sold here; now the Deruta-Ripabianca ceramics market is held here twice a week). An ancient well, with a diameter of 5.6m (18 feet) and lined with travertine blocks, plunges 36m (118 feet) below Palazzo Bourbon-Sorbello.

❸ Cattedrale San Lorenzo

Despite more than two centuries' work – from 1345 to 1569, the year of its consecration – the cathedral was never completed. Its left side is partially covered with pink and white marble, and forms one side of Piazza IV Novembre, behind the fountain. In the 17th century it was raised with bricks and the façade itself has remained incomplete. In the luminous interior you can admire an *Enthroned Madonna* (1484), a masterpiece by Luca Signorelli, and a *Deposition* (1567–9) painted by Federico Barocci. To the left the cathedral extends into a loggia built in 1423 by Braccio da Montone, then lord of Perugia, 'so that the nobility of Perugia may stroll there at its pleasure and conduct transactions'. Under the first arch are the remains of the 12-sided bell tower demolished in the 14th century in a search for the *palladium*, the mythical Homeric shield that made the city of Troy invincible.

❹ Palazzo dei Priori

The construction of this imposing building, the seat for the town's judiciary, lasted from 1293 to 1443. As was the case for many stately mansions in the region, adjacent tower-houses were bought from craftsmen and merchants and then converted

to the new requirements. Housed within are the Collegio della Mercanzia, Collegio del Cambio, Sala dei Notari and Galleria Nazionale dell'Umbria.

❺ Collegio della Mercanzia

In 1390, the merchants' guild took one of the properties on the ground floor of the Palazzo dei Priori. During the first half of the 15th century, the Collegio della Mercanzia audience chamber (entrance on Corso Vannucci) was covered with splendid inlaid pine and walnut panels. Visible in a lunette is the griffin of Perugia above a bale, the guild's emblem.

❻ Collegio del Cambio

Between 1452 and 1457, money-changers installed themselves in the rooms to the

right of the Collegio della Mercanzia. Their audience chamber became a Renaissance showcase, thanks to the frescoes painted by Perugino (1497–1507), which, in keeping with his humanistic approach, combined classical figures (pagan gods, sibyls, illustrious men) with Christian themes (virtues, prophets, the transfiguration and a crib). The painter may have availed himself of the assistance of, among others, the young Raphael (1483–1520). Apparently, both are portrayed on the walls of the chamber – the master from Città della Pieve in an explicit self-portrait and his pupil from Urbino as Daniel. This chamber leads to

Statue of Pope Julius III on the cathedral of San Lorenzo

SPECIAL TO...

The surviving rooms of the Rocca Paolina are the venue for the biennial City of Perugia Antiques Fair (October– November), and an antiques and collectables fair is held in the Carducci gardens, on the last weekend in the month.

the lovely chapel of San Giovanni Battista, entirely covered in frescoes by Giannicola di Paolo in 1515–18.

⁊ Sala dei Notari

In 1582 the notaries also moved into Palazzo dei Priori, occupying the Sala del Popolo, a large, vaulted room which they had sumptuously frescoed. It is reached through a doorway in front of the Fontana Maggiore. Hanging from the corbels, supporting the griffin of Perugia and the Guelph lion, are the chains and a long bar that the people of Perugia removed from the gates of Siena after defeating its militia in 1358. To the right of the portico, the narrow Via della Gabbia is a reminder of the times when wrongdoers were suspended in an iron cage and exposed to public ridicule.

⁸ Galleria Nazionale dell'Umbria

The Umbria National Gallery is the latest tenant of note in the mansion, where it was installed on the third floor in 1878. It exhibits works in well-ordered, chronological sequence, divided by schools. Duccio di Buoninsegna, Gentile da Fabriano, Beato Angelico,

Benozzo Gozzoli, Piero della Francesca, Perugino, Pinturicchio and Pietro da Cortona are among the painters, and Arnolfo da Cambio and the Pisano family among the sculptors. These few names show that this is one of Italy's richest museums, particularly important for its work from the Umbrian, Tuscan and Marche areas.

▶ *Return to Corso Vannucci and turn right into Via dei Priori.*

⁹ Via dei Priori

Descending along this major medieval thoroughfare, you come to the Torre degli Sciri (46m/151 feet), Perugia's tallest intact tower/fortress. Exploring the winding narrow side streets that lead off Via dei Priori, often with steps and covered with vaults, is like stepping back in time.

⑩ Piazzetta della Madonna della Luce

This irregular square is noteworthy for its mix of architectural styles – Gothic houses and the remains of a postern stand opposite the Renaissance façade of the church of the Madonna della Luce (1513–19). A few steps away, on its original

Strolling in Piazza IV Novembre, the social heart of the town

Etruscan columns, rises the Porta Trasimena (gate), the old exit on the route to Trasimeno and Tuscany.

⑪ Oratorio di San Bernardino

The medieval stone austerity of Via dei Priori brings you out into the Piazza San Francesco, which is a splendid setting for the masterpiece of Perugian Renaissance architecture across the lawn – the oratory of San Bernardino, with refined bas-reliefs on its polychrome façade, sculpted by Agostino di Duccio in 1457–61.

SPECIAL TO...

The Sandri pastry shop in Corso Vannucci is a Perugian institution, greeting customers in regal surroundings – old furnishings, a frescoed vault and crystal cases containing perfect pastries, the results of combining the original central European proprietors' recipes with regional tradition.

Above: looking out over Perugia
Below: detail from the Volumni
hypogeum

▶ *Return to the Sciri tower and take Via Francolina to the left, Via Vincioli to the right, Via della Pernice to the left and Piazza Morlacchi to the right, leading to Piazza Cavallotti, where you turn into Via Maestà delle Volte.*

🔟 Via Maestà delle Volte

The Via Maestà winds along one of Perugia's medieval streets, past 13th- and 14th-century houses and beneath dark vaults. A red-and-white banded Gothic arch is all that remains of the oratory built in 1335 to protect the *Majesty* fresco there.

▶ *Once in Piazza IV Novembre proceed through Piazza Danti, Piazza Piccinino and Via Buontempo, and turn right into Via Volte della Pace.*

🔟 Via Volte della Pace

Following the curve of the Etruscan walls is the picturesque covered Via Volte della Pace. In the Middle Ages, treaties with nearby towns were contracted here. It opens into the elongated Piazza del Sopramuro, now Piazza Matteotti, created in 1247 to house the market, fish-

---

SPECIAL TO...

In early July Perugia holds the important Umbria Jazz Estate, followed by Trasimeno Blues. A more specialised and experimental event is Umbria Jazz Winter, held between Christmas and New Year at Orvieto. Since 1986, Rockin' Umbria, a multimedia rock festival, has reviewed music, video, graphics, photography and cartoons in Perugia and Umb'rtide and other centres (June–July).

---

mongers and abattoir. Until the 15th century the inhabitants of Perugia flocked to this square to watch their favourite sport – violent stone fights between teams from the various districts.

▶ *From Piazza Matteotti continue along Via Baglioni to Piazza Italia, where the steps and escalators lead back to the car park. The following excursions can be made after a short drive following the signs (the hypogeum is southeast of the centre; the Città della Domenica to the northwest).*

EXCURSION 1

Ipogeo dei Volumni

An impressive row of house-shaped cinerary urns found in the surrounding necropoli dominates the steps descending into the underground tomb of the Velimna Etruscans. The 2nd century BC hypogeum reproduces the plan of a noble house. Three *cubicula* (bedrooms) open off each side of a large rectangular atrium with a pitched roof; at the end is the *tablinium*, the sitting room, with seven urns. The central urn shows the head of the Arunte family, watched over by funerary demons that guard the door to the next world; around this lie other members of the family, with Arunte's daughter Velia sitting on an elaborate seat.

EXCURSION 2

Città della Domenica

Step into Pinocchio's village, Snow White's house, Swan Lake, the Witches' Wood, Sleeping Beauty's Castle and the Far West. The amusement park, created in 1955 northwest of Perugia on the slopes of Monte Malbe, was planned as a mini Umbrian Disneyland. Other attractions include an aquarium, animals roaming free and a miniature railway that crosses the park.

Northeast
Umbria

This tour winds up and down the Umbria-Marche Apennine ridge, through hills, woods, valleys and harsh mountain gorges, encountering tantalising fragments of a distant past. Visits to isolated hermitages add a touch of mystery.

2 DAYS • 202KM • 126 MILES

[i] *Loggia dei Lanari, Piazza Matteotti 18, Perugia*

▶ *Take the SS298 towards Gubbio, passing Belvedere and then turning right for Biscina-Fratticciola Selvatica to the short, unsurfaced road, signposted on the right for the Castello di Petroia.*

❶ Castello di Petroia

Together with the castles of Biscina and Vallingegno to the north, the tiny fortified village of Petroia formed Gubbio's defence system in the Middle Ages on the right bank of the Chiascio river. In 1414 Duke Guidoantonio da Montefeltro, whose family controlled Gubbio from 1384, sold the castle to Matteo Accomandugi of Urbino. Eight years later, his grand-daughter, Elisabetta, lady-in-waiting to Duchess Rengarda in Urbino, chose remote Petroia to give birth to her lover Guidoantonio's illegitimate son Federico, the future duke and magnificent patron of Renaissance Urbino. The castle is now a hotel.

▶ *Back on the SS298, continue towards Gubbio to the sign on the right for the Abbazia di Vallingegno.*

❷ Abbazia di Vallingegno

St Francis' early biographers tell how the young man from Assisi, travelling to Gubbio after leaving his paternal home, stopped cold and hungry at a monastery along the way. This was probably Vallingegno Abbey, rebuilt by the Benedictines in the 13th century. In the crypt, a late imperial arch contains the remains of San Verecondo, stoned to death in the 5th century by local pagans, worshippers of Genius, the god who presided over the destiny of newborn babies. Slightly lower down is the medieval castle. The 'miraculous' spring on the side of the main road was apparently made to gush forth by Ubaldo Baldassini, the bishop-saint who controlled Gubbio between 1130 and 1160. It is now a working farm and *agriturismo*.

▶ *Return to the SS298 and proceed right to Gubbio.*

❸ Gubbio

Even from afar the grey calcareous stone buildings of Gubbio stand out, huddled at the foot of Monte Ingino. This was where the Umbrians constructed their Tota (town) Ikuvina, mentioned on seven bronze tablets (2nd–1st century BC), now in the Civic Museum. The Romans moved

---

RECOMMENDED WALK

Leaving Gubbio in the direction of Scheggia, you soon reach the Bottaccione basin, created in the Middle Ages to fuel the mills below. The presence of rare iridium in the rocks of the gorge has prompted theories of a huge asteroid falling and having catastrophic effects on the vegetation and climate. The upper town can be reached from the Bottaccione dam by walking 2km (1.2 miles) along the stones of the overhanging aqueduct (1327). Less precarious is the ascent to the Basilica di Sant'Ubaldo on Monte Ingino, which can also be reached by *funivia* or car.

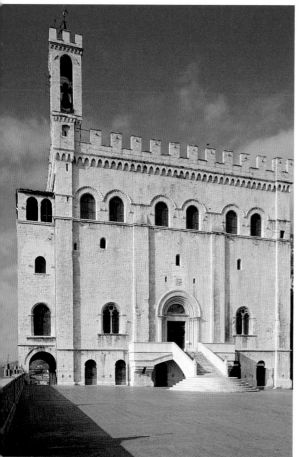

Gubbio's Palazzo dei Consoli

their town to the plain, where you will find the well-preserved remains of their 1st century AD theatre, and the urban nucleus did not return to the slopes of the mountain until the Middle Ages. On Piazza Quaranta Martiri stand Gothic San Francesco (1255; site of the home of the Spadalonga family, who welcomed St Francis on his arrival in Gubbio) and the 17th-century Loggia dei Tiratori (wool-workers responsible for ironing the cloth). From here climb to Piazza Grande, a windy, scenic balcony supported by arches. The *comune* started building this, their new centre of civic power, in 1321. Angelo da Orvieto and Gattapone built the tall, graceful Palazzo dei Consoli (1332–49), now a museum. Even higher up is the 15th-century Gothic Duomo (cathedral), near Palazzo Ducale, which the town donated to Federico da Montefeltro, Duke of Urbino, in 1480. The court of honour bears the mark of Francesco di Giorgio Martini, and is the only real Renaissance space in Gubbio.

This is an ancient town, proud of traditions such as the ancient and extremely popular Corsa dei Ceri (see below) and the Palio della Balestra (last Sunday in May), during which local crossbowmen in costume challenge those from

Sansepolcro. At the 14th-century Palazzo del Bargello you may see people walking three times around the fountain while some-one else splashes them with water from the basin – this is the 'madman's fountain' and the ceremony gives participants the right to adopt the honorary title of 'madman'.

i Via della Repubblica 18

▶ Follow the **SS298** to Scheggia and then the **SS360** towards Sassoferrato, turning left (towards Cantiano) for Chiaserna, where a road sign-posted for Monte Catria climbs to the grassy saddle between Monte Acuto and Monte Catria. Here the

The crowded Corsa dei Ceri in Gubbio

SPECIAL TO...

The Corsa dei Ceri is a race held in Gubbio every 15 May, featuring three *ceri* – wooden structures, each weighing 200kg (441 pounds) and standing 4m (13 feet) high. The statue of a different saint is attached to the top – Sant'Ubaldo, San Giorgio and Sant'Antonio. Each *cero* takes its eight carriers and their two team captains between 9 and 11 minutes to climb the course from the city gate to the Basilica of Sant'Ubaldo. During World War I, when there were no men, the *ceri* were carried by women.

SPECIAL TO...

Many of the 13th- to 14th-century ashlar stone houses that line the streets of Gubbio feature strange pointed doors, raised above street level, on the main entrance side (see those on Via dei Consoli and Via Baldassini).
According to tradition, this is the 'door of the dead', reserved for funerals. A more prosaic explanation is that they were raised for safety reasons and provided independent access to the upper floors.

The Fonte Avellana hermitage, a Camoldolensian abbey at the foot of Monte Catria

SCENIC ROUTES

The most spectacular part of this tour (in particular the ascent and descent of Monte Catria, on unsurfaced roads) requires caution. Rough, narrow roads run along the edge of unprotected precipices; it's best to stop if you want to enjoy the views. Always sound your horn on the narrow stretch between Isola Fossara and Scheggia that skirts the Sentino river gorge.

asphalt ends and you bear right at the next two forks to come, near the Vernosa shepherds' hut, to a path that leads in half an hour to the top of Monte Catria (1,701m/5,581 feet).

◢ Monte Catria
Views of Umbria and the Marche as far as the Adriatic Sea open out from the plateau on the summit of Monte Catria,

which is dominated by an enormous metal cross. Stretching out to the south is the regional park that culminates in the conical Monte Cucco (1,568m/5,144 feet), an ideal destination for keen hikers, hang-gliders and pot-holers.

▶ *Descend to the last fork and continue to the right along the unsurfaced road (bear left at a fork after 5km/3 miles) to Fonte Avellana (those who prefer surfaced roads can avoid the ascent of Monte Catria and remain on the SS360 as far as Isola Fossara before turning left for Badia di Sitria and Eremo di Fonte Avellana).*

◢ Eremo di Fonte Avellana
Founded in 979 in the woods at the foot of Monte Catria and prosperous in the Middle Ages,

RECOMMENDED EXCURSION

Monte Cucco is a hang-gliders' and pot-holers' paradise. The famous Cucco underground system extends for 30km (19 miles) to a depth of 922m (3,025 feet). It is reached from Sigillo (on the SS3 south of Scheggia) along a scenic road that leads in 9km (5 miles) to the beech woods and meadows of Val di Ranco (1,040m/3,412 feet). The entrance to the cave (no access) opens sheer above a gorge at a height of 1,390m (4,560 feet).

the Camaldolensian abbey of Fonte Avellana now comprises a Romanesque-Gothic church with presbytery, built over a dark crypt dating from the 11th century. As well as the cloister, chapterhouse and library, you can visit the *scriptorium*, where a barrel vault with 13 windows ensured plenty of even light for the scribes. The famous illuminated manuscripts of Fonte Avellana are now kept in the Vatican library. Dante was one of many visitors, and refers to it in the *Divine Comedy*.

▶ Leave the hermitage in the direction of Pergola, then turn right towards Scheggia to come to the Badia di Sitria.

6 Badia di Sitria

The abbey of Santa Maria di Sitria, a satellite of Fonte Avellana, was founded in the early 11th century by San Romualdo, a nobleman turned monk. Its interesting Romanesque church has a nave with barrel vaults and raised presbytery.

▶ Continue to Isola Fossara, where you turn right on to the SS360 for Scheggia and then take the SS3 (Via Flaminia) towards Rome to the turning for Gualdo Tadino.

7 Gualdo Tadino

Roman Tadinum lay on the plain, near the Via Flaminia; the town was moved to the hillside during the 12th century. San Benedetto cathedral, dating from 1256, has a lovely façade with three doorways and a rose window. A few steps away is Gothic San Francesco (deconsecrated), with frescoes by Matteo da Gualdo (*c*1430–1507). Notable triptychs by him and other Umbrian painters are exhibited in the picture gallery in the Rocca Flea, a massive fortress built by Federico II in the 13th century.

[i] Via Calai 39

▶ Continue along the SS3 southbound to Nocera Umbra.

8 Nocera Umbra

A disastrous earthquake in September 1997 destroyed large parts of this attractive hilltown. For many years reconstruction was slow, and much still needs to be done. But at the same time, tremendous efforts have succeeded in rebuilding some of the major structures. The church of San Francesco has reopened and the Pinacoteca holds some fine works by Matteo da Gualdo, and Niccolò Alunno. It also has some Roman mile markers. The 15th-century Duomo has also been restored, as has the tower of the castle. This is where, in 1421, the lord of the castle, Pasquale di Vagnolo, murdered his adulterous wife along with his feudal lord, Trinci di Foligno. A view of the valley and mountains opens up between cathedral and tower.

[i] Corso Cavour 126, Foligno

▶ Continue south on the SS3 to the slip road leading to the SS75 dual carriageway for Perugia.

The thrill of parascending. Monte Catria and Monte Cucco are well known to lovers of free flying

Shores & Hills
of Trasimeno

With its low shores, in places thick with reeds, lying amid gentle hills of olive trees, vines and castles, Trasimeno – Italy's fourth largest lake, though only 6m (20 feet) deep – has been poetically described as 'a veil of water on a meadow'.

1/2 DAYS• 128KM • 80 MILES

ITINERARY

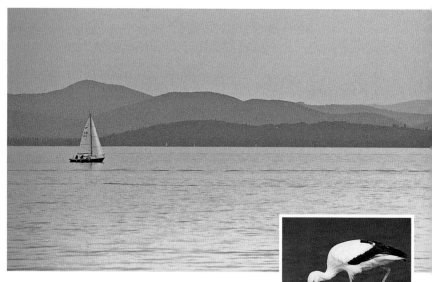

⌐*i*⌐ *Loggia dei Lanari, Piazza
Matteotti 18, Perugia*

▶ *Take the SS75 bis to the
turning signposted on the
right for Corciano.*

❶ Corciano

Within a turreted ring of 15th-
century walls, streets and alleyways follow the gradient of the
hill up to a typically Perugian
castle. The Palazzo Comunale
once belonged to the della
Corgna family, who assumed
control of Trasimeno in 1550.
Several residences used by
them include the 14th-century
castle of Pieve del Vescovo,
north of Corciano, which was
restored by Cardinal Fulvio
between 1560 and 1570. The
13th-century church of Santa
Maria holds a fine altarpiece
depicting the Assumption by
Pietro Vannucci, known as
Perugino.

⌐*i*⌐ *Via Cardinale Rotelli 21*

▶ *From Pieve del Vescovo return
to the SS75 bis and follow
this to the right to Magione.*

❷ Magione

At the entrance to the village
stands a 15th-century abbey, a
fortified mansion with corner

towers (not open to visitors),
originally a hostel erected by the
Knights Templar for pilgrims on
their way to Rome. In 1311–12,
after the Knights' possessions
had been seized by the State, the
building became a *mansio* (residence) of the Knights of Malta,
who still own it.

⌐*i*⌐ *Piazza della Repubblica
Italiana 30*

▶ *Take the provincial road
northbound, signposted for
Castel Rigone.*

SPECIAL TO...

The area to the south of Lake
Trasimeno is rich in works by
Perugino (Pietro Vannucci).
He was born around 1450
in Citta della Pieve, where
several of his pictures and
frescoes can be found, and
others are in Spello, Foligno,
Montefalco and Perugia.
On this tour you can see his
works at Corciano (Santa
Maria) and Panicale (San
Sebastiano). He died of the
plague in Fontignano (his last
fresco is in the Annunziata),
just east of Panicale in 1523
and his tomb is there.

Sails and aquatic birds, typical
scenes on Lake Trasimeno

❸ Castel Rigone

A climb past olive groves leads
to the site of this magnificent
natural observatory. In the
village are remains of a 1297
castle and the elegant sandstone
sanctuary of the Madonna dei
Miracoli, built in 1494 in the
hope that it would protect
against the plague. Its design
was inspired by the Renaissance
forms of the Madonna del
Calcinaio of Cortona.

▶ *Descend westwards to the
SS75 bis, which leads to the
right to Passignano.*

❹ Passignano sul Trasimeno

The alleyways of the ancient
Passum Jani (Oasis of Janus)
climb from the shores of Lake
Trasimeno towards the fortifications at the top of the headland,

Olive trees at Castiglione del Lago

with its striking triangular Ponente tower (14th century). An aircraft factory was established at Passignano in 1934, later converted into a shipyard. Today, the town's main activities focus on lakeside tourism, encouraged by the boat service for Isola Maggiore, the second largest island on the lake (Isola Polvese is the biggest) and the only one still inhabited.

i *Piazza Trento e Trieste 6*

RECOMMENDED EXCURSION

The tranquillity of Isola Maggiore, with its olive, ilex and cypress trees, prompted St Francis to retreat here during Lent in 1211–13. The island's village, dominated by the Gothic parish church of San Michele Arcangelo, consists of a single paved street leading past 14th- to 15th-century houses to Romanesque San Salvatore. Lying in a state of abandon is neo-Gothic Guglielmi Castle (also known as Villa Isabella), where, in 1904, a lace workshop was set up to teach the women – already experts at net-weaving – 'Irish stitch', still a local speciality.

FOR HISTORY BUFFS

On a foggy day in 217 BC Hannibal's forces bore down from the hills above Tuoro and ambushed the Roman legions. Trapped against the marshy lakeshore, many Romans drowned trying to escape the Punic swords. A route illustrating the crucial phases of this battle starts west of Toro.

▶ *Continue west, turning right on to the SS416 for Tuoro.*

5 Tuoro sul Trasimeno

Tuoro was the scene of a bloody battle in which Rome suffered its worst defeat at the hands of the Carthaginians (see above). The Renaissance Palazzo del Capra was built over the mausoleum of the consul Caius Flaminius, who died in the battle. Visit the Campo del Sole, on the lakeshore; 27 column-shaped sculptures executed by various artists between 1985 and 1989 form an enigmatic forest of stone around a solar symbol.

▶ *Return to the SS75 bis and follow it before turning left on to the SS71 for Castiglione del Lago.*

---

6 Castiglione del Lago

Overlooking Trasimeno from a high headland (in Etruscan and Roman times it was an island in the lake, which was then deeper and larger) are the beautiful Castiglione, the castle and cathedral, surrounded by walls. The fortunes of the della Corgna family, dukes of the town from 1550 to 1647, are reflected in their mansion, Palazzo della Corgna. Frescoes on the first floor celebrate family glories; the ground floor was reserved for social activities and conversation. A covered passageway links the mansion to the castle that Frederico II of Swabia erected in the mid-13th century. Events are now held within its pentagonal walls, guarded by four towers and a high, triangular keep (contact the tourist office for details).

FOR CHILDREN

Every year in spring, Castiglione del Lago hosts an international kite-flyers' meeting and the clear Umbrian sky is turned into an unforgettable, multicoloured palette.

---

i Piazza Mazzini 10

▶ *Continue south along the SS71 to the turning on the left for Paciano.*

7 Paciano
Seven towers and perfectly preserved 14th-century walls enclose the streets of Paciano, perched on a spur where a temple to two-faced Janus is said to have stood. The oak and chestnut trees of Monte Pausillo occupy 300 hectares (741 acres), along with deer, fallow deer, mouflons and a rich under-growth of mushrooms – a superb area for hiking.

▶ *Follow the signs for Panicale, bearing right at the two forks you come to.*

8 Panicale
In this scenic medieval village residents practice the rare craft of *ars panicalensis* – hand embroidery on tulle. Places of interest here include the collegiate church of San Michele, with its Renaissance doorways and frescoes by Perugino (*Martyrdom of St*

A traditional fishing net used on Lake Trasimeno

Sebastian, 1505), in the church of San Sebastiano.

i Piazza Umberto 11

▶ *Descend via Lemura and Casalini to the coastal SS599 and follow this to the right to the turning on the left for San Savino.*

9 San Savino
Dominated by a 14th-century castle, San Savino sits near the mouth of an outlet dug by Romans to halt the frequent lake floods. Numerous species of fish, protected by a ban on fishing, come to reproduce in the canebrakes of 'la Valle' nature reserve.

▶ *Skirt the lake northwards to San Feliciano.*

10 San Feliciano
This is a pretty little fishing village on Lake Trasimeno, with a Museum of Fishing featuring aquariums, aviaries and every-thing about the lake, its people and animals. A ferry to Isola Polvese, opposite, operates from April to September. From the 13th century onwards the island was colonised by various reli-gious organisations who built

their churches on it. Today, it is a protected nature reserve.

▶ *Continue to Monte del Lago, where you turn right towards Magione to come to Montecològnola.*

11 Montecològnola
The origin of this scenic village, defended by walls and towers, is revealed in the regular layout of its streets: it was founded and designed as a new town in 1293 by the inhabitants of Magione, who obtained Perugia's permission to create their new settlement.

▶ *Take the SS75 bis which leads back via Magione to Perugia.*

SPECIAL TO...

Trasimeno has always been Perugia's favourite lake. When Bonamico Buffalmacco was commissioned by the Perugians in the 14th century to paint their patron saint, Ercolano, he crowned him not with gold or gems but with 'a garland of dace (carp-like fish), the largest ever to come out of the lake'.

The Umbrian
Valley

Like balconies overlooking the historic route of the Via Flaminia, the towns in the Umbrian Valley face each other across two sides of the plain that stretches between Assisi and Spoleto. Rich with medieval and religious associations, particularly related to episodes in the life of St Francis, they also contain splendid works of art.

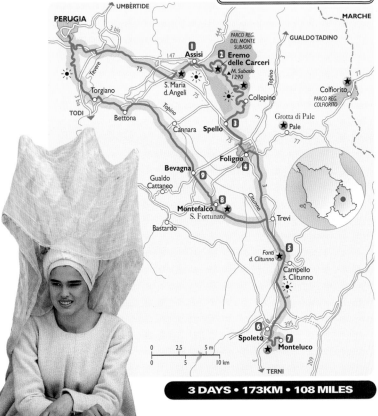

3 DAYS • 173KM • 108 MILES

▶ *After reaching the SS75*
dual carriageway, proceed
towards Foligno to the signs
for Santa Maria degli Angeli
and Assisi.

❶ Assisi

Lying on terraces on the slopes
of Monte Subasio, Assisi is inextricably bound to its most
famous son, St Francis. His life
and ideology have transformed
this medieval town into a monumental shrine, which draws
hosts of pilgrims and visitors.
Below town is the towering
basilica of Santa Maria degli
Angeli, begun in 1569 to incorporate the humble locations
where Francis chose to live and
die. Its vast dome is in startling
contrast to the little chapel of
the Porziuncola below, where
the Franciscan Order was
founded in 1208; and to the
simple cell (known as the
Transito Chapel) in which the
saint died on 4 October, 1226.

At one end of the town you
can climb on foot to the Basilica
di San Francesco, made up of a
crypt and two churches, one
built over the other. The style
combines Umbrian
Romanesque with French-
inspired Gothic. It took more
than a century to build the
whole complex, begun in 1228
under the direction of Friar Elia,
and to fresco the interior. In the
lower church, works by Giotto
and his assistants alternate with
paintings by Cimabue, Pietro
Lorenzetti and Simone Martini.

> #### SPECIAL TO...
>
> The ruins of the house of
> Francis' father, rich merchant
> Pietro di Bernardone, are
> concealed among the pillars of
> the Chiesa Nuova, erected in
> 1615 at the expense of Philip
> III, King of Spain. According to
> legend, in 1182 a mysterious
> pilgrim told the mother of the
> future saint to take refuge in a
> nearby stable to give birth, and
> this is where the oratory of
> San Francesco Piccolino
> now stands.

Rising from the massive basilica of
San Francesco is the great bell
tower of 1239

As well as Cimabue and Giotto,
the anonymous 'Master of
Isaaco' worked in the other
church. Together they produced
a prodigious decorative display,
which has been described by
some as representing the beginning of the history of western
European painting.

The main street climbs from
San Francesco past medieval
Piazza del Comune, on which
stands the Temple of Minerva
(1st century BC, one of the best-
preserved monuments of the
classical world), to reach the
secluded cathedral of San
Rufino, a 13th-century
Romanesque masterpiece.
Lower down, a tangle of narrow
streets leads to the Gothic basilica of Santa Chiara, where the
remains of this saint have rested
since 1260.

i Piazza del Comune 22

▶ *Follow the signs eastwards for*
the Eremo delle Carceri.

2 Eremo delle Carceri

The rural convent was built in the 14th and 15th centuries on the spots where Francis and his companions lost themselves in prayer. If you arrive early in the morning, you will still find silence and solitude, as well as a view of the thick ilex wood around it and the town. Go down steps and through narrow passages to visit the cave where the saint rested, the stone he sat on to meditate, the ilex tree where the birds are said to have listened to his famous sermon (although some say this was at Bevagna), and a stream that dried up so that the noise of its waters would not disturb the friars. In the park, lovely numbered paths lead to shelters used over the centuries by religious devotees.

Composition with flower petals for the flower festival at Spello

▶ *Cross Monte Subasio to Collepino; turn right for Spello.*

3 Spello

More than in any other centre in Umbria, the old town hall of *Hispellum* has retained important evidence of Roman presence. The 1st-century BC southern Consolare three-arched gate was integrated into the 14th-century ring of walls; a square tower near by is crowned, as it was in the 16th century, with an olive tree. The scenic Venere gate, to the west, is now enclosed by two majestic Romanesque towers. Between the two is the arch of the Urbica gate, flanked by walls of the Augustan era. Along the old Via Flaminia, you can see the remains of the amphitheatre. Spello's rare Renaissance masterpiece was funded by the Baglioni family, who, in 1501, commissioned Pinturicchio from Perugia to decorate a chapel in the church of Santa Maria Maggiore with frescoes, and there are some works by Perugino.

i *Piazza Matteotti 3*

▶ *Proceed southeast, following the signs for Foligno.*

View of the hilltown of Spello

SCENIC ROUTES

Fine views of sky and open spaces can be enjoyed from the road that crosses Monte Subasio from the Eremo delle Carceri, before descending to Collepino or Spello. In summer the meadows on the summit are a popular spot, where the local people seek relaxation.

SPECIAL TO...

The inhabitants of Spello prepare a memorable spectacle for Corpus Christi. After weeks of intense labour, in just one night the streets used by the procession are covered with brightly coloured floral designs on a holy theme. This tradition is also adopted in a number of other Umbrian towns.

4 Foligno

Lying in the valley of the Topino river, Foligno has one of the few old centres on flat ground in Umbria. Its excellent position and a manufacturing tradition dating from the 14th century have made it a busy town of commercial and industrial activity. Economic development, bombing and earthquakes (the last in 1997) have erased many traces of the past, although the Duomo (cathedral), with its bands of red and white stone, and the nearby Palazzo Trinci remain intact. The former has a fine side entrance (1201); its interior was transformed into neo-classical style by Giuseppe Piermarini of Foligno, royal imperial architect in Milan between 1779 and 1796. The Palazzo Trinci is one of the most interesting late-Gothic residences in central Italy; its fresco cycles constitute an encyclopaedia of the early 15th-century humanistic culture.

i Corso Cavour 126

▶ Take the **SS3** south to the sign for the Fonti del Clitunno.

FOR HISTORY BUFFS

Goldsmithery, silver-work, woodcarving, ceramics, yarns and hemp, wool and silk fabrics, paper-making, organ-making, metal-casting … the list of Foligno's output during its golden age (1310–1439) goes on and on. Its greatest pride dates from the period of papal rule. In 1472 Emanuele Orfini of Foligno and the German printer Johann Numeister produced 300 copies of Dante's *Divine Comedy*, the first book printed in Italy in the Italian language. Fourteen complete copies are known to exist; the press believed to have been used for that edition can be seen at the printing documentation centre in the oratory of the Nunziatella.

---

5 Fonti del Clitunno

This little river flows into the Teverone, but before it reaches its destination its springs form a magical sheet of water dotted with green, grassy islets and weeping willows. This spot is said to have been an early

---

The Clitunno springs

tourist attraction, at the time of Roman writer and orator Pliny the Younger (1st century BC), who refers to villas, inns and public baths built in the vicinity. The site was sacred to the god Clitunno; the pagan *sacellum* mentioned by Pliny inspired the early Christian church (thought to date some time between the 4th and 9th centuries), encountered on the right just before reaching the springs.

i Piazza Ranieri Campello 1

▶ Continue along the **SS3** to Spoleto.

6 Spoleto

Spoleto has a long history, evident everywhere, from the massive polygonal walls, raised by the Umbrians in the 4th

---

SPECIAL TO…

In June and September, ten horsemen representing the ten districts of Foligno race each other in the Giostra della Quintana.

RECOMMENDED WALK

In Spoleto you can visit the 'Torri' bridge-aqueduct (crossed on foot; actually there are no towers, but the two main pylons have rooms for sentinels). Pass beside the stronghold to reach the 230m (754 feet) structure, which crosses the Tessino chasm on ten pointed arches, resting on pillars up to 76m (249 feet) tall. Continuing to the right, descend to admire the Romanesque reliefs (12th–13th century) of the façade of San Pietro, before returning to the old centre. This splendid walk, with views of the town and Monteluco, can be prolonged to visit the church of San Paolo inter Vineas, which has a fine cycle of 13th-century frescoes in the transept.

century BC, to the 'inner thoroughfare' that, in the middle of the 19th century, tore into the steep winding streets of the lower town from north to south, to allow the passage of carts and carriages. The Roman colony founded in 274 BC survives near the Tessino river in traces of the amphitheatre and three arches of the Sanguinario, or 'bloody bridge', so called perhaps because Christians were martyred there. Further north is the basilica of San Salvatore, a remarkable early Christian construction with a nave and two aisles dating from the 4th to the 5th century. Along the Via Flaminia, place-names tell of a yet more eventful history. Via di Porta Fuga ('street of the escape gate') and the 13th-century Olio (oil) tower are thought to be references to the tale that Hannibal was seen off with boiling oil by the inhabitants of Spoleto in 217 BC. Higher up are the steps and orchestra of the theatre, the Druso arch, the remains of a temple and a luxurious residence said to have

belonged to Emperor Vespasian's mother. Nothing remains, though, from the thriving early Middle Ages. In 576 Spoleto became the capital of a powerful duchy, but Barbarossa destroyed all traces of this period in 1155, when he razed 'the well-fortified town defended by a hundred towers' to the ground. That's when the present Duomo (cathedral, consecrated in 1198) was built, a splendid Romanesque backdrop to the funnel-shaped square reached down Via dell'Arringo. The frescoes in the apse (1467–9) are by Filippo Lippi and his assistants; 30 years after their execution, Pinturicchio decorated the Eroli Chapel. In the meantime, Cardinal Albornoz had consolidated papal power over Spoleto (the Duchy formally ceased to exist in 1231). Spoleto has many

A detail of the façade of Spoleto's Duomo, its rich rose window adorned with tracery and mosaics

BACK TO NATURE

Heading east from Foligno along the SS77, after 24km (15 miles) you will come to the undulating Colfiorito plateaux. The most significant of the seven karst depressions is the Colfiorito marsh, an ecosystem of extraordinary importance for rare species of flowers and marsh vegetation, as well as migratory and aquatic birds, gastropods and amphibians. Remains of fortified Iron Age structures and the Roman city of Plestia are also found in the area, which forms part of a regional park.

The spectacular bridge of Torri di Spoleto which crosses the Tessino

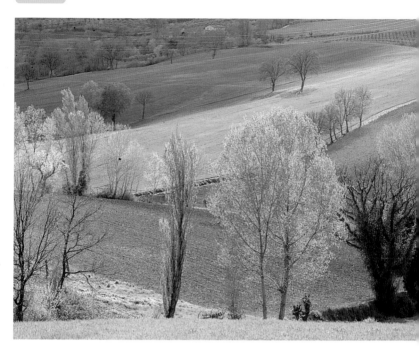

Above: the Umbrian landscape towards Montefalco
Right: frescoes in the church of Sant'Agostino, Montefalco

fascinating museums including the Galleria Civica d'Arte Moderna in Palazzo Collicola, with works by Alexander Calder, Henry Moore and several Italian

RECOMMENDED EXCURSION

Pale is a small village to the east of Foligno on the SS77 to Colfiorito. Tucked into the harsh, calcareous stone of the sheer Sasso di Pale rock is the Eremo di Santa Maria Giacobbe, built in the late 13th century and inhabited until 1963. Clearly visible from below – it is reached up a steep path across a scree – are the hermits' caves scattered around a little church (ask for the keys in the village), partially hewn into the rock and rich in votive frescoes of the 14th to 16th centuries.

▶ Follow the signs for Bevagna.

FOR CHILDREN

Children will certainly enjoy roaming through the stalls in the main square of Bevagna. Here, the old medieval trading traditions are revived during the Gaite market (second half of June), in a good-humoured challenge between the workshops of the districts responsible for guard duties (*gaite*) on the town walls.

---

masters. The theatres, Nuovo and Caio Melisso, date from the late 19th century and are famous for hosting the Festival dei Due Mondi (now the Spoleto Festival), first held by the composer Giancarlo Menotti in 1958.

ⓘ *Piazza della Libertà 7*

▶ *Follow the signs for Monteluco.*

7 Monteluco

Behind the Rocca, you can climb to the 773m (2,536 feet) sanctuary of Monteluco. The little chapel where Francis prayed, some cells and a well of cool water brought forth by the saint are all still there. Lovely scenic spots and small caves are scattered throughout the woods below. Monteluco wood was sacred to the Roman god Jupiter; as early as the 3rd century BC a special *lex spoletina* (Spoleto Law) prohibited tree-felling. Towards the end of the 5th century, it was inhabited by Syrian hermits, and later by Benedictines and Franciscans. A community of artists, painters and architects from Spoleto gathered here in the early 16th century, forming a religious community in 1547 which was dissolved two and a half centuries later, at the time of French occupation.

▶ *Descend to Spoleto and take the* **SS3** *northbound as far as Trevi, where you turn left for Montefalco.*

8 Montefalco

Just before reaching Montefalco you come to a church dedicated to San Fortunato, who died in 390. It has frescoes by Benozzo Gozzoli, and Franciscan stories and pictures painted by Tiberio d'Assisi in 1512 adorn the chapel that overlooks the courtyard. In the village, perched above the picturesque Topino and Clitunno plains, follow Via della Ringhiera Umbra, which descends from the main square to an opening in the walls commanding an outstanding view.

Halfway down, you can visit the former church of San Francesco, now the Civic Museum. This important church was used for public functions and assemblies; it was almost entirely covered in frescoes from the 14th century on. The artists who worked here include Perugino (*c*1450–1523), but its fame is due mainly to the fascinating cycle of the life of St Francis painted by Florentine Benozzo Gozzoli in 1452, on the walls of the central apse. This illustrious work influenced Umbrian painting for half a century.

ⓘ *Piazza del Comune*

9 Bevagna

Bevagna's charming asymmetrical main square, Piazza Silvestri, has hardly changed since its construction between 1195 and 1270. On one side, the Romanesque façade of San Michele has a doorway that reuses marble from classic times. The church of San Silvestro, opposite, crowned by a three-light window, is connected by a large arch to Palazzo dei Consoli, erected on the transepts of a loggia (the modern steps flanking it give access to a 19th-century theatre). Wander through the quiet streets of the town – already prosperous in Roman times – to discover the remains of a temple dating from the 2nd century BC, incorporated

A figure carved on the doorway of San Michele in Bevagna

into a deconsecrated church. These include a large mosaic, featuring the marine creatures of Porta Guelfa.

ⓘ *Piazza Filippo Silvestri 1*

▶ *Return to Perugia via Bettona and Torgiano.*

THE LEGEND OF
ST FRANCIS OF ASSISI

'Destroy all that has been written about Francis.' This was the order given in 1266 by Bonaventura da Bagnoregio, general minister of the Franciscan Order and author of the founding saint's 'official' biography (*Legenda maior*, 1263). His order was duly executed, although several Cistercian archives escaped the Franciscan friars' attention. A clash between 'rich' conventuals and 'poor' spiritual fathers was tearing the Order apart, and the message of evangelical poverty was in danger of being lost altogether. So da Bagnoregio considered it vital to eliminate all details of Francis' life that might open the Order to charges of subversion. As a result, the texts that trace Francis' steps through life are more intent on emphasising the stages of his sanctity than on describing the man's life.

Peter's house
It all started in Assisi (see Tour 22), in the home of Francis' father, a wealthy cloth merchant called Pietro di Bernardone. While Pietro was away on business, his wife Monna Pica, from Provence, gave birth in a nearby stable to a baby boy she called Giovanni (1182). On his return

from France, Pietro had the baby baptised as Francesco. Young Francis attended the school annexed to the church-hospital of San Giorgio. He grew to be a wealthy and ambitious but dissatisfied young man; despite being shut into the house, he persisted in visiting the poor and sick, and had an encounter with

lepers outside the Moiano gate. The 12th-century painted crucifix (now in Santa Chiara) of a country church in poor repair (San Damiano) spoke to Francis, saying: 'Go and repair my house, which, as you see, is all in ruin'. Francis obeyed. After publicly renouncing his wealth and possessions in the Vescovado at Assisi in 1206, he took up a nomadic life, travelling to Rome in 1210, and later to Spain and, in 1219, to Egypt, where he was greeted respectfully by the Muslim Sultan Malik-al Kamil.

First steps
Francis made countless visits to Umbria and Tuscany. On the first, having left his father's home in Assisi, he sought shelter in the abbey of Vallingegno (see Tour 20). From here he went on to Gubbio (see Tour 20), where he later tamed a ferocious wolf near the Vittorina Church. In San Francesco della Pace you can see the stone on which he stood to preach. Francis' first steps towards his destiny are retraced by the Assisi-Gubbio Sentiero Francescano della Pace, a splendid country excursion with an extension planned that will take visitors as far as Verna (contact tourist offices for details).

Stage in a life
At Cannara, south of Assisi, Francis founded the Third Order, for lay people of both sexes (Buona Morte Church).

The Eremo delle Carceri, Assisi

At Bevagna (see Tour 22) he preached to the birds on the Pian d'Arca (his stone podium is in San Francesco). At Vecciano, near Montefalco (see Tour 22) he made a spring gush forth. At Bovara, near Trevi, he prayed before a crucifix (now in San Pietro di Bovara). At Narni (see Tour 24) he cured a paralysed man. At Lugnano in Teverina (see Tour 24) he performed a miracle, depicted in a fresco in San Francesco Church. The oldest and perhaps truest likeness of the saint is a 1235 panel by Bonaventura Berlinghieri in San Francesco at Pescia (see Tour 5). Francis visited Siena (see Tour 15) and stayed at the Camàldoli hermitage (see Tour 13), in the convent of Monte Casale overlooking Sansepolcro (see Tour 14), in the Belverde caves above Cètona (see Tour 18), on Isola Maggiore on Lake Trasimeno (see Tour 21) and at Monteluco (see Tour 22). In 1220 he met Pope Honorius III in Orvieto (see Tour 23). The Duomo of Spoleto (see Tour 22) displays a letter he wrote to his friend Leo, who lived with him at the Verna hermitage (see Tour 13). This was a crucial phase in his life; in 1224 Francis was here when he received the stigmata, the first of many in the history of Christianity. The previous year, the Pope had officially sanctioned his rule.

Two churches for Francis

But by this time Francis was exhausted. In 1226, after a stay at the Celle hermitage of Cortona (see Tour 14), he died on the outskirts of Assisi in a small room (Transito Chapel); it's now incorporated into the basilica of Santa Maria degli Angeli. Immediately after his death, Friar Elia – minister-general of the Order between 1232 and 1239 – ordered the construction of an immense,

Francis receiving the oral confirmation of the Rule from Pope Innocent III, by Giotto, in the upper basilica, Assisi
Below: *The Stigmata* (Chapel of the Antico Tribunal, Anghiari)

T-shaped church in his honour. In fact, he built two – one above the other. Francis was canonised in 1228. In 1230 the lower church of the basilica of San Francesco became Francis' tomb: an incongruous resting-place for a man who had chosen to live in the hovel of the Porziuncola and on the remote crag of the Eremo delle Carceri (see Tour 22).

From Orvieto to
the Tevere Valley

Tempting food and wine, medieval surroundings, Renaissance highlights – as often happens in Umbria, past and present are inextricably entwined on this highly enjoyable tour.

2/3 DAYS • 187KM • 116 MILES

ITINERARY	
PERUGIA	▶ **San Sisto (5km-3m)**
SAN SISTO	▶ **Città della Pieve (38km-23½m)**
CITTÀ DELLA PIEVE	▶ **Orvieto (48km-30m)**
ORVIETO	▶ **Todi (41km-25½m)**
TODI	▶ **Deruta (34km-21m)**
DERUTA	▶ **Torgiano (7km-4m)**
TORGIANO	▶ **Perugia (14km-9m)**

[i] Loggia dei Lanari, Piazza
Matteotti 18, Perugia

▶ Take the **SS220** to San Sisto.

⓵ San Sisto
Just outside Perugia on the
SS220 (Via Pievaiola), the
Nestlé-Perugina chocolate
factory has an annexe housing
the Perugina History Museum.
Here, the company's products
and advertising campaigns,
going back to its foundation in
1907, reflect 100 years of Italian
life and habits. Intriguing
gimmicks include love letters
inserted into Baci Perugina
wrappings (1922) and a collection of figurines, which sparked
off a collecting craze in the
1930s.

▶ Continue along the **SS220**
and turn right on to the **SS71**
for Città della Pieve.

⓶ Città della Pieve
A turreted 1326 Rocca, or
stronghold, recalls the turbulent
days when this city's Perugian
and Guelph rulers had to
subdue the pro-Ghibelline
comune. Città della Pieve is striking for the colour of its bricks, of
which it was a renowned
producer in the Middle Ages.
Around it, the soft shades of the
hills fade into the distant blue of
the mountain contours, from the
Cimini to Pratomagno. The
same shades appear in the background of the *Adoration of the
Magi*, painted on the premises of

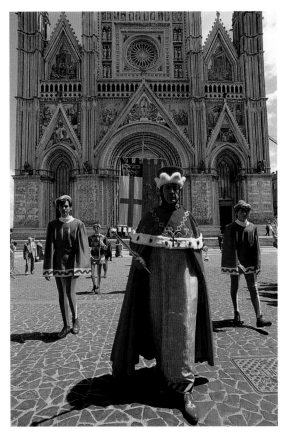

Historic procession against the
backdrop of Orvieto's Duomo

the Compagnia dei Disciplinati,
now the oratory of Santa Maria
dei Bianchi, in 1504 by Pietro
Vannucci. Although popularly
known as Perugino, the artist
was actually born in Città della
Pieve, in about 1450. On the
square, the fine Palazzo della
Corgna faces the Pubblico tower
(12th–14th century, in travertine
stone and bricks, 38m/125 feet
high) and the Duomo (cathedral), which houses a work
signed by Perugino in 1514.

In the northern third of the
town the Vescovo tower is a
reminder of the town's harsh
military past, with its large,
pointed arches designed to
accommodate war machines.
There's a more romantic
atmosphere in the picturesque

alleyway known as 'Baciadonne'
(kiss the ladies) because it's just
half a metre (1.5 feet) wide (a
person could lean out of the
window and kiss someone in the
opposite house).

[i] Piazza Matteotti 1

▶ Follow the **SS71** southbound
via Monteleone d'Orvieto and
Ficulle to Orvieto.

⓷ Orvieto
A small and orderly 'city of the
dead' – the Etruscan necropolis
of Crocifisso del Tufo – nestles
at the foot of an enormous tufa
rock; on its flat summit stands
Orvieto. As you climb to the
eastern edge of the town, you
reach the signs of a complex
historic stratification: a scenic
clearing, with the ruins of the
Etruscan temple of Belvedere

Piazza del Popolo, Orvieto

(late 5th century BC); the adjacent remains of the Rocca,
erected for Cardinal Albornoz in
1364; and a low, circular building, below which the San
Patrizio well plunges 62m
(203 feet). This was built
between 1527 and 1537 as part
of a project by Antonio da
Sangallo the Younger to give the
town a water reserve in the
event of a siege. Around the
central duct of the well, 13m
(43 feet) wide, 72 windows light
two spiral staircases with 248
steps each. Using these, the
beasts of burden could descend,
draw water, cross a bridge on the

bottom and climb up again without obstructing each other.

In the centre, the three
districts of the medieval town
are situated around the civic
tower and Palazzo dei Signori
Sette (seven lords – the consuls
representing the guilds). To the
north is the square overlooked
by the Palazzo del Popolo,
erected between the 13th and
14th centuries along with the
bell tower.

To the west is Piazza della
Repubblica, with the 13th-
century Palazzo del Comune,
renewed in the 1500s, and the
collegiate of Sant'Andrea, in the
shadow of a great tower. To the
southeast, enclosed between
the terraced canons' houses and
mansions housing major museums, stands the extraordinary
Duomo (cathedral), begun in
1290, developed by the Sienese
Lorenzo Maitani (1310–30) and
given a rose window and doorway by Andrea Orcagna. The
grandiose Gothic triptych on the
façade, completed in the 16th
century, shines with polychrome
marble, sculptures and mosaics.
Inside, in the chapel of San
Brizio, frescoes were painted
between 1477 and 1504 by Luca
Signorelli on the theme of the
end of the world; Fra' Angelico
also had a hand in their creation.
The cathedral's working hours
were sounded from the
Maurizio tower (a corruption of
ariologium de murriccio, 'the
works clock') by the 'robot' cast
in 1348.

In western Orvieto you pass
through medieval districts to
San Giovenale, built in 1004 on

SCENIC ROUTES

The best views, from the eroded clay furrows of the valley floor to high wooded hills, can be seen beyond Città della Pieve from the winding SS71. Those in a hurry can use the A1 motorway to reach Orvieto, instead. Between Orvieto and Todi, the lovely SS448, along Lago di Corbara, is the slow option; alternatively, the equally scenic (and far more demanding) SS79 bis runs high on the opposite bank of the Tiber.

the edge of a precipice. The frescoes inside (13th–16th century) feature an unusual 'tree of life', symbolising Paradise and the renewal of eternal life. Walking south along delightful streets such as Via Malabranca, Via della Cava (in Etruscan times the only access to the town) and Via Ripa

Piazza del Popolo in Todi, with Palazzo dei Priori behind

Medici, you reach the attractive Piazzale della Porta Romana, which commands a sweeping view of the valley crossed by the medieval aqueduct.

i Piazza del Duomo 24

▶ Continue along the **SS448** eastwards to the turning signposted on the right for Todi.

4 Todi

Romans called this Tuder, a name derived from the Etruscan Tular, or 'border' – referring to the division between the Etruscan world, west of the Tiber, and the Umbrian-Sabellian territories to the east, towards the Nera basin and the Piceno area. Today, Todi is another evocative medieval town, culminating in the rectangular Piazza del Popolo. Built over large Roman reservoirs, this surprisingly flat space in a town of steep gradients is enclosed and, until the 16th century, was reached through four corner gates. Between the 13th and 14th centuries it was the seat of civic power. At one end stand

Monument to Jacopone da Todi, Franciscan and poet, in Todi

the three seats of the town judiciary – the Palazzo del Popolo or Comune, Palazzo dei Capitani or Nuovo, built in 1293 with a

FOR HISTORY BUFFS

Impetuous poet Jacopo dei Benedetti, known as Jacopone, was born in 1230. He served as a notary in Todi until his wife's tragic death; only then did he discover that she wore a hair-shirt beneath her clothes. This threw him into a tormented state of penitence and mortification, so intense that the Franciscans were at first reluctant to accept him as a friar. Jacopone took up arms against Pope Boniface VIII to defend the spiritual rigour of the Order, and was incarcerated from 1298 to 1303. While in prison he composed part of his famous *Laudi*. He died in 1306 and was buried in the crypt of San Fortunato in Todi.

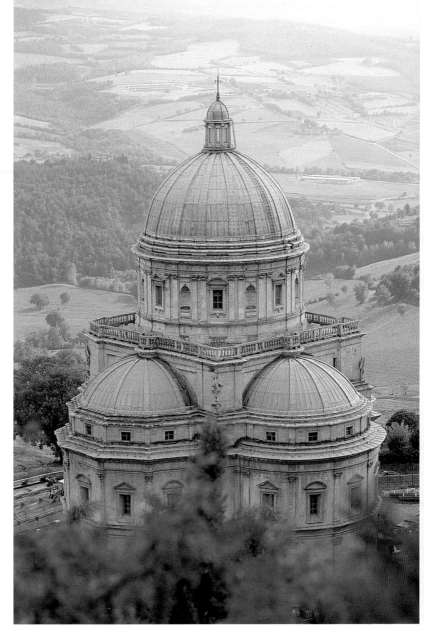

The dome of the church of Santa Maria della Consolazione in Todi

Gothic façade (picture gallery on the top floors of both buildings) and Palazzo dei Priori, of Gothic foundation, extended and completed in the 14th century, together with its trapezoid tower. On the opposite side, the Duomo (cathedral; 12th–14th century) has a carved wooden door beneath a magnificent 16th-century rose window.

Two of the three sculptures from the façade, kept in the crypt, are attributed to Giovanni Pisano (c1250–c1319. Set slightly apart is the Church of San Fortunato, at the top of a flight of steps. The incomplete façade has a fine Gothic doorway; inside are frescoes including one by Masolino da Panicale (c1383–1447).

The Renaissance seems to have found a place in Gothic Todi only outside the three

rings of walls (Etruscan, Roman and comunal), in the church of Santa Maria della Consolazione. Isolated and compact, this Greek cruciform building has four apses, a luminous interior and a high dome begun in 1508 but not completed until 1607. Its exemplary central plan led experts to attribute the design to Bramante (1444–1514), but records mention other masters, including Baldassarre Peruzzi, Vignola and Ippolito Scalza.

RECOMMENDED EXCURSION

About 12km (7 miles) east of Monteleone, past Montegabbione, with its walls and towers, you come to the former Franciscan convent of La Scarzuola, where architect Tommaso Buzzi created his 'ideal city' between 1960 and 1981. Seven theatre spaces – the open-air Arnie theatre, the Torre, the water theatre, the round and the never-ending patios, the sports theatre and, lastly, on the summit, the theatre of the Acropolis – create a fantastic maze, enriched with quotations and references to masters of the past (visit by appointment).

Majolica shop in Deruta

[i] Piazza del Popolo

▶ After reaching the **SS3 bis** dual carriageway, proceed towards Perugia to the exit for Deruta.

5 Deruta
A row of ceramics factories and displays gives away Deruta's main trade. By the 14th century residents were already exploiting the excellent local clay; the

A room in the Wine Museum in Torgiano

ceramics industry produced its greatest results in the first half of the 16th century. Antique specimens of iridescent majolica are on display in the Regional Ceramics Museum, set up in the former convent of San Francesco. Nearly 600 pieces of votive majolica, dating from the 16th to the 18th century, line the interior of the 17th-century sanctuary of the Madonna dei Bagni. Modern production is displayed in the pottery workshops in the lower part of town.

[i] Piazza dei Consoli 4

▶ Continue north via Ponte Nuovo following the signs for Torgiano.

6 Torgiano
This village on an outcrop at the confluence of the Tiber and the Chiascio was fortified in the 13th century. Its coat-of-arms – a tower enveloped by a scroll with bunches of grapes – indicates its principal attraction: a wine museum. Set up in 20 fine rooms in the 17th-century Palazzo Graziani-Baglioni, it gives a thorough review of vine-growing and wine-production. Torgiano produces an excellent red wine.

[i] Corso Vittorio Emanuele 23

▶ Continue north following the signs for Perugia.

SPECIAL TO...

The theme of Torgiano's Wine Museum is illustrated with a selection of Cycladic jugs and Hittite ceramics, Attic amphorae, Etruscan bronzes and Bucchero pottery, Roman glass, della Robbia ceramics, farming tools, 'waffle' irons and great presses. There's also a library for wine experts, and the annexed Osteria (inn) serves typical Umbrian wines and food.

Southern
Umbria

Terni has been an industrial centre since 1875–81, when the state set up the royal arms factory here. But there's a surprise in store here for romantic visitors: the Basilica di San Valentino, south of town, is the final resting place of St Valentine, the bishop who was executed in 270, and was to become the patron saint of lovers.

2 DAYS • 172KM • 107 MILES

ITINERARY	
TERNI	▶ **Càrsulae** (17km-10½m)
CÀRSULAE	▶ **Acquasparta** (5km-3m)
ACQUASPARTA	▶ **San Gèmini** (10km-6m)
SAN GÈMINI	▶ **Narni** (12km-7½m)
NARNI	▶ **Amelia** (13km-8m)
AMELIA	▶ **Lugnano in Teverina** (11km-7m)
LUGNANO IN TEVERINA	▶ **Alviano** (5km-3m)
ALVIANO	▶ **Baschi** (21km-13m)
BASCHI	▶ **Terni** (78km-49m)

i Via Cassian Bon 4, Terni

▶ *Take the SS79 towards San Gemini and turn right after Campitello to proceed via Cesi and San Gemini Terme to the Càrsulae archaeological site.*

❶ Càrsulae

Founded in the 3rd century BC along the western branch of the ancient Via Flaminia between Narnia and Tuder, the Roman town of Càrsulae flourished in Augustan times (27 BC–AD 14), but declined when the main thoroughfare was moved to the east. Having been abandoned, it was finally destroyed by

FOR CHILDREN

On the return journey on the motorway, a pleasant stop for young and old alike is a visit to the Mostri di Bomarzo Park, in Lazio, 6km (4 miles) east of the Attigliano exit on the A1. In 1552, Prince Pier Francesco Orsini, known as Vicino, created a trail amid the oak and chestnut trees and populated it with huge creatures sculpted in stone, half-hidden in the vegetation. While visiting this baroque fantasy, take time to test your sense of balance in the 'hanging house'.

RECOMMENDED EXCURSION

Dunarobba, 13km (8 miles) southwest of Acquasparta, has an extraordinary fossil forest, where sections of petrified sequoia trees, with diameters of up to 1.5m (5 feet) rise 5–10m (16–33 feet) from the ground. They stood more than a million years ago on the edge of Lake Tiberino, which extended over 120km (75 miles) between Sansepolcro and Spoleto, fed by a large river that periodically flooded the lands between Todi and the Terni depression.

barbarians and earthquakes. Among the remains scattered about the archaeological site are the forum with basilica, temples, tombs and a leisure complex with theatre and amphitheatre. Also found here is the church of San Damiano, erected in the 11th century reusing classical structures and materials.

▶ *Continue north to the SS3 ter, which leads to the right to Acquasparta.*

❷ Acquasparta

For many centuries Acquasparta administered its own territories, under the name Terre Arnolfe:

The extraordinary fossilised sequoia trees in Dunarobba forest

lands assigned by the Emperor Otto I in 966 to a nobleman, Arnolfo. In 1606, under Church rule, a new statute was issued delineating the Terre Arnolfe, after Pier Luigi Farnese had sold the lands to the Cesi family. Three years later, Prince Ferdinando Cesi founded Acquasparta's version of the glorious Lincei Academy, created in Rome six years earlier. Galileo Galilei was a guest here in 1624. Cesi money was also responsible for Palazzo Cesi, in the centre of the town. Built between the 16th and 17th centuries, it has splendid carved wooden ceilings and frescoes exalting the virtues of the owners. Ruins of the medieval castle walls and round towers survive.

i Corso Umberto 1

▶ *Take the SS3 ter southbound to San Gèmini.*

❸ San Gèmini

The centre of this village is dominated by Palazzo Pubblico (13th century), with its truncated tower and external steps protected by an arch. As well as the 14th-century Duomo (cathedral) note the fine

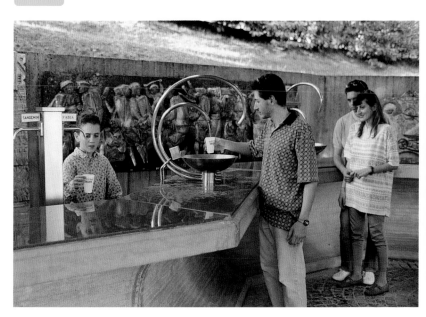

The Sangemini mineral water springs, close to the town of the same name

doorway of Gothic San Francesco, and the Romanesque one with mosaics of the parish church of San Giovanni Battista, founded in 1191. The remains of a tomb known as the Grotta degli Zingari, and of a villa with mosaics, testify to the Roman origin of this settlement.

⟦i⟧ Pizza San Francesco 4 (seasonal)

FOR HISTORY BUFFS

Nicknamed Il Gattamelata (the honeydew cat) for his shrewdness and smooth manners, Erasmo da Narni was one of the most valiant *condottieri* (mercenary leaders) of his time. Born in Narni in 1370 (probably in Via Gattamelata), he fought under Braccio da Montone and Piccinino, and from 1437 served as captain general of Venice, leading his troops against the Viscontis. He died in Padua in 1443; Donatello immortalised his stern expression in a famous bronze equestrian monument.

▶ Continue along the **SS3 ter** southbound then follow the signs for Narni.

⁴ Narni
Ancient Narni extends along a spur above the Nera gorge. From the northern district, with its regular streets dating from Roman times (299 BC), it climbs to two labyrinthine medieval districts and the spectacular Rocca, the papal stronghold,

erected in the late 14th century by Cardinal Egidio Albornoz. On the square, once called 'del Lago' after the reservoir below, stands the Duomo (cathedral), a grand Romanesque monument built in 1047. A further aisle was added to the original nave and two aisles in the 15th century, to incorporate the votive chapel of

The 14th-century Rocca (stronghold) of Narni

The rose window of the church of Santa Maria Assunta at Lugnano

the first bishops of Narni. The bell tower is built on Roman walls, with a Romanesque stone base and Renaissance upper section. Descend to the centre of medieval Narni, Piazza dei Priori, which features the arches of a 14th-century loggia attributed to Gattapone and the massive Palazzo del Podestà. Lower down, a church partially hewn from the rock beneath the complex of San Domenico (deconsecrated) provides access to the chamber where the Tribunal of the Holy Inquisition used to meet; the plaster of an adjacent cell still bears graffiti scratched by prisoners.

i *Piazza dei Priori 3*

▶ *After reaching the SS205, proceed northwest to Amelia.*

5 Amelia

Originally an Umbrian stronghold, Amelia later fell to the Romans and was taken over by the Church from 1307. Set on a hill on the ridge between the Tiber and Nera rivers, it has historic charm enhanced by beautiful countryside; the local willows, pears, figs and apples are much admired. Visible

beside the Roman gate, rebuilt in the 17th century and the only point of access permitted by the contours of the hill, are sections of pre-Roman polygonal walls (6th–4th century BC); a huge Roman reservoir, divided into ten vaulted chambers, extends beneath Piazza Matteotti. As well as fine 15th- and 16th-century mansions, you can visit an archaeological museum and the church of San Francesco (1287), with its red stone façade and Gothic doorway. A chapel houses six tombs of the Geraldini family; the tomb of Matteo and Elisabetta was made in 1477 by Agostino di Duccio. At the top end of the village, beside the Duomo (cathedral), stands a mighty 12-sided bell tower (1050).

i *Via Orvieto 1*

▶ *Follow the signs for Lugnano in Teverina, to the west.*

6 Lugnano in Teverina

High on its solitary hill, this village was fought over for many years by Todi, Orvieto and Amelia. Its pride is the 12th-century collegiate church of Santa Maria Assunta, one of the most significant Romanesque buildings in Umbria. A portico supported by spiral and smooth columns precedes the four-pitched façade and rose window. The interior, with a nave and two aisles, has a finely enclosed *schola cantorum*, iconostasis (decorated screen) and a presbytery raised above the crypt.

▶ *Proceed north on the SS205 and turn left for Alviano.*

7 Alviano

The medieval village of Alviano is set in a beautifully scenic position, overlooking the Tiber Valley and surrounded by hills. Its parish church has 15th-century frescoes; there's also a grandiose square-plan castle with corner towers and a Renaissance courtyard rebuilt by Bartolomeo d'Alviano (1455–1518), a captain in the service of the Venetian Republic. It now houses a fine Folk Museum.

▶ *Back on the SS205, continue left via Guardea, following the signs for Baschi.*

8 Baschi

A 16th-century parish church with a 15th-century polyptych dominates this little village scenically perched on a spur. If you're after a fine meal before returning to Terni, call in at Cannitello, on the main road for Todi, where you'll find chef Vissani, a star of Italian cuisine.

▶ *From Baschi, go to the A1 motorway at Orvieto and follow this to Orte before taking the SS204 back to Terni.*

BACK TO NATURE

About 8km (5 miles) north of Alviano Scalo, on the road along the edge of an artificial basin (formed by damming the Tiber), is a marsh area with nature trails and huts for watching migratory birds.

Valnerina & the
Sibillini Mountains

Along the lush Nera river gorges, this tour enters the lesser-known heart of southern Umbria, and ventures into the mountains that separate it from the Marche region. These are lands of mystics and saints, of hermitages and abbeys, and of the myths and legends of an ancient civilisation.

3 DAYS • 243KM • 151 MILES

The spectacular drop of the Màrmore waterfall

i Via Cassian Bon 4, Terni

▶ *Take the SS19 along the so-called Strada Inferiore (sign-posted, as is the Strada Superiore) to the Cascata delle Màrmore.*

❶ Cascata delle Màrmore

Only those arriving from below will be able to appreciate the roaring grandeur of the three falls of the Velino that plunge spectacularly 165m (541 feet) from the Màrmore plateau down to the Nera river. In mid-summer much of the water disappears, absorbed by the hydroelectric stations which have radically altered the land-scape. In fact, the falls are not even the work of nature. In 271 BC Roman consul Manlio Curio Dentato had a channel dug to reclaim the marshy Rieti plain. The source of constant discord between the people of Rieti, Terni and Valnerina, the falls underwent significant changes between the 16th and 18th centuries and were dammed up in the 1920s and 1930s.

RECOMMENDED WALK

A route at the Màrmore falls links the Strada Inferiore and the Strada Superiore to the Observatory, a small loggia built in 1781 so that visitors could admire the spectacle close up. Other impressive views can be enjoyed from the scenic points created along the paths that skirt the three falls; in certain weather conditions the spray creates amazing colour effects.

▶ *Continue along the SS79 and turn right for Piediluco.*

❷ Piediluco

Approximately 20m (66 feet) deep, lovely Lago di Piediluco – from the Latin for 'at the foot of the woods' – is now exploited as a reservoir for the area's hydro-electric plants (a 42km/26-mile channel carries the water of the Nera river). The lake's shores were already inhabited between the Bronze and Iron ages; boats and fishing equipment have

---

FOR CHILDREN

The famous echo that could repeat up to two 11-syllable sentences on the lakeshore opposite Piediluco no longer exists; it has been eliminated by newly built houses. What is left of it can be heard a few dozen metres off the shady shore, if you hire a boat.

---

been sculpted on the doorway of the Gothic parish church in the village of Piediluco, which is overlooked by the ruins of a 14th-century stronghold.

▶ *Proceed briefly along the SS79 then turn left and drive via Forca dell'Arrone to the SS209, following this to the right to Ferentillo.*

❸ Ferentillo

The two villages that form Ferentillo straddle the Nera river near a wooded gorge defended by two strongholds (one reduced to ruins, the other with towers and a keep). Thrill-seekers should visit the crypt (13th- to 14th-century) of San

Stefano Church. Resting on the walls and pillars are about 20 mummies, with hair, nails and body-hair intact, as well as traces of clothing. Their preservation is due to the sand, rich in nitrates and chloride, on which the corpses were laid, and constant ventilation from the windows.

▶ *Proceed along the SS209 to the turning on the left to the Abbazia di San Pietro in Valle.*

❹ Abbazia di San Pietro in Valle

The abbey was founded around 720 by Faraoldo, the Lombard Duke of Spoleto, after he had been granted a vision of St Peter (the scene is depicted in the left arm of the transept). After falling into ruin following Saracen incursions, the abbey was restored at the command of emperors Otto III and Henry II in the 10th to 11th centuries. Here you can admire several Roman sarcophagi, a rare

Above: St Paul sculpted on the jamb of a door of the Abbey of San Pietro
Below: the abbey of San Pietro in Valle

Lombard main altar and 15th-century frescoes in the apse. Most important of all is the fresco cycle painted on the walls of the nave, showing stories from the Old (left) and New (right) Testaments. Dating from the 12th to 13th centuries, it is a masterpiece of Romanesque painting in Italy.

▶ *Back on the SS209, continue right to Scheggino.*

❺ Scheggino

According to contemporary chronicles, the women of Scheggino covered themselves with glory when, in 1522, the castles of Valnerina rebelled against Spoleto, and the women's strenuous defence saved the triangular

The churches of Santa Maria and Sant'Agostino at Visso

run by the Benedictine abbey of Sant'Eutizio, the main political, economic and cultural centre in the area between the 10th and 12th centuries, and its surgeons had access to a well-stocked library. Inside the abbey complex, 3km (2 miles) south-east of Preci, you can visit the caves of hermits who, at the end of the 6th century, formed a community under the guidance of hermits Spes and Eutizio.

ℹ️ *Via Madonna della Peschiera, Casa del Parco*

▶ *Go back and turn right off the provincial road to travel via Saccovescio to the **SS209**, and take this to the right to Visso.*

8 Visso
An austere ancient village, Visso lies in the Marche, where the upper reaches of the Nera river flow. For a long time, Visso challenged Norcia for control of the high pastures on the Sibillini mountains. Towering inside the Romanesque-Gothic collegiate church of Santa Maria, on a fine square surrounded by 15th- and 16th-century houses and mansions, is a 14th-century St Christopher standing more than 10m (33 feet) high, among several fine frescoes.

stronghold from a memorable siege.

▶ *Continue on the **SS209** to the turning signposted on the right for Vallo di Nera.*

6 Vallo di Nera
Vallo di Nera is particularly noted for the integrity of its 13th-century spiral plan. Houses are propped against each other with the aid of arches, as a protection against earthquakes. Steep, narrow streets link the streets on level ground that adapt to the contours of the hill and lead to the 16th-century doorway of San Giovanni Battista (13th to 14th century, with an apse entirely covered in 16th-century frescoes). At the bottom, where the turreted ring of walls is interrupted, beautiful

votive frescoes of the 14th and 15th centuries by artists from Umbria and Marche adorn the interior of Santa Maria Church.

▶ *Back on the **SS209**, drive on to Pontechiùsita, where the provincial road to Preci branches off to the right.*

7 Preci
Repeatedly devastated by wars and earthquakes (the last in 1997), Preci has an unusual history. Between the 16th and 18th centuries, it had a flourishing school of surgery which specialised in the treatment of eye complaints (including cataract operations), hernias and kidney stones, as well as castrations performed on budding *castrato* singers in the 17th and 18th centuries. The hospital was

---

FOR HISTORY BUFFS

Desolate Pian Perduto ('lost plain') earned its name in 1522, when the people of Norcia fought in vain for it, hand to hand against the people of Visso. 'Norcia, with more forces, believes it will win,/But Visso, with trust in the saints, knows it will win' say the first lines of epic poem *La Battaglia del Pian Perduto*, composed before the 1800s by a shepherd-storyteller from Visso. Poetic challenges were a traditional way of passing the nights while guarding the flocks. Incidentally, Pian Perduto still belongs to Visso.

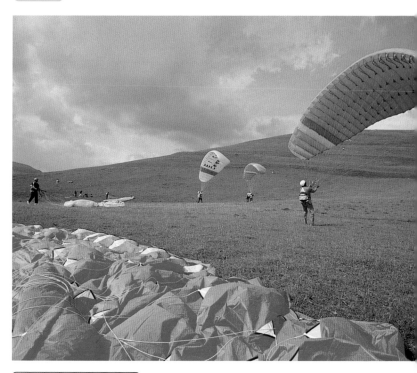

▶ Follow the signs for
Castelsantangelo sul Nera
and then turn right for
Castelluccio, a distance of
22km (14 miles).

BACK TO NATURE

Flower-lovers will enjoy the orchids (about 30 species) that grow in the grounds of Villa Franchetti, on the road to Forca dell'Arrone. Not to be missed in June is the spectacular carpet of flowers on the Castelluccio plain: violets, daffodils, tulips, gentian and gentianella, buttercups, red and yellow poppies, asphodel, peonies, saxifrage, lilies, crucifers, lily of the valley, nigritelle, dwarf juniper, alpine wall germanders, black whortleberry and bearberries are just some of the 1,800 species that brighten the meadows and slopes of the Sibillini mountains. Lake Pilato sits at 1,940m (6,365 feet), at the centre of Monte Vettore's amphitheatre. The *Chirocephalus marchesonii*, a tiny reddish crustacean (shrimp) that swims backwards with its abdomen upwards, lives in its waters – its only known habitat.

9 Castelluccio

High on a hill that separates Pian Perduto from Pian Grande, at the foot of the Sibillini, this mountain village (1,452m/4,764 feet above sea level), built by the people of Norcia to defend their eastern border, seems to float on the smooth basin of a dried-up glacial lake. It makes a good base for exploration.

Until the mid-20th century, this ancient site could only be reached on foot or on horseback. On winter evenings, long tolls of the bell guided wayfarers through the fog and snow that blanked out the fields, famous now for their tasty lentils. Bawdy words, written in lime and often in verse by bored shepherds far from home, are now fading on village houses, stables and shelters.

Hang-gliders in the mountain meadows around Castelluccio

▶ Follow the signs for Norcia,
always bearing right at the
four main forks in the road.

10 Norcia

Enclosed within its unbroken ring of walls (more than 2km/ 1 mile long), this elegant town – Vetusta Nursia to the Romans, who took it from the Sabines in 290 BC – stands on the edge of a fertile plain, dominated by the Sibillini mountain range. Wide streets, two-storey houses and walls reinforced with projected footings were all built to guidelines issued by the papacy in 1730 after yet another devastating earthquake. The main square is dominated by the powerful Castellina, built by Vignola in 1554 for the papal governors. The 14th-century façade of San Benedetto Church is flanked by a 16th-century portico, beneath which are the old measures for cereals, adapted in the 19th century to the metric system. According to tradition, a Roman chamber in the crypt below, the site of an ancient house, is where Benedetto (*c*480–547), founder of Western monasticism, and his twin sister, Scolastica, were born. Their stories are told in the 15th-century frescoes that adorn the church of Santa Scolastica, at the cemetery. There are several *norcinerie* here – pork butchers: the word was coined here. They overflow with salami, cheeses and black truffles (festival in February).

i | Via Solferino 22

▶ *Take the SS396 west, then the SS320 to the left to Cascia.*

⑪ Cascia

Cascia's old centre was changed by 20th-century development, designed to make room for the influx of devotees of Santa Rita (1381–1457, canonised in 1900). An enormous basilica was erected between 1937 and 1947 beside the monastery where Rita Lotti lived her last 40 years

as an Augustinian. A crystal urn contains her mummified body. Forced to marry at a very young age, for 18 years she suffered at the hands of a brutal husband and was only able to embrace the religious life after his death. She prayed that God would grant her twin children innocent deaths before they were old enough to repeat their father's sins – and her prayer was answered. To the left of the basilica is the convent where the saint lived much of her life. Other places to see are the Museo Civico, the church of Sant'Antonio Abate, and Rita's birthplace, Roccaporena.

i | Piazza Garibaldi 1

▶ *After visiting Cascia you could detour to Roccaporena to visit St Rita's birthplace. Otherwise drive south from Cascia following signs to Monteleone di Spoleto. At the crossroads*

below Monteleone turn right and follow signs to Borgo Cerreto and Poggiodomo.

⑫ Santuario della Madonna della Stella

From the bottom of a small, wooded valley, a path climbs steeply to a church partially hewn from the rock. The interior (ask for the keys in nearby Roccatamburo), with 14th-century frescoes, gives access to 20 or so monastic cells, also dug into the stone. Founded in 1308 by the Augustinians (although the cells date from Lombard times), the hermitage was abandoned in the 17th century and restored around 1830. No one has lived here since 1949.

▶ *Back on the asphalt road, continue left to the SS209, which leads left to Terni.*

A winter view of Lake Pilato, in the Sibillini mountains

MOTORING IN ITALY

ACCIDENTS

If you have an accident, place a warning triangle 50m (55 yards) behind the car and call the police (tel: 112 or 113). Do not admit liability or make statements which might later incriminate you. Ask any witness(es) to remain, make a statement to the police and exchange names, addresses, car details and insurance companies' names and addresses with other driver(s) involved. A report must be made to the insurance company. If the accident involves personal injury, medical assistance must be sought for the injured party.

On the *autostrada* there are emergency telephones that connect with the Automobile Club d'Italia (ACI).

BREAKDOWNS

If your car breaks down, put on hazard warning lights and place a warning triangle not less than 50m (55 yards) to the rear of the vehicle.

If you are driving your own car, call the Automobile Club d'Italia (ACI) 24-hour emergency number (tel: 116) and tell the operator your location, car registration and make of car. Roadside assistance will not be given. The car will be towed to the nearest ACI affiliated garage. The service is free to members of affiliated motoring clubs.

In a rental car, call the rental company on the emergency number included with the car's paperwork.

CARAVANS
Caravans and trailers

Take a list of contents, especially if any valuable or unusual equipment is being carried, as this may be required on arrival. A towed vehicle should be readily identifiable by a plate in an accessible position showing the name of the make of the vehicle and the production and serial number.

Brakes

Check that the caravan braking mechanism is correctly adjusted. If it has a breakaway safety mechanism, the cable between the car and caravan must be firmly anchored so that the trailer brakes act immediately if the two part company.

Lights

Make sure that all the lights are working (check that the flasher rate is correct: 60–120 times a minute).

Tyres

Both tyres on the caravan should be of the same size and type. Inspect them carefully: if you think they are likely to be more than three-quarters worn before you get back, replace them before you leave.

CAR RENTAL AND FLY/DRIVE

Many international firms operate this service. Rates generally include breakdown service, maintenance and oil, but not petrol.

Firms restrict rental to drivers over 21 years of age.

You must have had a valid licence for at least one year before applying.

CHILDREN

Children under four must not travel in the front or rear seats unless using a suitable fitted restraint system.

Children between 3 and 12 may only travel in the front seat if using such equipment.

Note: under no circumstances should a rear-facing restraint be used in a seat with an airbag.

COMPULSORY EQUIPMENT

A reflective jacket must be worn when getting out of the vehicle on intercity roads. Also carry spare bulbs and a warning triangle. Vehicles with an over-

hanging load (eg a bicycle carried at the rear) must display a reflectorised square panel.

CRASH HELMETS

All motorcyclists and their passengers must wear crash or safety helmets.

DIMENSIONS RESTRICTIONS

Private cars and towed trailers or caravans are restricted to the following dimensions:
height – 4m; width – 2.5m; length – 12m.

DOCUMENTS

Visitors bringing their own (foreign registered) car to Italy must be at least 18 years of age (also for motorcycles over 125cc or with a passenger) and carry the vehicle's registration documents (logbook) and a full, valid driving licence (*patente* in Italian).

Third party insurance is compulsory; an international green card, though not compulsory, is recommended. A green UK, red Eire or other foreign licence is acceptable accompanied by a translation, available free from the ACI or the Italian State Tourist Office in the country of origin. The translation is not required for the pink EU, UK or Republic of Ireland licence.

Carry documents with you whenever you are driving; if you are stopped by the *polizia stradale* or *carabinieri* they will want to see them.

DRINKING AND DRIVING

The permitted blood-alcohol level is 0.05%. Laws regarding drinking and driving are strict and the penalties severe, so if you drink don't drive.

DRIVING CONDITIONS

Italian traffic rules follow the Geneva Convention and Italy uses international road signs. Driving is on the right and you should give way at intersections to vehicles approaching from your right. You should keep close to the nearside kerb, even when the road is clear.

Vehicles travelling in opposite directions and wishing to turn left must pass in front of each other.

Motorcycles under 150cc are not allowed on motorways.

FINES
On-the-spot fines are very heavy for speeding offences. The police must give a receipt for the amount of fine paid. Cars parked illegally can be clamped or towed away, and a fine will be imposed.

FUEL
Petrol *(benzina)* in Italy is some of the most expensive in Europe. Diesel *(gasolio)* is cheaper. Carrying fuel in cans is prohibited.

Petrol stations are open 7–12.30 and 3–7.30 (mornings only at weekends), but 24-hour service is guaranteed on motorways.

Self-service and 24-hour pumps are common.

INSURANCE
Fully comprehensive insurance, which covers you for some of the expenses after a breakdown or an accident, is advisable. Third-party insurance is compulsory.

LIGHTS
If you are driving your own car, have the headlights adjusted for driving on the right.

Full-beam headlights can be used only outside cities and towns. Dipped headlights are compulsory on major roads and motorways, as well as in tunnels, even if well-lit. You must equip your vehicle with a spare set of light bulbs.

MOTORING CLUBS
The Touring Club Italiano (TCI) has its headquarters at Corso Italia 10, 20122 Milano. Tel: (02) 85261; www.touringclub.it.

The Automobile Club d'Italia (ACI) headquarters are at Via Marsala 8, 00185 Roma. Tel: (06) 49981 (116 for foreign language assistance); www.aci.it.

The ACI provides towage from a breakdown to the nearest affiliated garage. Call from telephone columns placed every 2km (1.2 miles) on the motorway.

PARKING
Parking is difficult as Italy's ancient towns and villages are not built to accommodate vehicles. Some pedestrianized historic towns allow cars in to deposit luggage – you may need a permit from your hotel.

Invest in a parking dial; these are used in permitted parking areas and are displayed in your windscreen to indicate when you arrived. Rental cars usually have one; they are also available at tourist offices.

Many cities have parking zones, indicated by coloured lines. Blue zones have a maximum stay of 1–2 hours. Pay the attendant or at the meter. White zones are free and unlimited in some cities, but reserved for residents in others. Yellow zones are generally reserved for residents only.

ROADS
Main and secondary roads are generally good. Mountain roads are usually well engineered. Italy has some 6,440km (4,000 miles) of motorway *(autostrada)* with tolls payable on most sections (see also **tolls**).

ROUTE DIRECTIONS
The following abbreviations are used for Italian roads:

A – *Autostrada* (motorway)
SS – *Strada Statale* (state road)
dir, ter, bis, q, qu – suffixes to state roads (**SS**) relating to links and extensions of major roads
minor roads – unnumbered roads

SPEED LIMITS
The speed limit in built-up areas is 50kph (31mph); outside built-up areas – 90kph (55mph) on ordinary roads, 110kph (68mph) on main roads and 130kph (80mph) on motorways. For cars towing a caravan or trailer the speed limits are 70kph (43mph) outside built-up areas and 80kph (50mph) on motorways.

Note: a maximum authorised speed sticker must be displayed at the rear by all vehicles, including caravans and trailers, whose maximum permitted speed is less than 130kph (80mph). The stickers are on sale at Italian fuel stations; fines are levied for failure to display.

In wet weather the speed limit on motorways is 110kph (68mph), and 90kph (55mph) on dual carriageways.

TOLLS
Tolls are payable on most motorways in Italy. Visiting motorists may purchase a motorway toll card (Telepass) from ACI offices and motorway toll booths.

As you approach the motorway take the ticket from the automatic box on the left-hand side of the car or press the red button to get one. The barrier will lift. Keep your ticket safe, as you will need it to pay when you leave the motorway.

Cash payment is normally made to the official in the booth; the amount is displayed on a screen outside the pay window. If you are using a pass or paying by credit card, follow the appropriate signs into the Telepass or credit card booth.

WARNING TRIANGLE/ HAZARD WARNING LIGHTS
The use of a warning triangle is compulsory in the event of an accident or breakdown. It should also be used to give advance warning of any stationary vehicle that is parked on a road in fog, near a bend or on a hill at night when the rear lights have failed. It must be placed on the road not less than 50m (55 yards) behind the vehicle.

Motorists who fail to comply with this are liable to an administrative fine.

ACCOMMODATION AND RESTAURANTS

Following is a selection of hotels
(◇), *agriturismi* (🛏) and camping
sites (Δ) that can be found along
the routes of each tour, with
suggestions for restaurants (🍴)
to take a break.

Accommodation prices
Accommodation is divided into
three price categories based on
the cost of a double room per
night:
€ – up to €70
€€ – €70–€150
€€€ – over €150

Restaurant prices
Restaurants are divided into
three price categories based on
the cost of a three-course meal,
excluding drinks:
€ – up to €30
€€ – €30–€50
€€€ – over €50

TOUR I
MASSA
◇ Excelsior €€€
Via C Battisti 1, Marina di
Massa. Tel: 0585 8601;
www.hotelexcelsior.it.
70 rooms.

◇ Maremonti €€€
Lungomare di Levante 19,
near Ronchi. Tel: 0585 241008;
www.hotelmaremonti.com.
26 rooms.
Open Apr to mid-Oct.

Δ International
Partaccia I
Via delle Pinete 394. Tel: 0585
780133; www.partaccia.it.
Open Apr–Sep.

🍴 Da Riccà €€€
Lungomare di Ponente.
Tel: 0585 241070.
*Fish dishes. Closed Mon and
Christmas.*

FORTE DEI MARMI
◇ Raffaelli-Villa Angela €€€
Via Mazzini 64. Tel: 0584 787472;
www.raffaelli.com.
38 rooms.
Closed period in Dec–Jan.

🍴 Lorenzo €€€
Via Carducci 61. Tel: 0584
84030.
*Creative fish cuisine. Closed Mon,
plus lunch daily Jul–Aug & period
between Dec & Jan.*

MARINA DI
PIETRASANTA
◇ Battelli €€
Viale Versilia 189, near Motrone.
Tel: 0584 20010;
www.albergobattelli.it.
38 rooms.
Open mid-May to mid-Sep.

VIAREGGIO
◇ Plaza de Russie €€€
Piazza d'Azeglio 1. Tel: 0584
44449; www.plazaederussie.com.
51 rooms.

🍴 Cabreo €€€
Via Firenze 14. Tel: 0584 54643.
*Classic Tuscan cuisine. Closed Mon
and Nov.*

🍴 Il Porto €€–€€€
Via M Coppino 118. Tel: 0584
383878.
*Fresh fish and seafood. Closed Mon
lunch, all day Sun, period in Jan
& Nov.*

TOUR 2
LUCCA
◇ Ilaria €€€
Via del Fosso 26. Tel: 0583
47615.
41 rooms.

◇ La Luna €€€
Via Fillungo ang, Corte
Compagni 12. Tel: 0583 493634;
www.hotellaluna.com.
29 rooms.
*Closed for period from early
Jan–Feb.*

◇ Piccolo Hotel Puccini €€
Via di Poggio 9. Tel: 0583 55421,
fax: 0583 53487;
www.hotelpuccini.it.
14 rooms.

🍴 Buca di Sant' Antonio €€
Via della Cervia 3. Tel: 0583
55881.
*Lucchese cuisine. Closed Sun
evening.*

🍴 Giulio €
Via delle Conce 45. Tel: 0583
55948.
*Closed Sun (except third in month),
Mon, period in Aug & Christmas.*

🍴 Puccini €€
Corte San Lorenzo 1–3.
Tel: 0583 316116.
*Traditional Lucchese cuisine.
Closed Tue.*

TOUR 3
BAGNI DI LUCCA
◇ Park Hotel Regina €€€
Viale Umberto I 157. Tel: 0583
805508.
14 rooms.
Closed mid-Jan to Feb

BARGA
◇ Villa Moorings €€
Via Roma, 18. Tel: 0583 711538;
www.villamoorings.it.
12 rooms.

🍴 L'Osteria €
Piazza Angelio 13–14. Tel: 0583
724547.
*Local cuisine. Closed Nov, Jan,
Feb.*

CASTELVECCHIO
PASCOLI
◇ 🍴 Il Ciocco €€€
Near Il Ciocco. Tel: 0583 7191;
www.ciocco.it.
187 rooms.

PIETRASANTA
◇ Pietrasanta €€€
Via Garibaldi 35. Tel: 0584
793726;
www.albergopietrasanta.com.
19 rooms.

TORRE DEL LAGO
PUCCINI
🍴 Del Lago
Via Cimarosa, near Frassetti.
Tel: 0584 359702.
Open all year.

TOUR 4
PISA

Novecento €€€
Via Roma 37. Tel: 050 500323;
www.hotelnovocento.pisa.it.
12 rooms.

Royal Victoria Hotel €€€
Lungarno Pacinotti 12.
Tel: 050 940111;
www.royalvictoria.it.
48 rooms.

Torre Pendente
Viale delle Cascine 86.
Tel: 050 561704;
www.campingtorrependente.it.
Open Apr to mid-Oct.

Da Bruno €
Via Luigi Bianchi 12.
Tel: 050 560818.
*Traditional Pisan cuisine. Closed
Mon evening, Tue.*

Osteria dei Calvieri €€
Via San Frediano 16. Tel: 050
580858.
*Excellent Tuscan 'slow food'. Closed
Sat lunch, Sun, & Aug.*

La Rota €
Via Aurelia 276, Madonna
dell'Acqua. Tel: 050 804443.
Tuscan cuisine. Closed Tue.

MARINA DI PISA
Internazionale
Via Litoranea 7. Tel: 050 35211.
Open May–Sep.

Foresta €€
Via Litoranea 2. Tel: 050 35082.
*Seafood. Closed Thu & Sun evening
in winter.*

SAN GIULIANO TERME
Granduca €€
Via del Brennero 13. Tel: 050
814111; www.hotelgranduca.it.
170 rooms.
Restaurant.

Ugo €€
Via Aurelia 310, near Arena-
Metato. Tel: 050 804455.
*Tuscan and classic Italian cuisine.
Closed Sun evening & Mon.*

TOUR 5
PISTOIA

Patria €€
Via Crispi 6–8. Tel: 0573 25187;
www.patriahotel.com.
28 rooms.

La Bottegaia €€
Via del Lastrone 17. Tel: 0573
365602.
*Tuscan cuisine. Closed Sun lunch,
Mon & period in Aug.*

ABETONE
Regina €€
Via Uccelliera 579. Tel: 0573
60007; www.albergoregina.com.
25 rooms.
Open Jul–Aug, Dec–Apr.

Da Pierone €–€€
Via Brennero 556. Tel: 0573
60068.
*Traditional cuisine. Closed Thu &
period in Jun & Oct.*

MONTECATINI TERME
**Antica Casa Le Rondini
B&B €€**
Località Colle di Buggiano, Via
M Pierucci 21. Tel: 0572 33313.
5 rooms.

Nuovo Excelsior €€
Viale Felice Cavallotti 115.
Tel: 0572 70212;
www.dormireintoscana.it.
39 rooms.
Open Apr–Oct.

La Torre €€€
Piazza Giusti 8, Montecatini
Alto. Tel: 0572 70650.
Tuscan cuisine. Closed Tue.

PRATO
Giardino €€
Via Magnolfi 4. Tel: 0574
606588; www.giardinohotel.com.
28 rooms.

TOUR 6
VOLTERRA
Villa Nencini €€
Borgo Santo Stefano 55.
Tel: 0588 86386, fax: 0588 80601.
35 rooms.

Tenuta Orgiaglia
Near Ponsano. Tel: 0588 35029;
www.orgiaglia.it.
Open all year.

Le Balze
Via di Mandringa, near Borgo
San Giusto. Tel: 0588 87880.
Open Mar to mid-Oct.

Del Duca €€–€€€
Via di Castello 2. Tel: 0588
81510.
*Tuscan cuisine. Closed Tue (except
Jul–Sep), various holidays.*

**Vecchia Osteria dei
Poeti €**
Via Matteotti 55. Tel: 0588
86029.
*Tuscan cuisine. Closed Thu and
mid-Jan to mid-Feb.*

PIOMBINO
Rooms Canessa Camere €
Baratti 43. Tel: 339 429 4506;
www.canessacamere.it.
3 rooms.

Pappasole
Via Carbonifera 14, near
Riotorto. Tel: 0565 20414,
fax: 0565 20346.
Open mid-Apr to mid-Oct.

CASTAGNETO CARDUCCI
I Ginepri €€–€€€
Viale Italia 13, Marina di
Castagneto Carducci. Tel: 0565
744029; www.hoteliginepri.it.
50 rooms.
Open Mar–Oct.

Da Ugo €€
Via Pari 3A. Tel: 0565 763746.
*Traditional cuisine. Closed Mon &
in Nov.*

TOUR 7
PORTOFERRAIO
Viticcio €€
Near Viticcio. Tel: 0565 939058;
www.hotelviticcio.it.
32 rooms.
Open Apr–Oct.

Casa Marisa
Near Schiopparello 12.
Tel: & fax: 0565 933074.
Open all year.

CAPOLIVERI
Dino €€
Near Pareti. Tel: 0565 939103;
www.hoteldino.com.
30 rooms.
Open Apr–Oct.

RIO MARINA
⚿ Pierolli €€
Lungomare Kennedy 1.
Tel: 0565 931109;
www.hotelpierolli.it.
22 rooms.
Open Apr–Sep.

🍴 La Canocchia €€–€€€
Via Palestro 2–4. Tel: 0565
962432.
*Tuscan and classic Italian cuisine.
Closed Mon (except in sumer). Open
mid-Feb to Oct.*

TOUR 8
CASTIGLIONE DELLA PESCAIA
⚿ L'Approdo €€€
Via Ponte Giorgini 29.
Tel: 0564 933466;
www.hotellapprodo.com.
48 rooms.

⚿ Aurora €€
Via Fratelli Bandiera 19.
Tel: 0564 933718;
www.aurora-albergo.it.
21 rooms.

⚿ Piccolo Hotel €€€
Via Montecristo 7.
Tel: 0564 937081;
www.hotel-castiglione.com.
24 rooms.
Open Easter and mid-May to Sep.

🍴 Da Romolo €€–€€€
Corso della Libertà 10. Tel: 0564
933533.
*Maremma cuisine. Closed Tue
(except late Jun–late Sep) & early
Nov to mid-Dec. Dinner only
Jul–Aug.*

MASSA MARÌTTIMA
⚿ Duca del Mare €€
Piazza Alighieri 1–2. Tel: 0566
902284; www.ducadelmare.it.
28 rooms.
Closed mid-Jan to mid-Feb.

TOUR 9
SCANSANO
⚿ 🍴 Antico Casale di Scansano €€€
Near Castagneta.
Tel: 0564 507219;
www.anticocasalediscansano.it.
32 rooms.

SATURNIA
⚿ Villa Clodia €€
Via Italia 43. Tel: 0564 601212;
www.hotelvillaclodia.com.
10 rooms.
Closed period in Jan.

🍴 Due Cippi–Da Michele €€
Piazza Vittorio Veneto 26A.
Tel: 0564 601074.
*Regional cuisine. Closed Tue &
8–28 Jan.*

SORANO
⚿ Della Fortezza €€€
Piazza Cairoli. Tel: 0564 632010;
www.hoteldellafortezza.it.
15 rooms.
Closed Jan.

PITIGLIANO
⚿ Relais Valle Orientina €€
Via Valle Orientina. Tel: 0564
616611; www.valleorientina.it.
15 rooms.

ORBETELLO
🌿 Podere Bengodi
Bengodi Alto, Talamonaccio.
Tel: 385 833 3108;
www.agriturismoevacanzeverdi.
com.
Open all year.

🅐 Voltoncino
Near Albinia, SS Aurelia Km
153. Tel: 0564 870158.
Open Easter to mid-Sep.

TOUR 10
FIRENZE
⚿ Hermitage €€
Vicolo Marzio 1.
Tel: 055 287216;
www.hermitagehotel.com.
28 rooms.

⚿ Morandi alla Crocetta €€€
Via Laura 50. Tel: 055 2344747;
www.hotelmorandi.it.
10 rooms.

⚿ Villa Le Rondini €€€
Via Bolognese Vecchia 224.
Tel: 055 400081;
www.villalerondini.it.
42 rooms.

🌿 Le Macine
Viuzzo del Pozzetto 1, near
Bagno a Ripoli. Te: 055 6531089.
Open all year.

🍴 Beccofino €€–€€€
Piazza degli Scarlatti 1/r
(Lungarno Guicciardini).
Tel: 055 290076.
*Creative Tuscan cuisine. Closed
Mon. Open evenings only.*

TOUR 11
CERTALDO
⚿ 🍴 Osteria del Vicario €€–€€€
Via Rivellino 3, near Certaldo
Alta. Tel: 0571 668228.
15 rooms.
*Creative Tuscan cuisine. Closed
Wed.*

SAN GIMIGNANO
⚿ L'Antico Pozzo €€€
Via San Matteo 87. Tel: 0577
942014; www.anticopozzo.com.
18 rooms.
Closed mid-Jan to mid-Feb.

⚿ Leon Bianco €€
Piazza della Cisterna 13.
Tel: 0577 941294;
www.leonbianco.com.
26 rooms.
*Closed mid-Jan–mid-Feb & period
in Nov–Dec.*

🌿 Fattoria Poggio Alloro
Near Sant'Andrea 23.
Tel: 0577 950276;
www.fattoriapoggioalloro.com.
Open all year.

🍴 La Mangiatoia €€
Via Mainardi 5. Tel: 0577
941528.
*Tuscan specialities. Closed 4–25
Nov and Tue.*

🍴 Ristorante Dorandò €€
Vicolo dell'Oro. Tel: 0577
941862.
*Dishes from the Middle Ages and
Etruscan times with a modern twist.
Closed Mon (except Easter–Oct),
10 Jan–1 Mar & 10–26 Dec.*

MONTERIGGIONI
🍴 La Leggenda dei Frati €€€
Piazza Garfonda 7, near Abbadia
Isola. Tel: 0577 301222.
Tuscan cuisine. Closed Mon, Nov.

TOUR 12
VICCHIO
◇ **Villa Campestri €€€**
Via di Campestri 19/22, 5km
(3 miles) from Campestri.
Tel: 055 8490107;
www.villacampestri.it.
22 rooms.
Open mid-Mar to mid-Nov.

FIÈSOLE
◇ **La Fattoria di Maiano €€€**
Via Benedetto da Maiano 11,
near Maiano. Tel: 055 599600;
www.fattoriadimariano.com.
22 rooms.

🍴 **La Reggia degli Etruschi**
€€
Via San Francesco 18. Tel: 055
59385.
Regional cuisine. Closed Tue.

TOUR 13
AREZZO
◇ **Patio €€**
Via Cavour 23. Tel: 0575 401962;
www.hotelpatio.it.
7 rooms.
Closed period in Jan.

◇ **Magnanini Massimo**
Via Fontebranda 47. Tel: 0575
27627.
Open all year.

🍴 **Cantuccio €–€€**
Via Madonna del Prato 76.
Tel: 0575 26830.
Tuscan cuisine. Closed Wed and
period in Jul.

POPPI
◇ **Casentino €€**
Piazza della Repubblica 6.
Tel: 0575 529090.
28 rooms.

CAMÀLDOLI
🍴 **Cedro €–€€**
Via Camaldoli 20, near
Moggiona. Tel: 0575 556080.
Casentino cuisine. Closed Mon &
holidays in autumn.

TOUR 14
ANGHIARI
◇ **La Meridiana €€**
Piazza IV Novembre 8.
Tel: 0575 788102;
www.hotellameridiana.it
22 rooms.

SANSEPOLCRO
◇ **La Ballestra €€–€€€**
Via del Montefeltro 29.
Tel: 0575 735151.
52 rooms.

🍴 **Fiorentino €€**
Via Luca Pacioli 60.
Local cuisine. Closed Wed & periods
in Nov & Jan.

CITTÀ DI CASTELLO
◇ **Tiferno €€**
Piazza Raffaello Sanzio 13.
Tel: 075 8550331;
www.hoteltiferno.it.
47 rooms.

🐾 **Villa Bice**
Via Villa Zampini 43/45, near
Cerbara. Tel: 075 8511430;
www.villabice.it.
Open all year.

🏕 **Montesca**
Near Montesca. Tel: 075
8558566.
Open mid-Apr to Sep.

🍴 **Il Postale di Marco e**
Barbara €€
Via Raffaele de Cesare 8.
Tel: 075 8521356.
Closed Sat lunch & Mon from
Oct–May and 15 days in Jan.

UMBÈRTIDE
🐾 **Nestore**
Località Verna di Umbertide.
Tel: 075 927 1001;
www.nestoreholidays.com.
Open all year.

CORTONA
🐾 **I Pagliai**
San Marco in Villa 2/a. Tel: 0575
605220; www.ipagliai.it.
Open all year.

🍴 **Osteria del Teatro €–€€**
Via Maffei 2. Tel: 0575 630556.
Tuscan cuisine. Closed Wed &
period in Nov.

CASTIGLION
FIORENTINO
◇ **Relais San Pietro in**
Polvano €€€
Near Polvano 3. Tel: 0575
650100; www.polvano.com.
7 rooms.
Open Apr–Oct.

🍴 **L'Archimboldo €€**
Località Brolio. Tel: 0575
652307.
Innovative Tuscan food. Closed
Mon & Jan to mid-Feb.

TOUR 15
SIENA
◇ **Santa Caterina €€€**
Via Piccolomini 7.
Tel: 0577 221105;
www.hscsiena.it.
22 rooms.

◇ **Piccolo Hotel Il Palio €€€**
Piazza del Sale 18.
Tel: 0577 281131;
www.piccolohotelilpalio.it.
26 rooms.

🏕 **Siena Colleverde**
Strada Scacciapensieri 47.
Tel: 0577 334080.
Open Mar–Dec.

🍴 **Al Marsili €€**
Via del Castoro 3. Tel: 0577
47154.
Sienese cuisine. Closed Mon.

🍴 **Osteria Le Logge €€**
Via del Porrione 33. Tel: 0577
48013.
Creative Tuscan cuisine. Closed
Sun & Jan.

TOUR 16
CASTELNUOVO
BERARDENGA
◇ **Posta del Chianti €€**
Near Colonna del Grillo.
Tel: 0577 353000;
www.postadelchianti.it.
21 rooms.
Closed peiod in Jan.

GAIOLE IN CHIANTI
◇ **Castello di Spaltenna €€€**
Via Spaltenna 13, near Pieve di
Spaltenna. Tel: 0577 749483;
www.spaltenna.it.
37 rooms.
Open Apr to mid-Dec.

RADDA IN CHIANTI
◇ **Relais Fattoria Vignale €€€**
Via Pianigiani 8. Tel: 0577
738300; www.vignale.it.
42 rooms.
Open mid-Mar to mid-Nov.

IMPRUNETA

◊ **Bellavista €€**
Via delle Croce 2.
Tel: 055 211 1083;
www.bellavistaimpruneta.it.
19 rooms.

🍽 **Osteria lo Ziro €€**
Via Roma 19/21. Tel: 055
2012232.
*Tuscan and classic Italian cuisine.
Closed Wed.*

CASTELLINA IN CHIANTI

◊ **Salivolpi €€**
Via Fiorentina 89. Tel: 0577
740484; www.hotelsalivolpi.com.
19 rooms.

🍽 **Antica Trattoria La Torre
€–€€**
Piazza del Comune 15. Tel: 0577
740236.
*Chianti cuisine. Closed Fri &
periods in Feb & Sep.*

**TOUR 17
BUONCONVENTO**

🌿 **Podere Salicotto**
Località Salicotto 73.
Tel: 0577 809087;
www.poderesalicotto.com.

MONTALCINO

◊ **Casa Degli Orsi B&B €**
Via Spagna 2. Tel: 0577 222140.
2 rooms.

◊ **Vecchia Oliviera €€**
Via Landi 1. Tel: 0577 846028;
www.vecchiaoliviera.com.
11 rooms.
Closed period in Dec and Jan–Feb.

🌿 **La Crociona**
Near La Croce. Tel: 0577
848007; www.lacrociona.com.

🍽 **Taverna dei Barbi €€€**
Località Podernuovi 170.
Tel: 0577 84111.
*Regional cuisine. Closed dinner
Sat & Sun.*

PIENZA

◊ **Relais il Chiostro di Pienza
€€€**
Corso Rosellino 26. Tel: 0578
748400, fax: 0578 748440.
37 rooms.
Closed Jan to mid-Mar.

MONTEPULCIANO

◊ **Il Marzocco €€**
Piazza Savonarola 18.
Tel: 0578 757262;
www.albergoilmarzocco.it.
16 rooms.
Closed for period Nov–Dec.

🍽 **La Grotta €€€**
Via di San Biagio 2.
Tel: 0578 757479.
*Good quality regional cuisine.
Closed Wed, & Jan–Feb.*

RAPOLANO TERME

◊ **Due Mari €€**
Via Giotto 1. Tel: 0577 724070;
www.hotel2mari.com.
59 rooms.
Closed period in Jan.

**TOUR 18
PIANCASTAGNAIO**

🌿 **Sant'Apollinare**
Via Traversa Cassia Aurelia 1.
Tel: 338 664 6897;
www.agriturismosantapollinare.it.

ABBADIA SAN SALVATORE

◊ **Adriana €€**
Via Serdini 76. Tel: 0577 778116;
www.paginegialle.it/
hoteladriana.
41 rooms.
Closed Nov.

RADICÒFANI

🌿 **La Palazzina**
Near Le Vigne. Tel: 0578 55771.

CETONA

🍽 **La Frateria di Padre Eligio
€€€**
Via San Francesco 2. Tel: 0578
238261, fax: 0578 239220.
*Creative Italian cuisine. Closed Tue,
period during Jan & Feb.*

CHIUSI

◊ **Casa Toscana B&B €**
Via E Baldetti 37. Tel: 0578
222227; www.bbcasatoscana.it.
6 rooms.
Closed between Jan & Feb.

🍽 **Il Zaira €€**
Via Arunte 12. Tel: 0578 20260.
*Regional cuisine. Closed Mon
(except holidays & period in
summer).*

**TOUR 19
PERUGIA**

◊ **Hotel Fortuna €€**
Via Bonazzi 19. Tel: 075 722845;
www.umbriahotels.com.
52 rooms.

◊ **Relais San Clemente
€€€**
Near Bosco, 12km (7 miles)
from Perugia. Tel: 075 5915100;
www.relais.it.
64 rooms.

🌿 **Il Covone €€**
Strada Fratticiola 2, near
Ponte Pattoli. Tel: 075 694140;
www.covone.com.

🏕 **Paradis d'Été**
Strada Fontana 29/G, near Colle
della Trinità. Tel: 075 5173121,
fax: 075 5176056.
Open Mar–Nov.

🍽 **Antica Trattoria San
Lorenzo €€**
Piazza Dante 19. Tel: 075
5721956.
Umbrian cuisine. Closed Sun.

🍽 **Enoteca Giò €**
Via R D'Andreotto 19. Tel: 075
5731100.
*Umbrian cuisine. Closed Sun
evening & Mon lunchtime.*

🍽 **Il Falchetto €€**
Via Bartolo 26. Tel: 075 573
1775.
Umbrian cuisine. Closed Mon.

**TOUR 20
GUBBIO**

◊ **Gattapone €€€**
Via Ansidei 6. Tel: 075 9272489,
fax: 075 9271269.
18 rooms.

🌿 **Marano**
Località Colonnata 18.
Tel: 075 927 1001;
www.maranoholidays.com.

🏕 **Villa Orto Guidone**
Near Orto Guidone. Tel: 075
9272037, fax: 075 9276620.
Closed Jan–Mar.

⬛ **Taverna del Lupo** €€
Via Ansidei 21. Tel: 075 9274368.
*Umbrian cuisine. Closed Mon
(except Aug–Sep).*

NOCERA UMBRA
⬛ **La Lupa**
Via Colpertana. Tel: 0742
813539.
Open all year. Booking required.

TOUR 21
CORCIANO
⬥ **Locanda Solomeo** €€€
Piazza Dalla Chiesa 1, near
Solomeo. Tel: 075 5293119,
fax: 075 5294090.
12 rooms.
*Closed Christmas and period
mid-Jun to mid-Feb.*

MAGIONE
⬛ **Rosso di Sera** €€
Via Fratelli Papini 81. Tel: 075
8476277.
*Local food and good lake views.
Closed Mon.*

PASSIGNANO
SUL TRASIMENO
⬥ **Florida** €
Via II Giugno 2. Tel: 075 827228.
8 rooms.

⬥ **Kursaal** €€
Viale Europa 24. Tel: 075
828055; www.kursaalhotel.net.
18 rooms.
Closed Jan & Feb.

⬥ **Europa**
Località San Donato 8. Tel: 075
827405.
Open Apr–Sep.

⬛ **Trattoria del Pescatore** €
Via San Bernardino 5. Tel: 075
8296063.
Local fish and regional cuisine.

CASTIGLIONE DEL LAGO
⬥ **Miralago** €€
Piazza Mazzini 6. Tel: 075
951157; www.hotelmiralago.com.
19 rooms.
Closed Jan to mid-Mar.

⬛ **Poggio del Sole**
Near Ceraso, Sanfatucchio.
Tel: & fax: 075 9680221.
Open all year.

⬛ **Cantina** €
Via Vittorio Emanuele 89.
Tel: 075 9652463.
*Umbrian & lake cuisine. Closed
Mon & Oct–Mar.*

PANICALE
⬥⬛ **Le Grotte di Boldrino** €€
Via V Ceppari 30. Tel: 075
837161;
www.grottediboldrino.com.
9 rooms.

⬛ **Lillotatini** €€–€€€
Piazza Umberto I. Tel: 075
837771.
*Umbrian and Tuscan cuisine.
Closed Mon, Epiphany–Feb.*

TOUR 22
ASSISI
⬥ **Fontebella** €€€
Via Fontebella 25. Tel: 075
812883; www.fontebella.com.
43 rooms.

⬥ **Il Palazzo** €€
Via San Francesco 8. Tel: 075
816841; www.hotelilpalazzo.it.
12 rooms.
Open Mar–Oct & Christmas.

⬥ **San Francesco** €€€
Via San Francesco 48.
Tel: 075 812281;
www.hotelsanfrancescoassisi.it.
44 rooms.

⬛ **La Castellana**
Near Costa di Trex 4.
Tel: 075 8019046;
www.agriturismolacastellana.it.
Open all year.

⬛ **Ristorante Medio Evo** €
Via Arco dei Priori 4. Tel: 075
813068.
Umbrian delicacies. Closed Wed.

SPELLO
⬥ **La Bastiglia** €€€
Via Salnitraria 15. Tel: 0742
651277; www.labastiglia.com.
33 rooms.
Closed 7–31 Jun.

SPOLETO
⬥ **San Luca** €€€
Via Interna delle Mura 21.
Tel: 0743 223399;
www.hotelsanluca.com.
35 rooms.

⬛ **Il Casale Divino**
Località Colle de Marchese 101,
Castel Ritaldi. Tel: 0743 252029;
www.ilcasaledivino.it.

⬛ **Monteluco**
Near San Pietro. Tel: & fax: 0743
220358.
Open Apr–Sep.

⬛ **Tartufo** €€
Piazza Garibaldi 24. Tel: 0743
40236.
*Regional cuisine revisited. Closed
Sun evening, Mon & period in Jun.*

MONTEFALCO
⬥ **Palazzo Bontadosi** €€€
Piazza del Comune 19. Tel: 0742
379357; www.hotelbontadosi.it.
10 rooms.

BEVAGNA
⬥ **Il Chiostro di Bevagna** €€
Corso Matteotti 107.
Tel: 0742 361987;
www.ilchiostrodibevagna.com.
14 rooms.
Closed Jan–Feb.

TOUR 23
ORVIETO
⬥ **La Badia** €€€
Località La Badia 8. Tel: 0763
301959; www.labadiahotel.it.
27 rooms.

⬥ **Valentino** €€
Via Angelo da Orvieto 32.
Tel: 0763 342464;
www.valentinohotel.com.
19 rooms.
Closed Jan–Feb.

⬛ **Grotto del Funaro** €
Via Ripa Serancia 41. Tel: 0763
343276.
*Wild boar and suckling pig. Closed
Mon (except Aug) and period in Jul.*

⬛ **Trattoria La Grotta** €€
Via Luca Signorelli 5. Tel: 0763
341348.
*Regional cuisine and "slow food".
Closed Tue.*

TODI
⬥ **Fonte Cesia** €€€
Via L. Leony 3. Tel: 075
8943737; www.fontecesia.it.
35 rooms.

◊ **Villa Luisa** €€
Via Cortesi 147. Tel: 075
8948571; www.villaluisa.it.
40 rooms.

🍴 **Cavour** €€
Corso Cavour 21–23. Tel: 075
8943730.
Closed Christmas–New Year.

TORGIANO
◊ **Le Tre Vaselle** €€€
Via Garibaldi 48. Tel: 075
9880447; www.3vaselle.it.
60 rooms.

TOUR 24
TERNI
◊ **Hotel de Paris** €€
Viale della Stazione 52. Tel: 0744
58047; www.hoteldeparis.it.
63 rooms.

◊ **Michelangelo Palace** €€€
Viale della Stazione 63.
Tel: 0744 202711;
www.michelangelohotelumbria.it.
78 rooms.

🌿 **La Prima Mela**
Strada di Collestacio 18, Cesi.
Tel: 0744 241255;
www.bellaumbria.net/
agriturismo-laprimamela.
Open all year.

🍴 **La Mora** €€
Strada San Martino 44. Tel: 0744
421256.
*Local cuisine. Closed Wed & period
July, Aug.*

🍴 **Villa Graziani** €€
Via Villavalle 11, near Papigno.
Tel: 0744 67138.
*Local cuisine. Closed Sun evening
& Mon, period in Aug.*

ACQUASPARTA
◊ **Castello di Casigliano** €€
Piazza Corsini 1.
Tel: 0744 943428;
www.castellodicasigliano.com.
20 rooms.

NARNI
◊ **Dei Priori** €€
Vicolo del Comune 4. Tel: 0744
726843; www.loggiadeipriori.it.
19 rooms.

AMELIA
◊ **Anita** €€
Via Roma 31. Tel: 0744 982146;
www.bellaumbria.net/albergo-
anita.
31 rooms.

◊ **Badia alle Grazie** €€€
Località Foce, Via della
Gabelletta 4. Tel: 0744 983926;
www.badiaallegrazie.com.
16 rooms.

🌿 **San Cristoforo**
Strada San Cristoforo 16.
Tel: 0744 988249; www.
agriturismosancristoforo.com.
Open all year.

TOUR 25
**CASCATA DELLE
MÀRMORE**
🅐 **Cascata delle Màrmore**
Near I Campacci a Màrmore.
Tel: & fax: 0744 67198.
Open Apr–Sep.

FERENTILLO
◊ **Abbazia San Pietro in
Valle** €€€
Località Macenano, Via Carse
Sparse 4. Tel: 0744 780129;
www.sanpietroinvalle.com.
19 rooms.
Open Easter–Oct.

🍴 **Il Cantico** €€
Via Case Sparse 4, near
Macenano. Tel: 0744 780005.
*Umbrian cuisine. Closed Mon, Jan
& Feb.*

SCHEGGINO
🍴 **Del Ponte Scataloni** €€
Via di Borgo 11. Tel: 0743 61523.
Local specialities. Closed Mon.

NORCIA
◊ 🍴 **Grotta Azzurra** ££
Via Alfieri 12. Tel: 0743 816513;
www.bianconi.com.
46 rooms.

🍴 **Trattoria da Francese**
€–€€
Via Riguardati 16. Tel: 0743
816290.
*Umbrian cuisine, with game. Closed
Fri & periods in Jun & Nov.*

CASCIA
◊ 🍴 **Cursula** €€
Viale Cavour 3. Tel: 0743 76206;
www.hotelcursula.com.
40 rooms.
Closed Jan–Feb.

🌿 **Casale Sant'Antonio**
2km (1.2 miles) from Cascia.
Tel: 0743 76819;
www.casalesantantonio.it.
Open all year.

PRACTICAL INFORMATION

TOUR 1

ⓘ Viale Vespucci 24, Marina di Massa.
Tel: 0585 2400463.

ⓘ Viale XX Settembre, Carrara.
Tel: 0585 844136.

ⓘ Via Achille Franceschi 28d, Forte dei Marmi.
Tel: 0584 83214.

ⓘ Via Donizetti 14, Marina di Pietrasanta.
Tel: 0584 20331.

ⓘ Viale Carducci 10, Viareggio.
Tel: 0584 962233.

❶ Carrara
Academy of Fine Arts
Palazzo Cybo Malaspina, Piazza Granisci.
Tel: 0585 71685.

Marble Museum
Viale XX Settembre 85.
Tel: 0585 845746.
Open May–Sep, Mon–Sat 9.30–1, 3.30–6; Oct–Apr, Mon–Sat 9–12.30, 2.30–5.

❸ Fantiscritti
Quarry museum
Tel: 0585 70981.
Open Apr–Nov, daily 9–7; Dec–Mar, Mon–Sat 10.30–1.30, Sun 11–5.

❺ Fosdinovo
Castle
Tel: 0187 68891.
Open Apr–Sep, Fri 4–7, Sat–Sun 10–12, 4–7;

Oct–Mar, Sat–Sun 10–12, 3–6.

❻ Sarzana
Museum of Stelae-Statues
Castello del Piagnaro, Pontrèmoli.
Tel: 0187 831439.
Open Apr–Sep, 9–12, 3–6; Oct–Mar, 9–12, 2–5. Closed Mon in winter.

❼ Luni
National Archaeological Museum
Tel: 0187 660266.
Open Tue–Sun 8.30–7.30.

For Children
Pitagora New Park
Lido di Camaiore.
Tel: 0584 611008.
Open Jun–Aug, daily 10am–midnight; Oct–May, 10–7.30.

❿ Viareggio
Galleria del Libro
Via Margherita 33.
Tel: 0584 962734.
Open Tue–Sun 9–1, 3.30–7.30.

TOUR 2

ⓘ Piazzale Giuseppe Verdi, Lucca.
Tel: 0583 583150.

❼ Casa dei Guinigi
Guinigi Tower
Via Sant'Andrea.
Open Tue–Sat 8.30–7.30, Sun 8.30–1.30

❽ Duomo di San Martino
Tomb of Ilaria del Carretto
Sagrestia del Duomo.
Open mid-Mar to Oct, Mon–Fri 9.30–5.45, Sat 9.30–6.45, Sun 11.20–11.50, 1–4.45; Nov to mid-Mar, Mon–Fri 9.30–4.45, Sat 9.30–6.45, Sun 11.20–12.50, 1–4.45.

TOUR 3

ⓘ Piazzale Giuseppe Verdi, Lucca.
Tel: 0583 583150.

ⓘ Via di Mezzo 45, Barga.
Tel: 0583 724743.

ⓘ Piazza delle Erbe 10, Castelnuovo di Garfagnana.
Tel: 0583 641007.

ⓘ Alpi Apuane Nature Visitor Centre, Piazza delle Erbe 1, Castelnuovo di Garfagnana.
Tel: 0583 65169.

ⓘ Piazza Statuto, Pietrasanta.
Tel: 0584 283375.

❶ Villa di Camigliano
Near Camigliano.
Tel: 0583 928041.
Open Mar–Oct, Wed–Mon 10–1, 3–6.30.

❷ Villa Mansi
Segromigno in Monte.
Tel: 0583 920234.
Currently closed.

❸ Villa Reale
Via Fraga Alta, Marlia.
Tel: 0583 30108.
Open for guided tours Tue–Sun 10–1, 2–6.

❹ Bagni di Lucca
Spa establishment
Piazza San Martino II.
Tel: 0583 87221.
Open monrings all year, afternoons in summer.

Recommended Excursions
Civic Museum
Via del Mangano 17, Coreglia Antelminelli.
Tel: 0583 709301.
Open May–Sep, Mon–Fri 10–1, Sat–Sun 10–1, 3–7; Oct–Apr, Mon–Fri 10–1.

Grotta del Vento
Tel: 0583 722024.
Open Apr–Sep for guided tours.

❻ Castelvecchio Pascoli
House of Giovanni Pascoli
Via Caprona 4.
Tel: 0583 766147.
Open Tue, Thu–Sun 10.30–1, 3–6.45, Wed 3.30–6.45. Closed Mon.

❼ Castelnuovo di Garfagnana
Exhibition on Ancient Ligurian Civilization
Rocca di Castelnuovo, Piazza Ariosto 1.
Tel: 0583 62746.
Visits by request.

TOUR 4

ⓘ Piazza dei Miracoli, Pisa.
Tel: 050 560464.

ⓘ Piazza Vittorio Emanuele II 16, Pisa.
Tel: 050 42291.

ⓘ Pisa Airport.
Tel: 050 502513.

ⓘ Via Lante 1a, Vicopisano.
Tel: 050 796276.

ⓘ Via Roma 9, Calci.
Tel: 050 9910638.

ⓘ Piazza P B Shelley, San Giuliano Terme.
Tel: 050 815064.

❶ Tenuta di San Rossore
Visitor Centre
Tel: 050 530101.
Open all year, Sat–Sun & holidays 9–7.

⑤ Marina di Pisa
Migliarino San Rossore
Massaciùccoli Natural
Park
Consorzio del Parco,
Via Aurelia Nord 4.
Tel: 050 525500.
Tours by appointment 8–2.

For Children
Fantasilandia
Viale del Tirreno 42,
Tirrenia.
Tel: 050 30326.
*Open Mar–end Sep, Mon–Fri
2.30–dusk, Sat–Sun
8.30–dusk.*

⑥ Certosa di Pisa
Via Roma, Calci.
Tel: 050 938430.
*Guided tours Tue–Sat 9–7,
Sun & holidays 9–1.*

Museum of Natural and
Territorial History
Certosa.
Tel: 050 2212970.
*Open mid-Jun to mid-Sep,
Tue–Fri 10–7, Sat 10–6, Sun
4pm–12am; mid-Sep to mid-
Jun, Tue–Sat 9–6, Sun 10–7.*

⑦ San Giuliano Terme
San Giuliano Hot Springs
Largo Shelley 18.
Tel: 050 88501.

TOUR 5

i Piazza del Duomo 4,
Pistoia.
Tel: 0573 21622.

i Via Marconi 70,
San Marcello Pistoiese.
Tel: 0573 630145 or
622300.

i Piazza Catalina,
Cutigliano.
Tel: 0575 68029 (seasonal).

i Piazza Piramidi 501,
Abetone.
Tel: 0573 60231.

i Piazza Castello 118,
Pescia.
Tel: 0572 408292.

i Viale Verdi 66–68,
Montecatini Terme.
Tel: 0572 772244.

i Piazza dei Medici,
Poggio a Caiano.
Tel: 0558 77012.

i Piazza Duomo 8,
Prato.
Tel: 0574 24112.

② Gavinana
Ferrucciano Museum
Piazza Francesco Ferrucci.
Tel: 0573 629068.
*Open Jul–Aug, daily 9–12,
4–7; Sep–Jun, Sat 3–6,
Sun 9–12.*

Back to Nature
Abetone Botanical Forest
Garden
Fontana Vaccaia.
Tel: 0573 607004.
*Open mid-Jun to mid-Sep,
daily 9.30–12.30, 3–6.30.
For bookings contact
Comando Forestale..*

⑤ Popiglio
Museum of Holy Art
Church of Santa Maria
Assunta.
Tel: 0573 97461.
*Open Jul–Aug, Tue–Sun 4–7;
Apr–Jun, Sep–Oct, Sat–Sun
4–7.*

⑧ Collodi
Villa Garzoni and Gardens
Tel: 0572 427314.
*Open Mar–Oct,
8.30–sunset; Nov–Feb,
Mon–Fri 9–12, 2–5, Sat &
holidays 8.30–sunset.
Butterfly House closed
Nov–Feb.*

Pinocchio Park
Tel: 0572 429342.
*Open Mar–Oct, daily
8.30–sunset; Nov–Feb,
Mon–Sat 9–sunset.*

⑨ Montecatini Terme
Hot Springs
(Tettuccio, Excelsior, Redi,
Torretta, Leopoldine,
Tamerici, La Salute spas).
Tel: 0572 778487.
*Open May–Oct. Excelsior all
year.*

⑩ Poggio a Caiano
Medici villa
Piazza dei Medici 14.
Tel: 0558 77012.

*Open Jun–Aug, daily,
8.15–7.30; Apr–May
Sep–Oct, daily 8.15–6.30;
Nov–Feb, 8.15–4.30; Mar,
daily 8.15–5.30. Closed
second & third Mon in the
month.*

⑪ Prato
Palazzo Datini
Via Ser Lapo Mazzei 13.
Tel: 0574 21391.
Open Mon–Sat 9–12.

TOUR 6

i Piazza Cavour 6,
Livorno.
Tel: 0586 204611.

i Piazza del Municipio 6.
Livorno.
Tel: 0586 204611.

i Porto Mediceo,
Livorno.
Tel: 0586 895320.
Open Jun–Sep.

i Via Aurelia 967,
Castiglioncello.
Tel: 0586 752291
(seasonal).

i Via G Turazza, Volterra.
Tel: 0588 86150.

i Via Roma, Campiglia
Marìttima, Venturina.
Tel: 0565 838958
(seasonal).

i Via de Amicis 23,
Piombino.
Tel: 0565 20808 (seasonal).

i Via della Marina 8,
Marina di Castagneto-
Donoràtico.
Tel: 0565 744276
(seasonal).

② Castiglioncello
National Archaeological
Museum
Rosignano Marìttimo,
Palazzo Bombardieri, Via
del Castello.
Tel: 0586 724288.
*Open Sep–May, daily 9–1;
Jun–Aug, 9–1, 5–10.*

⑤ Volterra
Mario Guarnacci Etruscan
Museum
Via Don Minzoni 15.
Tel: 0588 86347.
*Open mid-Mar to late Oct,
9–7; Nov to mid-Mar, 9–2.
Closed Christmas & New
Year.*

Art Gallery and Civic
Museum
Palazzo Minucci Solaini,
Via Sarti 1.
Tel: 0588 87580.
*Open mid-Mar to late Oct,
9–7; Nov to mid-Mar,
9–1.45. Closed Christmas &
New Year.*

⑥ Larderello
Museum of Geothermal
Energy
Piazza Leopolda.
Tel: 0588 67724.
*Open 15 Mar–15 Sep,
Mon–Fri 8–12, 1.30–5.30,
Sat–Sun 10–12, 1.30–6.30;
16 Sep–14 Mar, Mon–Fri
8–12, 1.30–4.30, Sun 9–12,
1–4.30. Closed Sat.*

⑦ Venturina
Terme di Caldana
Tel: 0565 851066.
*Open mid-May to mid-Oct,
Mon–Fri 7–12, 4–6, Sat
7–12.*

⑩ Rocca di San
Silvestro
Mining Park and Museum
Tel: 0565 226445.
*Open summer, Tue–Sun
10–7 (also Mon in Jul, Aug);
spring & autumn Sat–Sun
10–6.*

⑪ Castagneto
Carducci
Archive Museum
Via Carducci 1.
Tel: 0565 765032.
Open Mon–Fri 10–1.

Carducci Centre
Via Carducci 1.
Tel: 0565 763624 (Town
Hall).
Open Tue–Sun 10–1, 4–7.

13 Santuario di Montenero
Tel: 0586 57771.

TOUR 7

i Calata Italia 26, Portoferraio.
Tel: 0565 914671.

1 Portoferraio
Civic Archaeological Museum
Forte Linguella.
Tel: 0565 917338.
Open Easter to mid-Jun, Fri–Wed 10–1, 3.30–7.10; mid-Jun to mid-Sep, daily 9–2.45, 6–12; mid-Sep to Oct, Fri–Wed 10–1, 3.30–7.10,

Palazzina dei Mulini
Via Mulini 1.
Tel: 0565 915846.
Open Mon, Wed–Fri 9–7, Sat–Sun 9–1.

For Children
Elbaland
Near San Giovanni.
Tel: 0335 8194680.
Open Apr–Oct, daily 10–7 (later in high summer). Full details at www.elbaland.com.

3 Villa di San Martino
Villa Napoleonica
Tel: 0565 914688.
Open Tue–Sun 9–7.

11 Rio Marina
Elba Mineral Museum
Piazza Salvo D'Acquisto 1.
Open Mar–Oct, daily 9.30–6.30 (Jul–Aug 9–7.30).

TOUR 8

i Viale Monterosa 206, Grosseto.
Tel: 0564 454527.

i Piazza Garibaldi 6, Castiglione della Pescaia.
Tel: 0564 933678.

i Via Giacomelli 11–13, Follònica.
Tel: 0566 52012.

i Via Todini 3–5, Massa Maríttima,
Tel: 0566 904756.

1 Parco dell'Uccellina
Visitor Centre: Via del Fante, Alberese.
Tel: 0564 407098.
Open Mar–Sep, daily 8–5; Oct, daily 8–2; Nov–Mar, daily 8–1.

5 Centro Carapax
Vanelle.
Tel: 0566 940083.
Currently closed.

6 Massa Maríttima
Archaeological Museum
Palazzo del Podestà, Piazza Garibaldi.
Tel: 0566 902289.
Open Apr–Oct, Tue–Sun, 10–12.30, 3.30–7; Sep–Mar, Tue–Sun 10–12.30, 3–6.

Mining Museum
Via Corridoni.
Tel: 0566 902289.
Guided visits Apr–Oct, Tue–Sun 10–12.30, 3–5.30; Nov–Mar, Tue–Sun 10–12, 3–4.30.

13 Roselle
Archaeological excavations
Tel: 0564 402403.
Open May–Aug, 9–7; Sep–Apr, 9–dusk.

TOUR 9

i Viale Monterosa 206, Grosseto.
Tel: 0564 454527.

i Palazzetto dell'Archivio, Sovana.
Tel: 0564 614074.

i Piazza Busati, Sorano.
Tel: 0564 633099.

i Piazza Garibaldi 51, Pitigliano.
Tel: 0564 617111.

i Piazza della Repubblica 1, Orbetello.
Tel: 0564 861226.

i Via Caravaggio 78, Porto Ercole.
Tel: 0564 831019.

i Corso Umberto 55, Porto Santo Stefano.
Tel: 0564 814208.

i Piazzale del Porto (seasonal), Talamone.
Tel: 0564 887410.

3 Saturnia
Terme di Saturnia
Via della Follonata.
Tel: 0564 600111.

5 Sorano
Orsini Fortress and Museum of Medieval Art
Piazza Cairoli 1.
Tel: 0564 633767.
Open mid-Mar to Oct, daily 9–7; Nov to mid-Mar, Fri–Sat 9–5.

6 Pitigliano
Palazzo Orsini–Museums
Tel: 0564 616074.
Open summer, Tue–Sun 10–1, 3–7 (Aug daily until 8); winter, Tue–Sun 10–1, 3–6.

Museum of Civic Archaeology
Palazzo Orsini.
Tel: 0564 614067.
Open Mar–Nov, daily 10–1, 4–7; 26 Dec–6 Jan, daily 10–1, 3–6; Jan–Mar by appointment.

For Children
Giardino dei Tarocchi
Near Pescia Fiorentina.
Tel: 0564 895122.
Open Apr to mid-Oct, daily 2.30–5.30; mid-Oct to Mar, first Sat in the month.

7 Ponte dell'Abbadia
Vulci National Museum
Tel: 0761 437787.
Open May–Sep, Tue–Sun 9–1.30, 2.30–7 (6 in winter).

8 Ansedonia
Cosa ruins archaeological museum
Tel: 0564 881421.
Open Mar–Sep, daily 9–7; Oct–Apr, daily 9–2.

9 Orbetello
Talamone Aquarium
Via Nizza 24.
Tel: 0564 887173.
Open Tue–Sun 9–12.30, 3–5.30.

Laguna di Orbetello Natural Reserve
Tel: 0564 820297.

TOUR 10

i Via Cavour 1r, Florence.
Tel: 055 290832.

i Piazza della Stazione 4a, Florence.
Tel: 055 212245.

1 Piazza della Signoria
Palazzo Vecchio
Piazza della Signoria.
Tel: 055 2768325.
Open 9–7 (Thu & holidays 9–2).
Closed New Year, Easter, 1 May, 15 Aug & Christmas.

2 Galleria degli Uffizi
Piazzale degli Uffizi 6.
Tel: 055 2388651.
Open Tue–Sun 8.15–6.50.
For bookings tel: 055 294883 Mon–Fri 8.30–6.30, Sat 8.30–12.30.
Closed Mon & Christmas.

4 Palazzo Pitti
Royal Apartments
Piazza de' Pitti.
Tel: 055 294883.
Open Tue–Sun 8.15–6.50.

Costume Gallery
Tel: 055 294883.
Open Jun–Aug, 8.15–6.50; Apr, May, Sep, Oct, 9–6.30; Mar, 8.15–5.30; Nov–Feb, 8.15–4.30. Closed first & last Mon of the month.

Silver Museum
Tel: 055 294883.
Open Jun–Aug, daily 8.15–6.50; Apr, May, Sep, Oct, daily 8.15–6.30; Mar, daily 8.15–6.30; Nov–Feb, daily 8.15–5.30.
Closed first & last Mon of the month.

Practical • Information

Tourist Information Centre
12 Number on tour

Palatina Gallery
Tel: 055 294883.
Open Tue–Sun 8.15–6.50.

Recommended Walk
Bòboli Gardens
Tel: 055 294883.
*Open same hours as
Costume Gallery above.*

5 Cappella Brancacci
Piazza del Carmine.
Tel: 055 2768224 (pre-
booking required).
*Open Mon, Wed–Sat 10–5,
Sun & holidays 1–5.*

Museum of the Old
Florentine House
Palazzo Davanzati, Via Porta
Rossa 13.
Tel: 055 2388610.
*Open daily 8.15–1.50.
Closed first, third & fifth Mon
and second & fourth Sun in
the month.*

6 Orsanmichele
Via dell'Arte della Lana.
Tel: 055 284944.
Open Mon–Sat 9–12, 4–6.

7 Piazza del Duomo
Baptistery of San Giovanni
Tel: 055 2302885.
*Open Mon–Fri 12–7, first
Sat in the month 8.30–2,
Sun & holidays 8.20–2.*

Basilica of Santa Maria del
Fiore
Tel: 055 2302885.
*Open Mon–Wed, Fri 10–5,
Thu 10–3.30, Sat 10–4.45,
first Sat in the month
10–3.30.*

Museum of Works
Piazza del Duomo 9.
Tel: 055 2302885.
Open Mon–Fri 8–7, Sat 8–2.

Special to…
Brunelleschi's dome
Tel: 055 2302885.
*Open Mon–Fri 8.30–7, Sat
8.30–5.40. Closed Sun &
public holidays.*

Giotto's bell tower
Tel: 055 2302885.
Open 8.30–7.30.

**8 Palazzo
Medici-Riccardi**
Via Cavour 3.
Tel: 055 2760340.

Chapel of the Magi
*Open Thu–Tue 9–7. Booking
recommended.*

**9 Basilica di San
Lorenzo**
Piazza San Lorenzo.
Tel: 055 216634,
*Open 10–5.30.
Closed holidays.*

Medicea Laurenziana
Library
Piazza San Lorenzo 9.
Tel: 055 210760.
*Currently closed for
restoration.*

Medici Chapels (Cappelle
Medicee)
Piazza Madonna degli
Aldobrandini 6.
Tel: 055 294883.
*Open 8.15–1.50.
Closed second & fourth Sun
and first, third & fifth Mon in
the month, & holidays.*

Opificio delle Pietre Dure
workshop
Via degli Alfani 78.
Tel: 055 218705.
*Open Mon, Wed, Fri–Sat
8.15–2, first & third Tue &
Thu in the month 8.15–7.*

Special to…
Santa Maria Novella
Piazza Santa Maria Novella.
Tel: 055 219257.
*Open 9.30–5, Fri, Sun &
holidays 1–5.*

Museum of Santa Maria
Novella
Tel: 055 282187.
Open Mon–Thu, Sat 9–5.

**10 Chiesa e Museo
di San Marco**
Museum of San Marco
Tel: 055 294883.
*Open Mon–Fri 8.15–1.50,
Sat–Sun 8.15–4.50. Closed
first, third & fifth Sun &
second & fourth Mon in the
month.*

**11 Galleria
dell'Accademia**
Via Ricasoli 60.
Tel: 055 294883.
Open Tue–Sun 8.15–6.50.

**12 Piazza della SS
Annunziata**
Ospedale degli Innocenti,
picture gallery
Tel: 055 2491708.
*Open Mon–Sat 8.30–7, Sun
8.30–2.*

Basilica of SS Annunziata
Tel: 055 266181.
*Open daily 7.30–12.30,
4–6.30.*

Archaeological Museum
Via della Colonna 36.
Tel: 055 235750.
*Open Mon 2–7, Tue & Thu
8.30–7, Wed & Fri–Sat
8.30–2. Closed holidays
except Sun.*

13 Museo del Bargello
Via del Proconsolo.
Tel: 055 294883.
*Open daily 8.15–5. Closed
first, third & fifth Sun &
second & fourth Mon in the
month.*

**14 Chiesa di Santa
Croce**
Piazza di Santa Croce.
Tel: 055 2466105.
Open Mon–Sat 9.30–5.30.

Pazzi Chapel, Museum of
Works of Santa Croce
and cloisters
Piazza di Santa Croce 16.
Tel: 055 2466105.
*Open Mon–Sat 9.30–5.30,
Sun & holidays 1–5.30.*

Excursion
San Miniato al Monte
Via Monte Croci 34.
Tel: 055 2342731.
*Open summer, daily 8–7;
winter, Mon–Fri 8–12, 3–6,
Sat–Sun 3–6.*

TOUR 11

Via Cavour 1r,
Florence.
Tel: 055 290832.

Piazza della Stazione
4a, Florence.
Tel: 055 212245.

Piazza IV Novembre 8,
Lastra a Signa.
Tel: 055 8723749.

Via Baccio Sinibaldi 43,
Montelupo Fiorentino.
Tel: 0571 518993.

Piazza del Popolo 3,
San Miniato.
Tel: 0571 42745.

C/o railway station, Via
Ridolfi 1, Castelfiorentino.
Tel: 0571 629049.

Piazza Masini, Certaldo.
Tel: 0571 656721.

Piazza del Duomo 1,
San Gimignano.
Tel: 0577 940008.

Via Campana 43, Colle
di Val d'Elsa.
Tel: 0577 922791.

Piazza Roma 23,
Monteriggioni.
Tel: 0577 304810.

2 Artimino
Medici Villa,
Archaeological Museum
Viale Giovanni XXIII 5.
Tel: 055 8718124.
*Open Mon–Tue, Thu–Sat
9.30–12.30, Sun 10–12;
Nov–Jan, Sun 10–12,
Thu–Sat by appointment.*

**3 Montelupo
Fiorentino**
Archaeological and
Pottery Museums
Palazzo del Podestà,
Via Sinibaldi 45.
Tel: 0571 51352.
*Open Tue–Sun 10–6.
Closed Mon, New Year,
Easter & Christmas.*

**Recommended
excursion**
Leonardo Museum
Via Montalbano 2, Vinci.
Tel: 0571 56296.
*Open mid-Jun to Sep, daily
10–2.*

❺ Castelfiorentino
Church of Santa Verdiana, picture gallery
Tel: 0571 64096.
Open Sat 4–7, Sun 10–12, 4–7. Also by request.

Cultural Centre
Via Tieli 41.
Tel: 0571 64019.
Open Tue, Thu, Sat 4–7, Sun & holidays 10–12, 4–7.

❻ San Vivaldo
Tel: 0571 680114.
Open Apr–Oct, Mon–Fri 3–7, Sat–Sun 10–7; Nov–Mar, daily 2–5.

❼ Certaldo
Palazzo Pretorio
Piazzetta del Vicariato.
Tel: 0571 661219.
Closed for restoration.

Boccaccio House, Library and Study Centre
Via Boccaccio.
Tel: 0571 661265.
Open daily 9.30–1.30, 2.30–7 (6.30 in winter).

Special to…
Palazzo del Popolo, Civic Museum, Torre Grossa
Piazza del Duomo, San Gimignano.
Tel: 0577 990312.
Open Mar–Oct, 9.30–7; Nov–Feb, 10–5.30.

⓫ Certosa del Galluzzo
Tel: 055 2049226.
Open Tue–Sun 9–11, 3–5 (4 in winter).

⒤ Via Cavour 1r, Florence.
Tel: 055 290832.

⒤ Piazza della Stazione 4a, Florence.
Tel: 055 212245.

⒤ Palazzo dei Vicari, Scarperìa.
Tel: 055 8468165.

⒤ Villa Pecori Giraldi, Via Togliatti 45, Borgo San Lorenzo.
Tel: 055 8456230.

⒤ Via Garibaldi 1, Vicchio.
Tel: 055 8439220.

⒤ Via Portigiani 3/5, Fièsole.
Tel: 055 598720.

❶ Villa di Careggi
Viale Gaetano Pieraccini 21.
Tel: 055 4279753.
*Open Mon–Fri 9–6, Sat 9–12.
Closed Sun & holidays.*

❷ Villa della Petraia
Via della Petraia 40.
Tel: 055 2948834.
*Open Jan, Feb, Nov, Dec, daily 8.15–4.30; Apr, May, Sep, daily 8.15–6.30; Jul–Aug, daily 8.15–7.30; Mar, Oct, daily 8.15–5.30.
Closed second & third Mon in the month.*

❸ Villa di Castello
Via di Castello 47.
Tel: 055 452691.
Gardens open Apr, May, Sep, Oct, daily 8.15–6.30; Jun–Aug, daily 8.15–7.30; Oct & Mar, daily 8.15–5.30; Nov–Feb, daily 8.15–4.30. Last entry 30 mins before closing. Closed second & third Mon in the month.

Accademia della Crusca
Tel: 055 454277.
Open Mon, Wed 9–5, Tue, Thu–Fri 9–2.

❹ Sesto Fiorentino
'Montagnola' Etruscan tomb
Via Fratelli Rosselli 95.
Tel: 055 44891.
Open Tue, Thu 10–1, Sat–Sun 5–7pm; winter Sat–Sun 10–1.

'Mula' Etruscan tomb
Via della Mula 2.
Tel: 055 44891.
Open Tue 10–12, Sat 5–6.30pm; winter Sat–Sun 10–noon.

Special to…
Museum of Doccia Porcelain
Via Pratese 31.
Tel: 055 4207767.
Open Wed–Sat 10–1, 2–6. Closed Sun.

❺ Parco Demidoff
Villa Medici-Demidoff
Pratolino, Via Fiorentina 6.
Tel: 055 409427.
Open Apr–Sep, Thu–Sun 10–8; Mar, Oct, Sun & holidays 10–6.

❼ Villa di Cafaggiolo
Via Nazionale 16, Barberino del Mugello.
Tel: 055 8498103.
Open Sat–Sun all year 10–12.30, 2.30–6.30; end Mar to mid-Oct, Wed, Fri 2.30–6.30.

❽ Bosco ai Frati
Museum of the Convent of Bosco ai Frati
Tel: 055 848111.
Open Fri–Sun 11.30–12.30, 6–7.

❾ Sant'Àgata
Church of Sant'Àgata, collection of sacred art
Via della Pieve.
Tel: 055 8406853.
Open Sun & holidays 3–6.

For Children
Craft and folk exhibition
Tel: 055 8406750.
Open summer, Sun & holidays 3–6; winter, Sun & holidays 3–6. Rest of week by request.

❿ Scarperìa
Knife Museum
Palazzo dei Vicari, Via Roma.
Tel: 055 8468165.
Open Jun to mid-Sep, Wed–Fri 3.30–7.30, Sat–Sun 10–1, 3.30–7.30.

Mugello racing track
Senni. Tel: 055 8499111.

⓬ Vespignano
Giotto's House
Tel: 055 8439224.
Open summer, Thu 10–1, Fri–Sat 10–1, 3–7.

⓭ Vicchio
Museo di Arte Sacra 'Beato Angelico'
Tel: 055 8439224.
Open Thu 10–1, Fri–Sun 10–1, 3–7.

⓯ Fièsole
Archaeological site
Via Portigiani 1.
Tel: 055 59477.
Open Apr–Sep, Wed–Mon 10–7; Oct, Mar, Wed–Mon 10–6; Nov–Feb, Thu–Mon 10–4.

⒤ Piazza della Repubblica 28, Arezzo.
Tel: 0575 377678.

⒤ Via Cavour 11, Poppi.
Tel: 0575 529682 (seasonal).

⒤ Piazza Cavour 3, San Giovanni Valdarno.
Tel: 055 943748 (seasonal).

❶ Eremo della Verna
Tel: 0575 5341.
Open summer, 6.30am–9.30pm; winter 6.30am–7.30pm.

❷ Poppi
Castle of the Guidi Counts
Tel: 0575 520516.
Open mid-Mar, Sep–Oct, daily 10–6; Jul–Aug, daily 10–7; Nov to mid-Mar, Fri–Sun 10–5.

Parco Zoo Fauna Europea
Via Parco Zoo 16.
Tel: 0575 504541.
Open daily 9–sunset.

Foreste Casentinesi, Monte Falterona and Campigna National Park
Visitor centre, Badia Prataglia.
Tel: 0575 559477.
Open 9am–12.30pm. Apr, Wed–Sun; May, Tue–Sun; Jun, Oct, Fri–Sun; Jul–Aug, daily, also 3.30–6; Sep, Tue–Sun, also Sun 3.30–6; Nov–Mar, Sat–Sun & holidays.

④ Eremo di Camàldoli
Tel: 0575 556021.
*Open Mon–Sat 9–12, 3–6
(5 in winter).*

⑥ Pieve di Romena
Tel: 0575 5812060.
Open 9–12, 3–6.

⑦ Vallombrosa
Abbey of Vallombrosa
Tel: 055 862251.
*Open for guided tours Tue,
Fri 10.30, 12.*

**⑨ San Giovanni
Valdarno**
Museum of the Basilica of
Santa Maria delle Grazie
Piazza Masaccio.
Tel: 055 9122445.
*Open Mon–Sat 9–12.30,
3.30–7, Sun 9–10.30,
3.30–7.*

TOUR 14

ⓘ Piazza della Repubblica
28, Arezzo.
Tel: 0575 377678.

ⓘ Piazza Umberto I
(Town Hall), Monterchi.
Tel: 0575 70092.

ⓘ Corso Matteotti 103,
Anghiari.
Tel: 0575 749279.

ⓘ Piazza Garibaldi 2,
Sansepolcro.
Tel: 0575 740536.

ⓘ Piazza Matteotti, Logge
Bufalini, Città di Castello.
Tel: 075 8554922.

ⓘ Via San Francesco 1,
Montone.
Tel: 075 9306427.

ⓘ Via Nazionale 42,
Cortona.
Tel: 0575 630352.

ⓘ Piazza del Municipio
12, Castiglion Fiorentino.
Tel: 0575 65641 (seasonal).

❶ Monterchi
Madonna del Parto
Via della Reglia.
Tel: 0575 70713.
Open Apr–Oct, daily 9.30–1,

*2–7; Nov–Mar, daily 9.30–1,
2–5.*

❷ Anghiari
State Museum
Palazzo Taglieschi, Piazza
Mameli 1–2.
Tel: 0575 787023.
*Open Tue–Sat 8.30–7,
Sun & holidays 9.30–7*

❸ Sansepolcro
Civic Museum
Via Aggiunti 65.
Tel: 0575 732218.
*Open mid-Jun to mid-Sep,
9–1.30, 2–7; mid-Sep to
mid-Jun, 9.30–1.30, 2.30–6.*

❹ San Giustino
Bufalini castle
*For details of opening times
contact the town hall, tel:
075 856115.*

❺ Città di Castello
Centre of Popular
Traditions
Località Garavelle.
Tel: 075 8552119.
*Open summer, daily
8.30–12.30, 3–7; winter,
daily 8.30–12.30, 2–6.*

Picture Gallery
Palazzo Vitelli alla
Cannoniera, Via della
Cannoniera 22/a.
Tel: 075 8554202.
*Open Apr–Oct, Tue–Sun
10–1, 2.30–6.30; Nov–Mar,
10–1, 3–6.*

Burri Collection
Palazzo Albizzini,
Via Albizzini 1.
Tel: 075 8554649.
*Open Tue–Sat 9–12.30,
2.30–6, Sun 10.30–12.30,
3–6.*

Burri Collection
Seccatoi Tabacchi, Via
Pierucci.
Tel: 075 8559848.
*Open Tue–Sat 9–12.30,
2.30–6, Sun 10.30–12.30,
3–6.*

❻ Montone
Town Museum
Former Convent of San
Francesco, Via San
Francesco.

Tel: 075 9306535.
*Open Apr–Sep, Fri, Sat & Sun
10.30–1, 4–6.30; Oct–Mar,
Sat & Sun 10.30–1, 3–5.30.*

❼ Umbèrtide
Rocca
Piazza Fortebraccio.
Tel: 075 9413691.
*Open daily, 10.30–12.30,
4.30–7.*

❿ Cortona
Museo dell'Accademia
Etrusca e della Città
Cortona (MEAC)
Piazza Signorelli 9.
Tel: 0575 630415.
*Open Apr–Oct, daily 10–7;
Nov–Mar, Tue–Sun 10–5.*

Diocesan Museum
Piazza del Duomo 1.
Tel: 0575 62830.
*Open Apr–Oct, Tue–Sun
10–7; Nov–Mar, Tue–Sun
10–5.*

Recommended Walk
Girifalco fortress
*Contact tourist office in
Cortona for details.*

TOUR 15

ⓘ Piazza del Campo 56,
Siena.
Tel: 0577 280551.

❸ Palazzo Pubblico
Civic Museum
Piazza del Campo 1.
Tel: 0577 292614.
*Open mid-Mar to Oct, 10–7;
Nov to mid-Mar, 10–6.*

❺ Torre del Mangia
Piazza del Campo 1.
Tel: 0577 41169.
*Open mid-Mar–Oct, 10–7;
Nov–mid-Mar, 10–4.*

**❼ Pinacoteca
Nazionale**
Palazzo Buonsignori,
Via San Pietro 29.
Tel: 0577 281161.
*Open Mon 8.30–1.30,
Tue–Sat 8.15–7.15, Sun &
holidays 8.15–1.15.*

**❽ Spedale Santa
Maria della Scala**
Piazza del Duomo.
Tel: 0577 224811.
Open daily 10.30–6.30.

**❾ Duomo
dell'Assunta**
Piazza del Duomo.
Tel: 0577 283048.
*Open Mar–May, Sep–Oct,
Mon–Sat 10.30–7.30, Sun
1.30–5.30; Jun–Aug,
Mon–Sat 10.30–8, Sun
1.30–6; Nov–Feb, Mon–Sat
10.30–6, Sun 1.30–5.30.*

**❿ Museo dell'Opera
del Duomo**
Piazza del Duomo 8.
Tel: 0577 283048.
*Open Mar–May, Sep–Oct,
daily 9.30–7; Jun–Aug, daily
9.30–8; Nov–Feb, daily
10–5.*

⓫ Battistero
Piazza San Giovanni.
Tel: 0577 283048.
*Open Mar–May, Sep–Oct,
daily 9.30–7; Jun–Aug, daily
9.30–8.*

**⓬ Casa di Santa
Caterina**
Costa di Sant' Antonio,
Vicolo Turatoio 8.
Tel: 0577 221562.
Open daily 9–12.30, 3–6.

**⓮ Palazzo
Piccolomini**
State Archives and Museo
Via Banchi di Sotto 52.
Tel: 0577 247145.
*Open same times as
Duomo dell'Assunta above.*

TOUR 16

ⓘ Piazza del Campo 56,
Siena.
Tel: 0577 280551.

ⓘ Via del Chianti 61,
Castelnuovo Berardenga.
Tel: 0577 355500.

ⓘ Via Galilei 11, Gaiole in
Chianti.
Tel: 0577 749411.

i Piazza del Castello,
Radda in Chianti.
Tel: 0577 738494.

i Piazza Matteotti 11,
Greve in Chianti.
Tel: 055 8546287.

i Piazza Buondelmonti
30, Impruneta.
Tel: 055 2313729.

i Piazza del Comune 1,
Castellina in Chianti.
Tel: 0577 742311.

**❶ Castelnuovo
Berardenga**
Landscape Museum
Tel: 0577 355500.
*Open Apr–Oct, Tue–Sat
10–1, 3–6; Nov–Mar,
Fri–Sat 10–1.*

❷ Castello di Brolio
Tel: 0577 7301.
*Open summer, Sat–Thu
9.30–1, 3–6.30, chapel and
gardens only.*

Barone Ricasoli cellars
Tel: 0577 7301.
*Open summer, Sat–Thu
9.30–1, 3–6.30.*

Special To…
Chianti Sculpture Park
Pievasciata.
Tel: 0577 357151.
Open Apr–Nov, 10–sunset.

❺ Radda in Chianti
Volpaia Castle
Tel: 0577 738066.

❼ Impruneta
Museum of the Treasures
of Santa Maria
all'Impruneta
Piazza Buondelmonti.
Tel: 055 294883.
*Open Sat–Sun 9.30–12.30,
3.30–7.*

❽ Castellina in Chianti
Museum of Etruscan
remains
Piazza del Comune.
Tel: 0577 742090.
Phone for times.

TOUR 17

i Piazza del Campo 56,
Siena. Tel: 0577 280551.

i Via delle Fonti, Asciano
(seasonal).
Tel: 0577 718811.

i Costa Municipio 8,
Montalcino.
Tel: 0577 849331.

i Via San Giovanni,
Castiglione d'Orcia.
Tel: 0577 888986.

i Via Dante Alighieri 33,
San Quìrico d'Orcia.
Tel: 0577 898303.

i Corso Rosselino 30,
Pienza.
Tel: 0578 749905.

i Via Don Minzoni,
Montepulciano.
Tel: 0578 757341.

❶ Asciano
Museum of Holy Art and
Collegiate of Sant'Agata
Corso Matteotti 122.
Tel: 0577 718811.
*Open Mar–Oct, Tue–Sun
9.30–12, 3–6.30; Nov–Feb,
Fri–Sat 10.30–1, 3–5.30.*

**❷ Abbazia di Monte
Oliveto Maggiore**
Tel: 0577 707611.
*Open daily 9.15–12, 3.15–5
(6 in summer).*

❸ Montalcino
Fortress
Piazzale della Fortezza.
Tel: 0577 849211.
Open daily 9–6.

❹ Sant'Àntimo
Abbazia di Sant'Àntimo
Tel: 0577 835659.
*Open Mon–Sat
10.15–12.30, 3–6.30, Sun
9.15–10.45, 3–6.*

❺ Rocca d'Orcia
Rocca di Tentennano
Tel: 0577 887363.
*Open Easter–May, Oct,
Tue–Sun 10–1, 3.30–6.30;
Jun–Sep, daily 10–1,
3.30–6.30.*

---

❻ Bagno Vignoni
Bagno Vignoni Hot Springs
Piazza del Moretto.
Tel: 0577 887365.

For Children
Val di Sole swimming pool
c/o Hotel Posta Marcucci,
Via Ara Urcea 43.
Tel: 0577 887112.
*Open Apr–Sep, Fri–Wed
9.30–1, 2–6; Oct–Mar,
Fri–Wed 10–5.*

**❼ San Quìrico
d'Orcia**
Horti Leonini Gardens
Tel: 0577 899771.
Open 8–8.

❽ Pienza
Cathedral
Piazza Pio II.
Tel: 0578 749071.
Open daily 7–1, 3–7.

Palazzo Piccolomini
Museum
Piazza Pio II.
Tel: 0578 748503.
*Open Tue–Sun 10–12.30,
3–6. Closed Mon and mid-
Nov to mid-Dec.*

❾ Montepulciano
Palazzo Comunale
Tel: 0578 717300.
Tower only: call for times.

Duomo (cathedral)
Open 9–6.

Church of San Biagio
Open 9–1, 3–7.

Back to Nature
San Giovanni Battista Spa
Pool
Tel: 0577 724030.

TOUR 18

i Piazza del Campo 56,
Siena.
Tel: 0577 280551.

i Abbazia di San
Galgano, Chiusdino.
Tel: 0577 756738..

i Piazza Garibaldi 39,
Santa Fiora.
Tel: 0577 775200.

---

i Via Adua 25, Abbadia
San Salvatore.
Tel: 0577 775811.

i Via R Magi 59,
Radicòfani.
Tel: 339 1235906.

i Via San Cassiano
11, San Casciano dei Bagni.
Tel: 0578 58141.

i Piazza Garibaldi 63,
Cetona.
Tel: 0578 239143.

i Piazza del Duomo 1,
Chiusi.
Tel: 0578 227667.

**❶ Abbazia di San
Galgano**
Tel: 0577 756738.
Always open.

Church of Montesiepi
*Open summer, 9–8; winter
9–6.30.*

❷ Bagni di Petriolo
Bagni di Petriolo Spa
Tel: 0577 757104.
*Open Jun–Nov, 8–6 by
appointment only.*

Back to Nature
Monte Amiata Fauna Park
Arcidosso, Podere dei
Nobili.
Tel: 0564 966867.
*Open 7.15am–sunset.
Closed Mon.*

**❻ Abbadia San
Salvatore**
Mineral Museum
Piazzale Renato Rossaro 6.
Tel: 0577 778324.
*Open Jun–Oct, daily
9.30–12.30, 3.30–6.30. By
request at least 10 days in
advance rest of year.*

Church of the Abbey
of San Salvatore
Tel: 0577 778083.
Open 10–7.30.

❼ Radicòfani
Rocca
Tel: 0578 55700.
*Open Apr–Oct 10–7;
Jan–Mar, Fri–Sun 10–5.*

8 San Casciano dei Bagni
San Casciano dei Bagni Spa
Via del Giardino.
Tel: 0578 58023.
Open Wed–Mon 9–7, Tue 9–3.

9 Cetona
Hermitage of Santa Maria a Belverde
Tel: 0578 2391143.
Open Jul–Sep 9.30–12.30, 4–7.30.

Civic Museum
Via Roma 37.
Tel: 0578 237632.
Open Jun–Sep, Tue–Sun 10–1, 4–7; Oct–May, Sat 3–6, Sun 10–1.

10 Chiusi
Cathedral museum, catacombs, labyrinth of Lars Porsena
Piazza del Duomo.
Tel: 0578 226490.
Open Jun to mid-Oct, daily 9.45–12.45, 4–6.30; mid-Oct to Dec, daily 10–12.30; Jan–Mar, Tue, Thu, Sat 10–12.30; Apr–May, Mon–Sat 10–12.30, Sun 4–6.30.

National Archaeological Museum
Via Porsenna 93.
Tel: 0578 20177.
Open daily 9–8.

i Loggia dei Lanari, Piazza Matteotti 18, Perugia.
Tel: 075 5736458.

1 Via Baglioni
Rocca Paolina
Access from Porta Marzia, Piazza Italia, Via Masi.
Open 8–7.

2 Fontana Maggiore
Etruscan well
Palazzo Bourbon-Sorbello, Piazza Dante 1.
Tel: 075 5733669.
Open Apr–Aug, daily 10–1.30, 2.30–6; Nov–Mar 11–1.30, 2.30–5.

5 Collegio della Mercanzia
Palazzo dei Priori, Corso Vannucci 15.
Tel: 075 5730366.
Open Mar–Oct & 20 Dec–6 Jan, Tue–Sat 9–1, 2.30–5.30, Sun & holidays 9–1; Nov–Feb, Tue, Thu & Fri 8–2, Wed & Sat 8–4.30, Sun & holidays 9–1. Closed Mon, Christmas & 1 Jan.

6 Collegio del Cambio
Palazzo dei Priori, Corso Vannucci 25.
Tel: 075 5728599.
Open mid-Mar to Oct, Mon 9–12.30, Tue–Sat 9–12.30, 2.30–5.30

7 Sala dei Notari
Palazzo dei Priori, Piazza IV Novembre.
Tel: 075 5722339.
Open 9–1, 3–7.

8 Galleria Nazionale dell'Umbria
Palazzo dei Priori, Corso Vannucci 19.
Tel: 075 5721009.
Open daily 8.30–7.30. Closed New Year, 1 May & Christmas.

Excursion 1
Volumni Hypogeum
Via Assisana 53.
Tel: 075 393329.
Open Mon–Sat 9.30–12.30, 4.30–6.30, Sun 9.30–12.30.

Excursion 2
Città della Domenica
Tel: 075 5054941.
Open late Mar to mid-Sep, daily 10–6; mid-Sep to early Nov, Sat–Sun 10–dusk.

i Loggia dei Lanari, Piazza Matteotti 18, Perugia.
Tel: 075 5736458.

i Via della Repubblica 15, Gubbio.
Tel: 075 9220693.

i Via Calai 39, Gualdo Tadino.
Tel: 075 912172.

i Corso Cavour 126, Foligno.
Tel: 0742 354459.

3 Gubbio
Civic Museum and Picture Gallery
Palazzo dei Consoli. Piazza Grande.
Tel: 075 9274298.
Open Tue–Sat 8.30–7.30.

Roman Theatre
Via del Teatro Romano
Tel: 0759 220922.
Open Apr–Sep, 8.30–7.30; Oct–Mar, 8–1.30.

Palazzo Ducale and Museum
Via Federico da Montefeltro.
Tel: 075 9275872.
Open Tue–Sun 8.30–7.30.

4 Monte Catria
Monte Cucco Regional Park
Sigillo.
Tel: 075 9177326.

7 Gualdo Tadino
Rocca Flea, Picture Gallery
Tel: 075 916078.
Open Apr–May, Thu–Sun 10.30–1, 3–6; Jun–Sep, Tue–Sun 10.30–1, 3.30–7; Oct–Mar, Sat–Sun 10.30–1, 2.30–5. Also open 1–2 Nov, 8 Dec, 23 Dec–6 Jan.

i Loggia dei Lanari, Piazza Matteotti 18, Perugia.
Tel: 075 5736458.

i Via Cardinale Rotelli 21, Corciano.
Tel: 075 5188260.

i Piazza della Repubblica Italiana 30, Magione.
Tel: 075 843859.

i Piazza Trento e Trieste 6, Passignano sul Trasimeno.
Tel: 075 827635.

i Piazza Mazzini 10, Castiglione del Lago.
Tel: 075 9652484.

i Piazza Umberto 11, Panicale.
Tel: 075 837319.

2 Magione
Castle of the Knights of Malta
Tel: 075 8373078.
Visits by request.

4 Passignano sul Trasimeno
Lake Trasimeno Regional Park
Tel: 0758 28059.
Always open. (Including the comunes of Castiglione del Lago, Magione, Panicale & Tuoro sul Trasimeno.)

5 Tuoro sul Trasimeno
Outdoor Museum of Campo del Sole
Near Punta Navaccia-Lido di Tuoro.
Tel: & fax: 075 825220.

Centre of Documentation for Hannibal and the Battle of Trasimeno
Via Ritorta 1. Tel: & fax: 075 825220.
Open Mon–Sat 9–12, 3.30–6.30, Sun 9–12.

6 Castiglione del Lago
Palazzo della Corgna
Piazza Gramsci 1.
Tel: 075 9658210 (Town Hall) or 075 951099.
Open mid-Mar to Apr, daily 9.30–1, 3.30–7; May–Aug, daily 10–1.30, 4–7; Sep–Oct, daily 10.30–1.30, 3.30–7; Nov to mid-Mar, Sat–Sun & holidays 9.30–4.30.

8 Panicale
Church of San Sebastiano
For information on times contact the tourist office, tel: 0758 857319.

9 San Savino
'La Valle'
Tel: 075 8476007.
Open daily 9–1, 4–8.

⑩ San Feliciano
Lake Trasimeno Museum of Fishing
Via Lungolago della Pace e del Lavoro 20.
Tel: & fax: 075 8479261.
Open Tue–Sun 10.30– 12.30, 2.30–6.

TOUR 22

ⓘ Loggia dei Lanari, Piazza Matteotti 18, Perugia.
Tel: 075 5736458.

ⓘ Piazza del Comune 22, Assisi.
Tel: 075 812534.

ⓘ Piazza Matteotti 3, Spello.
Tel: 0742 301009.

ⓘ Corso Cavour 126, Foligno.
Tel: 0742 354459.

ⓘ Piazza Ranieri Campello 1, Campello sul Clitunno.
Tel: 0743 275558.

ⓘ Piazza della Libertà 7, Spoleto.
Tel: 0743 238921.

ⓘ Piazza del Comune, Montefalco.
Tel: 0742 512200.

ⓘ Piazza Filippo Silvestri 1, Bevagna.
Tel: 0742 361667.

❶ Assisi
Basilica of Santa Maria degli Angeli
Tel: 075 80511.
Open daily 6.15–12.50, 2.30–7.30.

Museum of Porziuncola
Tel: 075 8051430.
Open summer, 9–12.30, 3.30–6.30; winter, 9–12.30, 3–6.

Basilica of San Francesco
Tel: 075 819001.
Open summer; 6–6; winter, 6am–6.45pm.

Temple of Minerva
Open 8–sunset.

Cathedral of San Rufino
Tel: 075 812287.
Open daily 7–1, 2.30–6.

Basilica of Santa Chiara
Tel: 075 812282.
Open 6.30–12, 2–7.

❷ Eremo delle Carceri
Colle San Rufino.
Tel: 075 812301.
Open 6.30am–7pm.

❹ Foligno
Palazzo Trinci and Picture Gallery
Piazza della Repubblica.
Tel: 0742 357697.
Open Tue–Sun 10–5.

❺ Fonti del Clitunno
Tel: 0743 521141.
Open Jan–Feb, 10–1, 2–6.30; Mar, 9–1, 2–6; Apr, 9–7.30; May–Aug, 8.30–8; 1–15 Sep, 8.30–7.30; 16–30 Sep, 9–7.30; Oct, 9–1, 2–6; Nov–Dec, 10–1, 2–4.30.

Tempietto del Clitunno
Tel: 0743 275085.
Open Apr–Oct, 9–8; Nov–Mar, 8–6.

Back to Nature
Colfiorito Regional Park
Tel: 0742 349715.

❻ Spoleto
Roman theatre and archaeological museum
Via Sant'Agata.
Tel: 0743 223277.
Open 8.30–7.30. Closed 25 Dec, 1 Jan.

Casa Romana
Via Visiale.
Tel: 0743 223277.
Open Apr–Sep, Mon–Thu 11–6, Fri–Sun 10.30–7; Oct–Mar, Wed–Mon 10.30–5.

Duomo
Piazza del Duomo.
Tel: 0743 44307.
Open Apr–Oct, daily 8.30–12.30, 3.30–7;

Nov–Mar, daily 8.30–12.30, 3.30–6.

Galleria Civica d'Arte Moderna
Palazzo Collicola.
Tel: 0743 46434.
Open mid-Mar to mid-Oct, 10.30–1, 3–6.30; mid-Oct to mid-Mar, 10.30–1, 2.30–5.

❽ Montefalco
Civic Museum of San Francesco
Via Ringhiera Umbra 6.
Tel: 0742 379598.
Open Jun–Jul, 10.30–1, 3–7; Aug, 10.30–1, 3–7.30; Mar–May & Sep–Oct, 10.30–1, 2–6; Nov–Feb, 10.30–1, 2.30–5. Closed Mon Nov–Feb.

❾ Bevagna
Roman mosaics
Via delle Terme Romana 2a.
Tel: 0742 360031.
Open Apr–May, Sep, daily 10.30–1, 2.30–6; Jun–Jul, daily 10.30–1, 3.30–7, Aug, daily 10.30–1, 3–7.30; Oct–Mar, Tue–Sun 10.30–1, 2.30–5.

TOUR 23

ⓘ Loggia dei Lanari, Piazza Matteotti 18, Perugia.
Tel: 075 5736458.

ⓘ Piazza Matteotti 1, Città della Pieve.
Tel: 0578 299375.

ⓘ Piazza del Duomo 24, Orvieto.
Tel: 0763 341772.

ⓘ Piazza del Popolo, Todi.
Tel: 075 8945416.

ⓘ Piazza dei Consoli 4, Deruta.
Tel: 075 9711559.

ⓘ Corso Vittorio Emanuele 23, Torgiano.
Tel: 075 985297.

❶ San Sisto
Historical Museum of Perugia Perugina
Nestlé Italiano Establishment.
Tel: 075 5276796.
Open Mon–Fri 9–1, 2–5.30.

❷ Città della Pieve
Oratory of Santa Maria dei Bianchi, Palazzo della Corgna, Church of San Pietro
Tel: 0578 299375.
Open daily 8.30–12.30, 3.30–6.30.

Recommended Excursion
Buzzi's 'ideal city'
Exconvent of Scarzuola.
Tel: 0763 837463.
Visits by appointment only.

❸ Orvieto
Necropolis of Crocifisso del Tufo
Tel: 0763 343611.
Open daily 9–7.

San Patrizio well
Viale Sangallo.
Tel: 0763 343768.
Open Jan–Feb, Nov–Dec, daily 10–5; Mar–Apr, Sep–Oct, daily 9–7; May–Aug, daily 9–8.

Civic tower
Corso Cavour 87.
Tel: 0763 344567.
Open May–Aug, 10–8; Mar–Apr & Sep–Oct, 10–7; Nov–Feb, 10.30–1, 2.30–5.

Duomo (Cathedral)
Piazza del Duomo.
Tel: 0763 341167.
Open Apr–Sep, 7.30–12.45, 2.30–7.15; Mar & Oct, 7.30–12.45, 2.30–6.15; Nov–Feb, 7.30–12.45, 2.30–5.15.

Chapel of San Brizio
Piazza del Duomo 26.
Tel: 0763 343592.
Open Mar, Oct, Mon–Sat 10–12.45, 2.30–6.15, Sun 2.30–5.45; Apr–Jun, Mon–Sat 10–12.45, 2.30–7.15, Sun 2.30–5.45; Jul–Sep, Mon–Sat 10–12.45, 2.30–7.15, Sun 2.30–6.45;

*Nov–Feb, Mon–Sat
10–12.45, 2.30–5.15, Sun
2.30–5.45.*

Special to…
**National Archaeological
Museum**
Papal Palaces, Piazza del
Duomo.
Tel: & fax: 0763 341039.
Open daily 8.30–7.30.

Emilio Greco Museum
Palazzo Soliano, Piazza del
Duomo.
Tel: 0763 344605.
*Open Apr–Sep, Mon–Sat
10.30–1, 2–6.30, Sun
10.30–1, 2–7; Oct–Mar,
daily 10.30–1, 2–5.30.*

**Museum of Civic
Archaeology**
Palazzo Faina, Piazza del
Duomo 29.
Tel: 0763 341511.
*Open Apr–Sep, daily 9.30–6;
Oct–Mar, daily 10–5. Closed
Mon Nov–Feb.*

Special to…
Orvieto Underground
Piazza Duomo 23.
Tel: 0763 344891.
*Open daily 11, 12.45, 4,
5.15. Guided visits.*

4 Todi
Picture Gallery
Palazzo del Popolo, Piazza
del Popolo.
Tel: 075 8944148.
*Open Apr–Oct, Tue–Sun
10–1, 3–6; Nov–Mar,
Tue–Sun 10.30–1, 2.30–5.*

Duomo (Cathedral)
*Open Apr–Oct, 8.30–4.30;
Nov–Mar, 8.30–12.30,
3–6.30.*

Church of San Fortunato
*Open Apr to mid-Oct,
Tue–Sun 8.30–12.30, 3–7;
mid-Oct–late Mar, Tue–Sun
9.30–12.30, 3–5.*

**Church of Santa Maria
della Consolazione**
*Open Apr–Oct, daily
9–12.30, 2.30–6.30;
Nov–Mar, daily 9.30–12.30,
2.30–5.*

5 Deruta
**Regional Ceramics
Museum**
Largo San Francesco.
Tel: 075 9711000.
*Open Apr–Jun, daily
10.30–1, 3–6; Jul–Sep, daily
10.30–1, 3.30–7; Oct–Mar,
Tue–Sun 10.30–1, 2.30–5.*

**Sanctuary of the Madonna
dei Bagni**
Tel: 075 973455.

6 Torgiano
Wine Museum
Palazzo Graziani-Baglioni,
Corso Vittorio Emanuele II.
Tel: & fax: 075 9880200.
*Open Apr–Oct, daily 9–1,
3–7; Nov–Mar, daily 9–1,
3–6.*

TOUR 24

🛈 Via Cassian Bon 4,
Terni.
Tel: 0744 423047.

🛈 Corso Umberto 1,
Acquasparta.
Tel: 0744 944800.

🛈 Piazza San Francesco
4, San Gèmini.
Tel: 0744 630130
(seasonal).

🛈 Piazza dei Priori 3,
Narni.
Tel: 0744 715362.

🛈 Via Orvieto 1, Amelia.
Tel: 0744 981453.

1 Càrsulae
Archaeological site
*Open Apr–Oct, 8.30–7.30;
Nov–Mar, 8.30–5.30.
For information, tel: 0744
334133.*

For Children
Mostri di Bomarzo Park
Bomarzo, Villa Orsini
Tel: 0761 924029.
Phone for opening times.

2 Acquasparta
Fossil Forest of Dunarobba
Viale Matteotti 9, Avigliano
Umbro.
Tel: 0744 940348.
Open Apr–Oct, Tue–Sun

*10–1, 3.30–6.30; Jul–Aug,
Tue–Sun 9.30–1, 3.30–7.30;
Nov–Mar, Tue–Sun 10–1.*

4 Narni
**Complex of San
Domenico**
Tel: 0744 722292.
*Irregular opening. Contact
tourist office for current
details.*

5 Amelia
Archaeological Museum
Palazzo Boccarini, Piazza
Augustovera.
Tel: 0744 978120.
*Open Oct–Mar, Fri–Sun
10.30–1, 3.30–6; Apr–Jun,
Sep, Tue–Sun 10.30–1, 4–7;
Jul–Aug, Tue–Sun 10.30–1,
4.30–7.30.*

7 Alviano
Folk Museum
Piazza Bartolomeo
d'Alviano, Castello 10.
Tel: 0744 905028.
*Open Apr–Jul, Sep, Sat 4–7,
Sun 10.30–12.30,
4.40–7.30; Aug, Tue–Sat
4.30–7.30, Sun 4.30–7.30;
Oct–Mar, Sun 10.30–12.30,
3–6.*

Back to Nature
Alviano marsh area
Madonna del Porto,
Alviano.
Tel: 0744 904224.
*Open Sep to mid-May,
Sat–Sun 10–sunset.*

8 Baschi
Vissani
SS448 Civitella del Lago.
Tel: 0744 950206.
*Closed Wed, Thu lunch, Sun
dinner & 15 Jul–15 Aug.*

TOUR 25

🛈 Via Cassian Bon 4,
Terni.
Tel: 0744 423047.

🛈 Via Madonna della
Peschiera, Casa del Parco,
Preci.
Tel: 0743 937000.

🛈 Via Solferino 22,
Norcia.
Tel: 0743 828173.

🛈 Piazza Garibaldi 1,
Cascia.
Tel: 0743 71147.

**1 Cascata delle
Màrmore**
Piazza G Byron.
Tel: 0744 62982.
*Open Jan, Sat–Sun 12–1,
3–4; Feb, Sat–Sun 11–1,
3–5; Mar, Mon–Fri 12–1,
4–5, Sat–Sun 11–1, 4–7;
Apr–May, Mon–Fri 12–1,
4–5, Sat–Sun 11–1, 4–7
(8 in May); Jun–Aug,
Mon–Fri 11–1, 4–6, 9–10,
Sat–Sun 10–1, 3–10; Sep,
Mon–Fri 12–1, 8–9,
Sat–Sun 10–1, 3–9; Oct, Fri
3–5, Sat–Sun 11–1, 3–7;
Nov–Dec, Sat–Sun 12–1,
3–4.*

3 Ferentillo
Museum of Mummies
Via della Torre, ex-Chiesa
di Santo Stefano.
Tel: & fax: 0744 780708.
*Open Apr–Sep, daily
9–12.30, 2.30–7.30; Mar,
Oct, daily 9.30–12.30,
2.30–6; Nov–Feb, daily
10–12.30, 2.30–5.*

**4 Abbazia di San
Pietro in Valle**
Tel: 0744 780708.
Phone for opening times.

7 Preci
Abbey of Sant'Eutizio
Piedivalle.
Tel: 0743 99659.
Phone for opening times.

10 Norcia
Civic Diocesan Museum
Piazza San Benedetto,
Castellina.
Tel: 0743 817030.
*Open Jun, daily 10–1,
4–7.30; Jul–May, Tue–Sun
10–1, 4–6.*

INDEX

Index

Index & Acknowledgements

The Automobile Association
wishes to thank the following libraries and photographers for their assistance in the preparation of this book.

AA PHOTO LIBRARY 17, 18–19, 45b, 54, 69, 121, 122a, 140, 144–5, 147a; G ANDREINI 8, 34, 96, 99, 128, 131, 141a; ARCHIVI ALINARI 85; F BINI 26b; S CELLAI 9, 10, 13, 16, 19a, 23, 33a, 36, 37, 66, 67, 68, 70–71, 72b, 74, 75, 76, 77, 78, 79, 81, 84, 89a, 100, 101, 102a, 107b, 110, 115a, 147b; C CIABOCHI 73b, 97b; R CONTI 118, 119a, 120, 123; CORTE/CARDONE 112; P DEL DUCA 107a, 108; G FIESOLI 97a; M FRASCHETTI 115b, 145, 149, 150a; S GALEOTTI 73a, 94, 113a; M MARCHETTI 109; T MIYAOKA 64–5; M. MORETTI 72a; L PESSINA 24, 28, 29; M PEZZOTTA 46; REALY EASY STAR 12a, 26a, 59a, 70, 125, 136, 154b; REALY EASY STAR/M ANDREINI 53b; REALY EASY STAR/P BENINI 124; REALY EASY STAR/E CARLI 14a, 57b, 65, 80, 92, 102b; REALY EASY STAR/C CONCINA 5, 60, 62, 83a, 93, 137, 144; REALY EASY STAR/G CORTE 111a; REALY EASY STAR/DI PAOLO 51, 55, 114; REALY EASY STAR/F FERRARIS 35b; REALY EASY STAR/D FRACCHIA 63b; REALY EASY STAR/G FURGHIERI 156a; REALY EASY STAR/S GALEOTTI 95b, 132, 143, 155, 156b; REALY EASY STAR/GLAMOUR INTERNATIONAL 40; REALY EASY STAR/F IORIO 146; REALY EASY STAR/M MARCHETTI 6; REALY EASY STAR/T MIYAOKA 52, 63a, 105b, 106; REALY EASY STAR/L PESSINA 10–11, 14b, 25, 127b, 151, 152, 153, 154a; REALY EASY STAR/A PICONE 7a; REALY EASY STAR/G RODANTE 45a, 105a, 117, 134a, 157; REALY EASY STAR/M RUBINO 133; REALY EASY STAR/L A SCATOLA 41, 43; REALY EASY STAR/T SPAGONE 7b, 12b, 15, 21, 33b, 35a, 38, 39, 47, 48, 49, 56, 58, 59b, 61, 86, 87, 88–9, 90, 91, 95a, 98, 103, 104, 116, 119b, 122b, 126–7, 129a, 130, 134b, 135, 138, 141b, 142, 148, 150–1; REALY EASY STAR/R VALTERZA 20, 22, 30, 57a, 82, 111b, 129b; REALY EASY STAR/C A ZABERT 53a, 83b; L A SCATOLA 31, 42; G P SENZANONNA 27; F SPANO 113b.

The publishers would also like to thank the Italian State Tourist Office for their help in updating this book.

Touring Map
1:500 000

Index to map pages

Legend

Cinquale

Forte dei Marmi

Pietrasanta

Marina di Pietrasanta

le Focette

Lido di Camaiore

Querceta

Valdicastello
Carducci

Cásoli

S. Rocco
Colognora
Pescáglia

Camaiore

Fiano

PIEVE DI B

475

1220

S. Donato

S. Martino
in Freddana

Ponte

Villa Fórci

Viaréggio

Bozzano

Massarosa

Nocchi

Bargecchia

Valpromaro

Piazzano

S. Macário
in Piano

Quiesa

20 **439**

LUCCA

Torre del Lago Puccini

Massaciúccoli

ARLIANO
Nozzano

Massáciuccoli
di

22

Marina di Torre d.Lago Puccini

15

Filéttole
Ripafratta
C. Quattro
Venti

Migliarino

Vecchiano

Cim.
di V

**S. Giuliano
Terme**

M.Faeta
831

Ascianc

PISA

Mezzana

Tenuta

C.ne
Vécchia

Gombo
di

MAR

S. Rossore

Arno

224

GALILEO
GALILEI

LÍGURE

Marina di Pisa

Cá

Tenuta
di

Arnáccio

21

32

Tirrénia

Tómbolo

Tenuta
di Coltano

570

26

carello

Calambrone

Stagno

555

Guastice

Colles

16

Faugl

TORRE D.
MARZOCCO

LIVORNO

Torre

T.RE D. MELÓRIA

S. Martino

Parrana

Loren

Salviano

S. Giusto

Ardenza

Marmigliaid

Antignano

Montenero

Gabbro

42

SANTUÁRIO

T.RE D. BOCCALE

Nibbiáia

33

di

Calafúria

275

Í. DI GORGONA
(Livorno)

Querciánella

Castelnuovo
Misericórdia

35

Tre Nuova Scalo
255

**PARCO NAZ.
DELL' ARCIPÉLAGO TOSCANO**

Rosignano
Maritt

Castiglioncello

Rosignano
Solvay

Golfo Arenci

Vada

C

S. Pietro
in Palazzi

Marina
di Cécina

Óbia Basita

Marina di Bibbona

Forte di Bibbona

Marina di Castagneto
-Donorático

D

P. d. Téia

Í. DI CAPRÁIA
(Livorno)

S. Vincenzo

Riva d. Etruschi

Capráia Ísola
447
FORTEZZA DI
S. GIÓRGIO

S. STÉFANO

**PARCO NAZ.
DELL' ARCIPÉLAGO TOSCANO**

P. d. Zenóbito

Í. d'Elba

Palermo

Golfo di Bara

Populónia

TOMBE
ETRUSCHE

472 · Canneto
295

Marina di Castagneto-
Donorático
Bámbolo
Donorático
Monteverdi
Maríttimo
329

Castagneto
Carducci
572 · 312
Capo di Monte Sassetta

S. Vincenzo
M. Calvi
646
Riva d. Etruschi
S. Carlo
MAD. DI
FUCINAIA
Suvereto
231 Campíglia
Maritt.

Terme di Caldana
Ventúrina
Casalappi
Montión

Goffo di Baratti
22
Populónia
181
Com 25
TOMBE
ETRUSCHE
Riotorto
50

Marina di Salivoli
Prato Ranieri
Follónica

Piombino
G. di
Follónica
Port

Canale di Piombino

C. Vita L. D. TOPI
Cavo
I. PALMAIOLA
I. CÉRBOLI

PARCO NAZIONALE
DELL' ARCIPÉLAGO TOSCANO
M. Serra 10
Rio
nell'Elba

C. d'Énfola
135
Portoférráio
Rio Marina

S. Andrea
TORRE
MEDICEA
Marciana
Marina
Scaglieri
Bagnáia
MAD. D. MONSERRATO
P. Ala
SC. D. SPÁRVIERO
le

P. Polveráia
Marciana
Biódola
Prócchio
VILLA NAPOLEÓNICA
Martino
Porto
Azzurro

P. Nera
1018
M. Capanne
S. Piero in C.
Marina
in Campo
Pila
Lacona
2
Naregno
Capoliveri
Camp
nell' El
10
G. Stella
M. Calamita
413
Fetováia
Cávoli
Marina di Campo
Pareti

P. di Fetováia
ISOLA D'ELBA
(Livorno)
P. dei Ripalti

P. d. Marchese
Í. PIANOSA
(Livorno)
P. Libéccio
Pianosa
PARCO NAZ.
DELL' ARCIPÉLAGO TOSCANO
P. Brigantina

MAR   TIRRENO

SCÓGLIO D'ÁFFRICA
(FORMICA DI MONTECRISTO)

ÉREMO DI
S. MAMILIANO
Í. DI MONTECRISTO
(Livorno)
645
la Villa
PARCO NAZ.
DELL' ARCIPÉLAGO TOSCANO
P. Rossa

Atlas Index

Atlas Index

198

Atlas Index

Index

Atlas Index

Town Plans

Index to town plans

Legend

Highway and thoroughfare	Monuments and buildings - Exceptional interest
Main road	Monuments and buildings - Very interesting
Other roads	Monuments and buildings - Interesting
Pedestrian zone	Church
Railway line and station	Tourist information office
Hospital	Principal parking area
Gardens and parks	Contour map showing elevation and gradient

Carrara

CAMPO CECINA km 17

CAVE DI COLONNATA

CAVE DI COLONNATA km 7

Chiesa delle Grazie

Via Lunigiana

P.za Alberica

Duomo

P.za Sacco e Vanzetti

P.za Gramsci
Pal. Cybo

P.za Manzoni

Accad. di Belle Arti

Municipio

P.za Battisti

P.za S. Martino

P.za Matteotti

Posta e T

P.za Salvator Allende

P.za XXVII Aprile

S. Francesco

P.za Don Minzoni

Via Don Minzoni

P.za Lodovici

Via San Francesco

AUTOSTRADA km 7,5

MASSA km 7

Prato

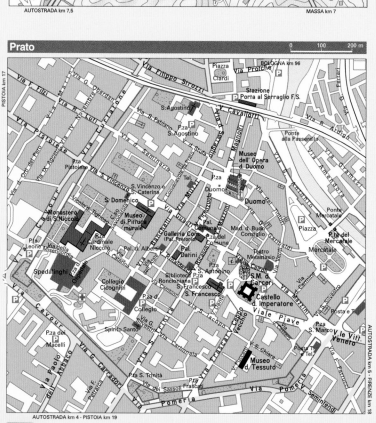

PISTOIA km 17

Via Filippo Strozzi

Piazza Ciardi

BOLOGNA km 96

Via Proliche

Stazione Porta al Serraglio F.S.

Via Cavallotti

S. Agostino

P.za S. Agostino

Ponte alla Passerella

Museo dell'Opera d. Duomo

P.za Pistoiese

Via IX Agosto

Via S. Vincenzo

Tel.

S. Vincenzo e S. Caterina

P.za Duomo

Duomo

S. Domenico

Monastero di S. Niccolo

Museo di Pittura murale

Galleria Con. (Pal. Pretorio)

Pal. Comunale

Mad. d. Buon Consiglio

Ponte Mercatale

Piazza

R. ta del Mercatale

P.za Cardinale Niccolo

Pal. d. Alberti

Pal. Datini

Teatro Metastasio

Spedalinghi

Collegio Cicognini

Biblioteca Roncioniana

S. Francesco

P.za Antonino

S. M. d. Carceri

Castello d. Imperatore

P.za d. Collegio

Spirito Santo

Posta e T

P.za dei Macelli

Viale Piave

S. Marco

V. le Vitt. Veneto

Via Cavour

P.ta S. Trinita

V. S. Chiara

Museo d. Tessuto

P.ta T. Tel.

P.za Frascati

Via Pomeria

AUTOSTRADA km 4 - PISTOIA km 19

AUTOSTRADA km 5 - FIRENZE km 18

204

Montecatini Terme

PISTÓIA km 15 - AUTOSTRADA km 3

Volterra

AUTOSTRADA km 36 - SIENA km 52

Fièsole

0 150 300 m

FIRENZE km 8   MAIANO km 2

Spoleto

0 100 200 m

TERNI km 8

Foligno

Gubbio

Todi

0   150   300 m

ORVIETO km 41

TERNI km 43
PERUGIA km 49

Orvieto

0   150   300 m

VITERBO km 41 · BOLSENA km 22

BOLSENA - VITERBO

208